ADVENTURES OF A SOUL

ADVENTURES OF A SOUL

Psychics, Mediums, the Mystical, and Me

ANNE NEWGARDEN

Star Garden Press
NEW YORK

Cover design by Laura Duffy
Interior design and page composition by Karen Minster
Author photo on page 363 by Albert Newgarden

PRINTED IN THE UNITED STATES OF AMERICA

978-1-7365369-0-2 (paperback)
978-1-7365369-1-9 (ebook)

FIRST EDITION

STAR GARDEN PRESS
Staten Island, New York
StarGardenPress.com

TO THE JOYFUL MEMORY
AND ENDURING SPIRIT OF
DAVID MARC FISCHER . . .
WITH LOVE AND GRATITUDE

Our own life is the instrument with which we experiment with truth.

— THICH NHAT HANH

Contents

Introduction

Some people talk about their first love as an experience they'll never forget. That's how I feel about my first psychic.

Her name was Patricia Masters.

A little more than twenty years ago, she sat across a table from me and quietly blew my mind, telling me things she shouldn't have—couldn't have!—known, but somehow did.

As interested as I was in hearing Patricia's accurate and insightful take on me, myself, and I—everything from my family relationships, to my health, to my writing and career, to my so-called love life—I found myself even more intrigued by how she was able to do what she was doing.

"How do you receive your information?" I eventually asked her—little knowing this would be the first of many times I'd ask this question, to many different intuitives (another term for psychics—preferred by most of those I met) in later years. Did she see images, hear voices, feel sensations? Or did she perceive things in some way that didn't involve the five senses at all?

"I don't normally talk about that to my clients," she replied. "But I'm going to talk about it to you. Because you're going to write about people who do what I do. And about what are called 'the invisible realms' . . ."

Well! I *was* an aspiring writer. But I was writing plays, screenplays, and short stories about very earthly, human subjects. And while I had, since childhood, been fascinated by things mystical and unexplained, or *"weird stuff"* as I called it back then, the metaphysical world wasn't something I'd ever considered writing about at all.

As it happened, Patricia was right. In my late forties, after a one-two punch to the heart and gut—a pair of devastating personal losses—I experienced a life crisis, and then a sort of a soul-level calling. The result? I plunged down my own personal rabbit hole on an exploratory quest, investigating the "invisible realms" Patricia had so long ago described. And Reader, what a life-changing journey it was!

This book is a chronicle of those explorations—into psychic intuition, mediumship, past lives, spirit guides . . . and other *"weird stuff."* I use the term now with affection because, the way I've come to see it, none of it is really weird at all. It's simply part and parcel of a Universe with more going on than what meets the eye—far more, I am certain, than any of us having this human experience can even imagine.

But why take my word for it? If you, too, have wondered about the existence of invisible realms, about truths that might be out there, or astonishing powers you might possess (and I'm here to tell you, you *do*!)—consider this book an invitation and let that "wonder-lust" be your guide. Crank your mind wide open, strap on your own personal bullshit detector, and join me as I share these, my first adventures in my ongoing exploratory expedition. My fondest hope is that they'll inspire you to set out on an exploration of your own.

Oh, and Reader, fasten your seat belt: It's going to be a *wild*—and wonderful—ride!

ADVENTURES OF A SOUL

ADVENTURES WITH
A PSYCHIC
✳ OR ✳

On a "Clair-" Day, You Can See Forever

SOMETIMES LIFE IS LIKE A FLEA MARKET. YOU GO IN WITH something specific in mind. You don't find what you came in looking for. But you *do* end up going home with something—something totally unexpected.

I was in my early thirties and living in Manhattan's Greenwich Village. One sunny afternoon, I sat drinking wine with my friend Maurice on his nearby building's rooftop, abloom with pots of pink impatiens and rosy begonias. Maurice and I had met shortly after college, when we'd both taken jobs at the Public Theater, an Off-Broadway theater complex in the East Village, to support ourselves while pursuing our art: for me, writing; for him, dancing and choreography. Even these many years later, I'd often turn to Maurice and his rooftop—not to mention his abundant supply of very good wine—when in the throes of unrequited love, which, alas, was quite often.

This particular day, I was drowning my sorrows about Leo, a tall, dark, and sad-eyed sax player I'd been seeing off and on. Leo was the closest I'd come to having a real love relationship. A very late bloomer—I'd struggled with my weight since childhood and had always been extremely shy with romance—I'd dated a bit in college and my twenties, but had never been able to develop a love connection that stuck. My "relationships," such as they were, had a distinctive pattern: I'd develop a friendship with a man, which always came easily to me as I had four brothers; fall for him, hard; sit with those feelings for an interminable amount of time, too fearful of rejection to admit to them or make a move; and finally, when I could bear it no longer, screw up my courage and express my feelings, only to be told by said man that he valued me greatly . . . but just didn't feel the same way.

Leo, though, had been willing to go there with me. While I'd been the pursuer—I was, at this point, hell-bent on experiencing a romantic relationship that lasted more than a few dates—he met me more than halfway, and we had some happy times together. Leo loved old movies and theater as much as I did, so along with the jazz clubs and other off-the-beaten-path music venues where he'd play, we regularly hit the Film Forum, the Thalia, and theaters from Broadway to "Off-Off-Off." Leo went biking with me on Manhattan's streets, which I'd been terrified to do alone. He even got me past my fear of pit bulls— instilled by my mother, who hyperventilates at the mere mention of the breed to this day—which was necessary, as he had a rescue pit he adored whom he'd dubbed "Laszlo," after the character Victor Laszlo in *Casablanca*, his favorite film. It was a favorite of mine as well, and we watched it together on his worn leather couch one night, with Laszlo—always well behaved, and in fact "a bit of a mush," as Leo had promised—sandwiched like a sausage between us.

Leo had told me he loved me—a first, for me—and shown it in many ways, though I was always aware that his feelings never quite matched mine. As months passed and we grew closer, though, he began to feel anxiety. He became uncharacteristically critical, never actually breaking things off with me, but saying and doing things to push me away: He'd tell me he disliked something I was wearing, or that I needed to learn to flirt more, in a way that made me feel that who I was, was somehow not enough. Rather than stand up for myself or tell him off, I'd shrink into my insecurity, grow cool, and retreat, and a period of mutual silence would inevitably ensue. Each time this happened, though, we'd eventually admit that we missed each other, and end up on the couch, sandwiching Laszlo, once again.

Over time, I came to see that Leo, despite being talented, smart, and handsome—he'd had no shortage of women interested in him—didn't feel good about himself, something I understood. Being constantly pushed away and pulled back was hurtful and confusing, but I could feel Leo's pain. I wasn't sure if it was because I'd grown up in a big, dysfunctional family, most of whom seemed perpetually unhappy, but I'd always had the sense that I could feel other people's feelings, especially their pain—I thought everyone could! And I always felt compelled to try and help. I knew, for example, that Leo had had a difficult time growing up; his father, who died when Leo was in his thirties, seemed to have been very critical, and, Leo had confided, had never once told him he loved him. Having found help on a therapist's couch myself, I'd suggested that Leo seek the same. Sensing, too, his lack of self-esteem, particularly about his finances, I'd helped him find venues for performing, as I had a number of friends who worked as musicians too.

I knew I should worry less about Leo's feelings and issues, and more about my own—and that I should definitely end things between us. But ending things felt like abandoning him. I couldn't seem to let go.

"I'm so tired of crying into my wine over men," I said to Maurice. "Why is this love stuff so ridiculously hard for me? Is something wrong with me? No one I know has such a horrible track record with men!"

I was looking for sympathy, consolation; Maurice, who was gay, had gone through difficulties of his own with men, and always had some words of empathy. But he was quiet for a moment, sipping his pinot noir.

"I have a story to tell you," he finally said, with one of his elfin smiles. He set his glass down on the picnic table between us. "Maybe it can help."

Maurice had recently been in class with a fellow dancer named Patricia Masters. During class, he'd been worrying about the severe headaches his mother was having, wondering if she should get a brain scan or other medical test. After class, Patricia asked him about his mother's headaches. Startled, as he'd told no one, he admitted his concern. "No need to worry," Patricia had said. "Tell her to get her eyeglasses checked. The prescription's too strong." Then she'd explained: Psychic advising was her "other job."

Intrigued, Maurice spoke to his mother, and all went as Patricia had predicted. The prescription *was* off. His mother got new glasses. And the headaches, to his amazement, went away.

When Maurice had told Patricia how accurate she'd been, she'd offered him a free reading. It had, he said, been *fascinating*.

As he lifted his glass again to take a sip, I set mine down with a resounding *plunk*. Maurice's story had touched something deep within me, a part of myself with which I'd not connected in a very long time. As a child, I'd been extremely curious about things metaphysical, which I'd collectively filed under the mental heading "*weird stuff.*" At ten, I'd been fascinated by a book about Dutch psychic Peter Hurkos, whose abilities emerged when he toppled off a ladder and bonked himself on the head; written a school paper on "ESP"; and bought a special deck of cards to test my own. Though my results with the cards proved no better than average, the deck nonetheless held an allure for me: an acknowledgment of hidden aspects of the mind, hidden realms, perhaps, of the soul.

I recall holding a séance with my younger sister and a teddy bear or two, in which I made the tabletop magically rise with the aid of a wooden spoon tucked up my sleeve. And then there was the Ouija board. My brothers and I loved asking it questions, placing our fingertips on the wedge-shaped pointer as it skimmed over the board on little felt-tipped feet. I was captivated by the idea of channeling answers from somewhere "out there." Because it had always seemed quite natural to me that there *was* an "out there." And I wanted to find out what it was.

Despite all this, though, at the time of that conversation with Maurice, I'd never actually experienced any sort of psychic reading for myself. In the wilds of Staten Island, where I was born and bred, there were no storefront psychics or tearooms where leaves or palms were read. Commuting to Stuyvesant, my math-and-science specialized high school in "the city"—as we Islanders called Manhattan—I'd seen fortune-tellers sitting in windows, crooking a bejeweled finger at passersby. But I'd never been tempted; I never felt they were for real. And I'd certainly never met anyone at the University of Virginia, that bastion of Southern tradition and prep-dom—at least, back in the early Eighties when I attended—who'd shown the slightest curiosity about such things. After that . . . well, the challenges and pressures of adulthood—making a living, trying to write, and searching endlessly for love—had afforded me little time to ponder things "beyond the beyond."

Now Maurice's words woke my slumbering inner child with all the impact of a soldier playing reveille at dawn.

"*So* . . . ?" I asked him, practically panting. "What was it like? What did she say?"

He flashed me another dimpled smile. "I'll tell you about it. But my own psychic two cents? You're going to want to have a reading with her and see for yourself."

MAURICE HAD BEEN absolutely right. A few weeks later, I found myself headed into the lobby of Patricia's small brick apartment building. I was excited at the prospect of finally experiencing a bona fide psychic reading. But my hopes ran far deeper than that.

More than a decade out of college, I still felt like a daydreaming girl, living mostly in my head and waiting for my real life to begin. And though my thirty-plus years on the planet had delivered more heartbreaks than a rom-com film festival, it wasn't just about men. I'd had a few interesting editorial jobs after leaving my gig at the Off-Broadway theater, but I kept getting laid off. I was trying to write plays and short stories, but lately I'd become totally blocked. Writing felt like breathing; when I wasn't doing it, I was miserable, disconnected from myself. On top of it all, I often couldn't sleep. When I did manage to drift off, I frequently had bizarre nightmares of soldiers climbing over my windowsill, brandishing machine guns, and other disturbing combat scenarios.

Was it possible that Patricia could help with any of that?

Walking through her building's entrance, I found myself feeling slightly anxious. Despite my excitement, meeting new people and trying new things always made me feel shy. As I waited for the elevator, a mural of the sky and clouds on the lobby's ceiling caught my eye. Its colors—soft aquas, pinks, and golds—were like a soothing balm. I stood lost in them until the elevator arrived.

My anxiety quickly evaporated, though, as Patricia opened the door, a ceramic mug in hand. She smiled warmly and ushered me in. Reed-slim and graceful, with short-cropped red hair, she had a voice that put me in mind of the swish of silk or the rustle of wind through leaves. She invited me to sit at a small table, offering me coffee. As she went into her tiny kitchen and returned with a steaming, fragrant cup, I told her that I'd loved the lobby's cloud mural, and that this was my first-ever reading, but shared nothing else.

Patricia switched on a tape recorder, which sat on the tabletop alongside a pad and pen, a stack of pale blue index cards, and something rectangular swaddled in a purple-and-blue paisley silk scarf, which turned out to be a well-worn deck of tarot cards. She began the reading by explaining the nature of her particular abilities. "There are people that are called 'psychic,'" she said, "but their sense of psychic is knowing the events in your life and how they will happen. And usually, with someone who gets things like that, it's because time is out of sequence. So what is future for *you* is not future for *them*."

Now, that, to me, was fascinating, and she hadn't even gotten started! As I digested this provocative statement, she picked up the pad and pen. "What *I* do is something very different." She drew a circle, with spokes radiating out from a central point. "If this is a wheel, the person who knows the events of a person's life knows *these* parts of the wheel." She pointed to the spokes. "But what *I* see is the central point"—she pointed to the axle—"or what's called the 'essential nature' of someone. Why they're here. From that, I can see the connection to the things they're doing in this life."

"In this life." Hmmmm, so Patricia believed in past lives! As a Catholic, I hadn't been raised to believe in reincarnation, but for some reason I'd always felt very open to and curious about the idea.

"Sometimes, the reason why people are here—this essential nature—and the form their life is taking are totally different. That's usually when they come to me, because something is off somewhere, and they feel it," she said. "Now, there's nothing I can tell you that you don't already know. You just may not be . . . fully aware of it."

Patricia set aside the pen and paper, and placed the stack of index cards in front of her—she referred to them from time to time—and for the next hour and a half, went on to give me her unique take on . . . *me*. Not predicting my future so much as telling me, or as she put it, *reminding* me, of who I was.

She told me that, first and foremost, I was a "sensualist of the imagination": "This is someone—and it comes out most strongly in your writing—who lives fully in the imagination. It is a poetic nature. It is not someone who can write long novels."

I was shocked. I hadn't told Patricia that I was a writer—when I'd made the appointment, I'd given her only my name and date of birth. Nor had Maurice. I'd checked. And this was 1994, well before the Internet was part of daily living, so there was no such easy way to search for details about a person's life. I was coming to Patricia for a psychic reading, and yet, here I was, honestly a bit startled by her first psychic "hit." I had to laugh at myself.

I told her I'd tried to start a novel but couldn't get it off the ground. And that I was currently trying to write a screenplay, but I kept hitting a big fat block.

"Yes, and calling it *writer's block* isn't helping. Call it *a writer's distinguishing-that-that's-not-where-you're-supposed-to-be-headed.* The writing you can do is truly poetic in nature. It does what a haiku does. Your writing has sensuality, it has *smell*. It also has touch, *sensation*. What I find interesting is that you're the first person I've met who has sensation that does not connect to the external world. When you're writing, you will *smell* what you're writing about. But it's not a smell that you might have actually smelled; you've *created* it. For instance, I got this image before you came." She picked up an index card on which she'd jotted down some words: "*You're someone who can go swimming without going swimming*," she read. "And no need to. It would in fact be more fully felt when you did it in your imagination."

Reader, if I hadn't been sitting, her words would have stopped me in my tracks. To hear her pinpoint so well something I'd actually experienced time and time again, but had never quite found the words for . . . it was a relief, a validation, an indescribable feeling of being on some profound, superhuman level, *understood*.

I flashed back on one of the first stories I'd ever written, a children's story I'd colorfully illustrated for a high school English class. In one scene, the main character had been walking in the rain. As I'd written it, I'd *felt* it—the moisture in the air, the patter of the droplets; *seen*, in my mind's eye, the surprising pink of a worm wriggling on wet gray cement. I remembered, as I wrote, the sensation of living it in some deeper way than I'd ever experienced such a walk myself.

"I don't know what this is," she said, breaking into my thoughts, "but they're showing me something to do with a worm."

What?! "They"—whoever *they* were—knew such a tiny detail about a story I'd written back in high school?! Who were these invisible beings, and how much did they know about me? Or was Patricia simply reading my mind? Not that there was anything simple about that.

I took a sip of coffee, feeling the need to ground myself in the familiar robust and slightly bitter, real-world taste and scent. "So, in order to make a connection between your inner world and the outer world," she continued, "like a child in the womb, there has to be some kind of cord. For you, the cord is writing. So the fact that you get blocked is a very real problem."

Next, she asked what type of writing I was presently doing. I mentioned playwriting, screenwriting, fiction writing, and, almost as an afterthought, the two children's books I'd once written and illustrated—I'd done a second one for a class I took in college.

Patricia flashed a smile, lifting her eyebrows, a sudden gleam of recognition in her eyes. "Yes. *This* is where you should be writing. Any type of work to do with children, and you'll be successful."

Reader, it wasn't really what I wanted to hear. People had always told me I should work with kids, and I knew I had an ability for that. And yes, when I'd been younger, I'd fancied being a children's book author. But I'd long since given that idea up—belittled it, really, maybe because it came so easily to me—and now had my sights fervently set on doing writing of other, more "sophisticated" types.

Further, she saw me doing children's writing *that involved a screen.* She told me to think about the idea of a "collective imagination"—like the *collective unconscious,* as conceived by the Swiss psychologist Carl Jung. It was an intriguing notion, though I couldn't imagine what that meant.

"Now, with your writing"—she tilted her head, as if listening—"*yes, thank you,* and with men as well, you've thought you had to use your

will and be strong. But no, I would say, allow yourself to be more fragile. Your nature has a very fragile aspect."

Fragile? I balked at the word. I was often fearful, yes. Even in my
sleep: Case in point those combat-zone nightmares. I'd gotten that
fearfulness from my mother, who had fears and phobias up the wazoo.
In any situation, her reflex reaction was to imagine all the things that
could possibly go disastrously wrong. She'd phone me if she heard
about anything bad that had happened anywhere in Manhattan to
make sure I was still alive. Growing up surrounded by so much anxiety
had felt stifling and restrictive, and left me with many crippling fears
and phobias of my own, which I was constantly trying to overcome:
pushing myself to take plane trips when I had a fear of flying; to ride a
zip line when I had a fear of heights; to learn to drive, when I had a fear
of speed . . . and killing people.

"And in relationships, you have not chosen someone who could
take care of you." She paused. *"Yes, thank you,"* she said again, tilting
her head. *Who or what was she talking to?* "The reason you don't let
yourself choose this is because, unbelievably so, your mother was very
sheltering. It was appropriate when you were a child, because of who
you are, but now as an adult it can feel controlling."

"Yes!" I shouted, practically launching myself out of my seat. I loved
my mother, and she'd been wonderfully supportive in many ways, but
I was having a mother lode of mother stuff coming up in therapy lately,
and Patricia's words were right on point.

But what did my mother's overprotectiveness have to do with me
picking men?

I didn't even have to ask. She cocked her head again. "Choosing
a man who can take care of you does not have to be a reemergence of
what your mother did. It's simply taking care of yourself."

I took that in, along with another mouthful of coffee, which went
down with a gulp of pleasure and surprise. I was picking men who
were unable to commit because I was afraid of feeling smothered, or

controlled, as I'd often felt with my mother? I'd never thought of that, but it made perfect sense! Patricia was connecting dots here that my therapist never had!

"Now . . . in addition . . . there are people who have what I call *alarms*, which tell them when something's dangerous, or off. You're not one of them."

It was true. Leo's behavior was definitely "off," as many of my friends, in no uncertain terms, had pointed out. But caught up in feeling his pain, and understanding where his actions came from, I hadn't really acknowledged it.

"And on some level, your mother knew that—your lack of alarms— very well. For you, living in the world, it's like looking at a snake, and sensing the movement and the color, and you get lost in the beauty and the wonder of it. But the snake can also bite you. You don't see it. You don't know that way of thinking. The perfect example: You walked into my building, looked up at the ceiling, and had the extraordinary sense of the clouds. Now, most people who see that also see that the plaster needs fixing, and the placement of the lights is off. That's called an 'alarm.' You have none of that. What *you* have is the extraordinary sensation of the clouds."

She paused. "Now, to think there's something wrong with that is wrong thinking. Because what would the world be without the poets, who would turn someone's head and remind them to look up at the beauty of the sunset, of the clouds? *The poet. That's who you are.* Now, do you want more coffee?"

Boy, did I! My mind needed a few more jolts of caffeine to absorb it all. Given that Patricia seemed to have crawled inside there and made herself at home, she could probably tell. She and her "helpers" had extraordinary insight on my life . . . or was it my soul? It felt like they were reading me like a book, peeling back my layers. I might have felt exposed, except that it was so extraordinarily helpful. If anything, I felt grateful, and touched.

"Eventually, you should be living by the water," she continued, as she refilled my cup.

"I've always wanted to live by the ocean!" I replied, with a hint of longing.

"Then you *should*!" She said it almost sternly. "These are not just silly thoughts; these are important things! Also, I'm being told you must live in places that do not have heights, but have scope. Horizons."

I found myself picturing vast swaths of sand, sea, and bright blue sky. I *could*, so easily, *sense* it: the briny smell of seaweed, the cry of the gulls, the hot sand under my feet.

"Now, metaphorically, we would like you to collect glass. Colored glass."

"I do!" I said. Since childhood, I'd scavenged for bits and pieces of sea glass, worn cloudy by the waves and smooth between my fingers, hoarding them like treasures on our summer vacations at the Jersey Shore, my happiest times. In college, I'd collected old colored-glass bottles—sea-foam green, cobalt blue, amber, and violet—lining them up on my windowsill so that the light shone through, like stained-glass windows, which I loved.

"You see, the way you would take care of a piece of glass, which is very fragile, is the way a man needs to be able to take care of *you*. You can't put glass in something that's going to allow it to break. So why not wish for someone who can protect you? Why think there's something wrong with meeting someone who can do that?"

She was right; but the feminist in me bridled at that. "I'm not sure about being taken care of," I said. "I want to be strong, independent. So that feels . . . contradictory."

"That's all in your mind," she said, with the barest hint of an eye-roll. "Listen, when you have this beautiful glass, someone needs to put it on the appropriate shelf for it to be seen. What would the world be without it? And someone would need to know how to take care of it.

Not everyone can. It's the way that *you* know how to take care of others! People feel safe in your kindness.

"There's a reason for both the glass itself and the person who takes care of it," she said. "It supplies something for both. To say that the glass should not exist or should make itself stronger is foolish thinking. But for the glass to feel safe with the appropriate person is a skill. And metaphorically, you can do it for yourself by taking good care of glass. In fact, I'm being told you'll have quite a collection of it, eventually. Do you know *The Glass Menagerie?*" she asked.

"Funny, I was just thinking of that." I didn't say that what I was thinking was that Laura, the character in that Tennessee Williams play who collected glass, was pretty much Froot Loops. Still, I had to admit, Patricia was right. In pursuing and even nurturing men who weren't nurturing *me*, I wasn't taking care of myself.

"And for you, taking good care of yourself means getting your footing on the ground . . . by being published and gaining a reputation."

Well, I liked the sound of *that*!

"And the outcome will be very secure, safe things in the world." She paused. "Now, have you ever watched how glass is *made*?"

I said that I had. When I was young, there'd been a glassblowing shop at the brand-spanking-new Staten Island mall, to which I always gravitated. There, several hirsute young men had used a blowpipe to turn molten glass the consistency of honey into delicate figurines in a rainbow of colors. I'd found it magical.

"A friend of mine's a glassblower, and actually, it's a very masculine form. It's the opposite of what you'd think, given what glass is like. It's like working with steel; it takes tremendous strength. So to think that saying someone is fragile means they're not *strong* . . . No. Not at all."

I smiled, somewhat mollified. If I was going to be glassware, at least I could be a beer stein rather than a brandy snifter. I supposed I could live with that.

Patricia's very powerful, insistent words about glass and glassblow-ing that day stayed with me. Metaphorical as they were—to some extent—they would haunt me decades later, when I'd meet a glass-blower whose particular brand of magic would, for better or worse, change my life.

✳

PATRICIA SPOKE, with astonishing detail and accuracy, about many other things that day, including my mother's high blood pressure and kidney issues, and my father's tendency toward depression and reclu-siveness. Then she asked me for questions.

Of course, I wanted to know about Leo. She asked only for his name and date of birth. Her sense was that Leo's anger and inner tur-moil were keeping him from fully appreciating who I was. It was good, she said, that I was having this experience. If I could think of it as a moment, I could enjoy and appreciate what we two shared simply for what it was.

"I have this strong feeling of wanting to *help* him. Or *save* him," I said.

"When you have the feeling of wanting to *save* someone, know that it's not about them. It's about saving yourself. If you work out your own life, then when it comes to meeting a man, it's not about that. And think of it this way: If you attempt to save someone, you're denying them the experience of saving themselves."

I let that sink in. That I might be *hurting*, when I was so sure I'd been *helping*—I'd never thought of it like that. But it made immediate sense, and was definitely something I needed to hear.

"So no need to end it with Leo," Patricia went on. "You two *have* helped one another. Is this love? Yes. But is this *divine* love? No. I would wish more for you in terms of that."

I knew it was true, though it was still hard to hear it.

"The story will be over when it's over. And you two will always be friends."

There was comfort in that, but even so, I felt a sliver of sadness embedding itself in my heart.

"Why have I had such a hard time with love, Patricia?" I asked, tearing up a little.

"There are a number of reasons," she said. "There's such a longing in you for male protection and care. But the male figure, in your psyche, is represented in a convoluted way. For you, that male figure, that strength, did not happen." She explained that because I'd not had that in my father—*true!*—I had to create it in myself. "Therefore, *you're* the one who's always trying to protect *them*—the men."

Oh. My. God. *More dots connected!* "But what can I do about it now?"

"You can say, 'Well, that was the picture with my father. But it doesn't have to be that way with men.' And listen well on this: You're so busy wondering what's *wrong* with you, you're not seeing what's *right* with you. Also, they're telling me"—she cocked her head again— "you're too shy. It's as if, with a man, energetically, it's too much for you. Actually, though, I would say that *most men would be afraid of you*, because they can get lost in that imagination, and in that sensual aspect of you."

Well, that would explain a lot.

She assured me that I'd be meeting many men, and eventually have a partner—but now it was all about *experiencing*—experiencing the joy of being alive.

As our session drew to a close, Patricia pulled a tarot card. "The Six of Pentacles is someone being generous, and someone *receiving* that generosity," she said. "And after a while, the roles—who's being generous and who's receiving—are reversed. That's you and me."

After thanking Patricia and hugging her goodbye—feeling as if I'd known her for years, rather than just a few hours—I rode the elevator back to the ground floor. I found myself wondering about that last statement of her reading. How might I become the generous one in relation to her? I couldn't imagine.

As I walked back through the lobby, still processing the new insights, the incredible "hits," and all that Patricia had said, I looked up at the cloud mural. There were the peeling plaster and the misplaced fixtures, just as she'd said. Caught up earlier in the wonder of the clouds, I hadn't even noticed them.

Had the fact that I'd told Patricia I liked the cloud mural when we'd first met tipped her off to my lack of "alarms," as she put it? The questioning, skeptical part of me realized that this might have been so. And yet Patricia had been so shockingly accurate about so many things. Nothing I'd told her could have tipped her off to my father's depression and reclusiveness, for example, or my mother's specific health concerns. Nor to that image of the worm!

As I stepped onto the sidewalk again, I felt an odd sensation. The world as I'd known it up till meeting Patricia seemed to have expanded, and shifted. Everything I was experiencing with my five senses suddenly felt more like a huge theatrical set than like finite reality. As if there was something *behind* it; *beyond* it. Something more enduring, and though invisible to my eye, somehow more real.

And I wanted to know what it was.

I HAD A SECOND READING with Patricia about a year later. By that point, several things she'd "seen" had come to pass. I'd started working as a writer for kids in a brand-new medium that involved a screen, just as she'd predicted—a little thing called the "World Wide Web." It wasn't as if I'd been looking for a job that fit her vision; I'd answered an ad in the *New York Times* for a writer for the kids/educational department of a new media venture that didn't include the word *Internet*— a medium still in its infancy, which I'd actually never experienced.

The goal of the department was to create just what she'd described: an online space of "collective imagination" in which kids could play, create, and share. Writing and editing for children's online media, to my surprise, became the way I made my living—and a very good, very enjoyable one, at that—for more than ten years.

This time, I wanted to ask Patricia about her abilities and process. I was curious if she was able to read other people in my life as well as she'd read Leo, so I inquired about several friends, giving only their names. With one, a lawyer, she pinpointed his kind, loving nature and ability to rifle through data, zeroing in on pertinent facts. She also *smelled wood* in connection to him, suggesting I ask him about it. I did, and was completely surprised to learn that he'd done a lot of wood-working and had actually considered becoming a cabinetmaker. With another, an art student who painted, Patricia picked up on her incredible sense of color. She said that my friend needed to work larger, and that she'd eventually teach college, both of which came to pass.

In the spirit of full disclosure, I must admit that Patricia was not infallible in her predictions. For example, she saw that I'd win a lawsuit involving my apartment, which I did—though I later lost it on an appeal. She also saw me married and raising kids, which, as of this writing at least, hasn't happened. Then again, she'd said that predicting wasn't really her gift. Still, when it came to people's abilities and talents, she was always spot on.

Finally, I asked her how she received her intuitive information. As much as I loved hearing the insights and advice that Patricia delivered, I was even more curious to learn how she did what she did.

"My process starts when I get a client's name," she said. "I immediately begin to get a sense of the person. Each day, I get a bigger view of their soul, going deeper and deeper, from layer to layer." Often, she explained, this came as a symbolic picture. For instance, she'd gotten an image of me as a child, putting flowers on my own grave—which, she said, meant an ending of one phase of my life and the beginning of another. She would note all of this information as she received it, on index cards.

"And when you seem to be listening and you say, 'Thank you,' is it actually a voice, or voices, that you hear?"

She nodded. "It happens in sound, and it's very direct, very fast."

"Do you know where it's coming from?"

"Yes, and that's the nice part of being psychic," she said. "You get to see where it's all coming from." She paused, then continued in her whispery, almost *silvery* voice. "I don't normally talk about this to my clients but I'll talk about it to you, because you're going to be writing about people who do what I do, and what are called 'the invisible realms.' Guardian angels, ghosts. These kinds of heavenly subjects and enlightened feelings . . . to help people realize there's much more going on than what meets the eye.

"You are entering the period of what's called 'puberty of the soul,' a period of spiritual guidance," she continued. "You're taking on a new family . . . of different realms. I see them, and other people like me do too. There truly is a realm of beings who are helping you constantly. During this time, you'll get the sense that everything's being taken care of. Also, there's going to be so much *synchronicity* going on, where you think of something"—she snapped her fingers—"and then it's there, you're going to realize that there's something else going on. It's all about the invisible world and becoming conscious of it."

Intrigued and delighted as I was to hear her words, and despite all that I'd experienced, a part of me remained slightly incredulous. An invisible realm of beings helping me constantly? Did such things really exist? Still, I'd gotten some very useful advice, and helpful explanations now, from a woman who to all appearances spoke to invisible *beings* . . .

I wanted to believe her words, to believe that the world I knew was only a small piece of a far larger reality, as I'd sensed back in my childhood. But could I really? Was I nuttier than a jar of Skippy to even consider that the invisible world she spoke of was real? Reader, I didn't know.

✳

I HAD MORE READINGS with Patricia over the years, and many of my friends did too. They told their friends, and *they* told *their* friends . . . *and so on, and so on, and so on*, to quote an Eighties shampoo commercial that has obviously embedded itself in my brain. This, I came to feel, was part of what Patricia had seen as *my* becoming the one who was generous to *her*.

Many of these friends, to my great satisfaction, reported being deeply, even profoundly affected by what she had to say. One of these was Griffin. Another friend from my theater days—when he'd been studying lighting and sound—Griffin, a highly intelligent, self-described "science-and-technology-oriented rationalist," was one of the most skeptical people I knew about things spiritual or New Age. All that changed, however, when after hearing about Patricia, he uncharacteristically decided to have a reading with her himself. Though he had shared that experience with me at the time, years later, while visiting him in his native Virginia, where he'd eventually returned to live, I asked him about it again.

"I went into my first reading with Patricia very skeptical," he said, as we sat eating Chinese noodle soup on the small but lovely outdoor patio of a local eatery, with a stunning view of the nearby mountains. "I was expecting a goofy psychic who'd prompt me and read facial expressions. Or a garden-variety medium, who'd maybe tune in some dull dead people. When I was younger, I'd actually had some very odd experiences I didn't know how to define, and had tried to ignore. Later, I learned they were usually known as *out-of-body experiences* and *lucid dreaming*—being conscious in the dream state. But I'd never talked to anyone about them. I'd also never talked to anyone—other than a therapist—about the bizarre, nuthouse environment I'd grown up in.

I was this weak, sickly child of alcoholic parents, one of them mentally ill."

He paused. "In trying to make that sickly child into a functioning, 'normal' adult, I spent years toughening myself up physically, forcing myself to do what I thought you were *supposed* to do—getting out, being social, all that. I had a job that involved a lot of human-contact-heavy work. I was good at it, but inside I felt exhausted. I was constantly trying to push down my feelings and build a sort of armor, to protect myself from the onslaught of other people's . . . what you might call *vibrations*. On top of it all, I felt like it was my own fault I was so disappointed with my life, like I just wasn't trying hard enough."

I remembered him well in those days. It was after he'd moved back to the South, but we'd stayed in close touch. Griffin was gay; I'd had a crush on him when we first met, before he came out. Once he had, he was even less successful than I in finding love. He'd struggled with depression, chronic illnesses, and addictions as well.

"The only thing that kept me going was spending as much of my time as possible alone and in nature, living a very solitary life."

"And that was about the time you first saw Patricia?" I asked, sipping my iced tea.

"Yes. She started off with, 'They had a lot to say about you,' and went on for a half hour straight, no fishing for clues at all. I said nothing; I was trying to be as inscrutable as possible." He smiled sheepishly. "But my purposeful silence just kind of morphed into this feeling of *I can't even react, because I am so deeply dumbfounded.*"

Griffin related how Patricia had told him that he'd come into this life with a very harsh image of the world, the result of many violent, brutal past lives. Because of this, he had created and attracted circumstances that would fit that image of the world. He had nothing left to do here; he'd done it all, in literally thousands of lives. Moreover, it was almost painful for him to be around other people, as there weren't many "tuned" like him.

"She said that most people had a life task that involved 'learning in relationship with others,' but that I'd done all of that already."

His purpose in this life, she told Griffin, was *inward*: He needed to create a safe, quiet place and learn to be alone to do the inner work he was here to do.

"To have this stranger relay this deeply true, *non*trivial information about my thoughts and feelings . . . well, it got my attention," he said. "Little by little, it became clear that her 'sources' were right. But you know, *they* don't have Earth bodies. *They* don't have to pay rent . . . or deal with being lonely, or horny . . . or try to act normal to get along in the world."

I chuckled. "So," I asked, "where are you now?"

"I guess I'd say I'm on a '*journey*,' to use that very clichéd term." He smiled, taking the final swig from his bottle of alcohol-free beer. "One that's pretty solitary. Not being religious and having pretty much zero tolerance for New Age hooey, there aren't any churches, or groups, or gurus to lean on." He paused. "I *have* had what you might call *answers from within*. Found things I needed to find at the right times. I left the big-city rat race for a simpler, less ambitious life. One that leaves me time and energy to pursue"—he squinted into the half-set sun's softening rays—"for lack of a better word, *spiritual* exploration."

I looked at Griffin. Outwardly, he'd barely changed an iota from the guy I'd met more than twenty-five years before. His thick, dirty-blond hair was a bit grayer. He'd developed a few wrinkles around his bright, hazel eyes. Yet I'd witnessed such dramatic inner changes in him. As he'd avidly studied in the realms of the metaphysical, this once-staunch skeptic became my go-to guy, as I, too, arrived at the place where I embarked on my own explorations.

✳

ABOUT TEN YEARS after I met Patricia, I heard the alarming news that she had cancer. She faced it bravely, and we, her friends, rejoiced when it went into remission. Patricia, who had long wanted children but been unable to have them, eventually adopted two infants from Africa, as a single mother . . . which made it all the more tragic when she became ill again. She passed away, leaving her young son and daughter in the loving care of some relations who would raise them as their own.

I felt for Patricia, for the pain she must have experienced upon realizing that she would leave her children behind. And I mourned the loss of this remarkable woman, who had opened up my mind so persuasively to the idea of an invisible world of divine wisdom, guidance, and love, and taught me that it was not only something to which I had access, but *to which I was always connected*. Patricia brought home to me the importance of trusting my own feelings, my own psychic sense—though I might not have been ready to call it that at the time. She taught me to value my own "essential nature"—the combination of qualities that made me uniquely who I was, and which I'd been given to help me on my own particular life path.

I wondered where she'd gone and whether she'd joined those beings she spoke to; whether she now knew all that they knew. I wondered if she was still helping others, wherever she was now.

Little did I know that, not so very many years later, I would find a way to speak to Patricia again, to ask my questions and hear her answers for myself.

2

ADVENTURES WITH

A MEDIUM

✳ OR ✳

"Papa, Can You Hear Me?"

I WAS TELLING MY GOOD FRIEND FRANKIE, A COMEDY WRITER and one of the most ardent skeptics I knew, a story I'd heard from a mutual friend. This friend worked at a publishing house that was putting out a book by Allison DuBois, the real-life medium on whom the TV show *Medium* had been based. Our friend told me that when his staff had met Ms. DuBois in their conference room one day, she'd tossed off some impromptu readings about their dead loved ones that were shockingly on target. It had, he told me, quickly transformed his own firmly skeptical point of view about mediumship and the afterlife.

As I finished, Frankie smiled. "I'd love to see this Allison person try one of those 'readings' on me. I know faking when I see it. I've been going to bed with women for twenty-three years."

LOL, Frankie. And I do take his point. Still, of those who claim that all psychics and mediums are charlatans and hucksters, I would ask this: What if a *friend* appeared to have these abilities—someone who didn't ask for money? What if you witnessed her abilities over and over? Would you believe in them then?

When I was in my late thirties, I joined a writing group that met in the stylish Battery Park City home of Paul and his wife, Katarina. Paul, a charismatic man with a thatch of jet-black hair and a disarming smile, was a criminal lawyer who, like most lawyers I knew, harbored a yen to be a screenplay writer. Katarina, a petite woman with a mane of long blond curls, wasn't a writer, but was intelligent and fun, so no one minded her chiming in about our work.

One night, I was hanging out in their living room, enjoying wine and cheese on their camel-colored sectional couch. Katarina wasn't her usual upbeat self, so I asked her about that.

"I just need a change," she said, sighing. Katarina, born in Poland, had done very well as a retail buyer, but had left that career to help with Paul's practice. "Paul has his law and his writing. I wish I had something that would satisfy me like that."

I told her I'd recently had several readings with a wonderful psychic named Patricia Masters. "Her specialty is helping people learn their purpose in this lifetime . . . Why they're here."

Katarina immediately lit up. "You've got to give me her number!"

Soon, she phoned to let me know that she'd booked a reading with Patricia. I asked her to call me afterward and tell me all about it. But a few weeks passed with no word. When she finally called again, her tone was strained. "It's hard to talk about," she said. "She started off telling me all this stuff about Paul." She related how Patricia, with no input from Katarina, had described a specific situation involving Paul's father, giving details that were right on the mark. Patricia had gone on to talk about Paul's writing, and some personal struggles in his past— again, very specific and accurate stuff.

Finally, Katarina related, Patricia's focus had shifted. "You must be wondering why I'm talking so much about your husband," she said, "when *you're* the one who's here. I wanted to show you that I know what I'm doing, so you'll believe what I'm about to tell you. You've come to see me as a psychic, but the truth is, *you're* a psychic too. Your gift is actually more powerful than mine."

I drew in a breath, astonished.

According to Patricia, Katarina wasn't just highly psychic, she was also a medium; she could contact people who had died, or, as Patricia put it, who had passed to the "Other Side." All mediums were psychic, she explained, though not all psychics were good mediums. But Katarina was both. And this was truly her life's purpose. The reason she hadn't been fully aware of it until now was that she hadn't been ready. And though it might seem scary at first, when Katarina saw how much comfort her gift could bring to those who'd lost loved ones, she'd find it extremely fulfilling. It was what she was here to do.

I was stunned. I was elated! And, Reader, I was a wee bit envious, too. Could it be true? Katarina, my very normal-seeming friend, highly psychic . . . and a *medium?*

"Of course, it was shocking," Katarina said. "But it was like hearing something a part of me always knew." Afterward, she said, she'd called her mother in Poland, from whom she was somewhat estranged. Her mother wasn't surprised; she reminded Katarina how, as a child, she'd dreamed several times of a relative's death just before it happened.

After delivering this potentially life-changing news, Patricia had proposed a test: She gave Katarina a man's name and asked her to see what she could pick up. As Katarina described it to me now, it was as if a male presence had become superimposed on her own body. She sensed that he was African American. And in his arms, she could feel tremendous strength.

As Katarina had related all of this, Patricia seemed visibly stirred.

"What's he saying? Are you getting words?" Patricia asked.

"Yes," Katarina told her. "But they don't make sense. He's saying . . . '*I want to lift you up.*'"

As she'd said it, Katarina related, tears had filled Patricia's eyes. This man had apparently been a dear friend of Patricia's, a fellow dancer, and yes, African American. The day of the reading had been the anniversary of his death, and he'd been very much on Patricia's

mind. Oh, yes—and whenever he would see Patricia, he had a particular greeting: He would take her in his arms and lift her up.

I got actual chills hearing that last part. Later, I checked with Maurice. He'd known this man from dance class too, and confirmed everything Patricia had said.

A short silence ensued. Frankly, I was at a loss for words, despite
my excitement at Katarina's news. I mean, what did one say upon
learning a friend could talk to dead people? "*So . . .*" I managed finally.
"*Now* what are you going to do?"

"Well, it was *completely exhausting*," Katarina said. She wasn't eager
to do it again. Moreover, she didn't like the idea of taking money for
readings, or reading for strangers at all. It was a lot of responsibility.
And what if she got everything wrong?

She and Patricia were supposed to talk again soon. "And she gave
me the name of an ex-boyfriend of hers who died," Katarina said.
"Everyone thought it was a suicide, but *she* thinks it was an accident.
She wants me to contact him and find out." She faltered a bit as she
said it, as if she really wasn't sure she was up to the task. "She also
said I should start doing readings"—she paused—"beginning with *you*,
because I'd be comfortable with you."

Yes!!!! I did a mental fist pump. I'd never had a medium reading,
though I had many loved ones who'd died, whom I sorely missed.
Would Katarina actually be able to do this—to put me in touch with
them? I couldn't wait to try.

I CALLED KATARINA the following week, curious about her "assignment" from Patricia. She said that indeed, she'd been having a recurring vision of a man. She could see his hair clearly; his face, less so.
This was a peculiarity of her gift, at least at first: She would see the
hair of the dead person in question, and sometimes the hands, but the

face would remain out of focus. Day by day, though, the man's face had grown clearer. Soon, she could see his clothing, too—a plaid shirt and corduroy pants. It was odd, she said; he was actually *pointing out* the pants. He affirmed that his death had in fact been accidental, and that he was helping addicts now who'd also "crossed over."

When Katarina had described the ex-boyfriend's appearance to Patricia, she'd verified it all. When Katarina had mentioned the corduroy pants, Patricia had flipped. Apparently, this man had worn *nothing but corduroy* when it came to pants, a subject of amusement to all his friends.

After Katarina had finished, Patricia showed her a photo. Now it was *Katarina's* turn to flip. It was the very man she'd seen in her mind's eye.

Again, though, rather than sounding pleased by this remarkable feat she'd accomplished, Katarina sounded almost perturbed. But I wasn't going to let that stop me. "So, remember, Patricia said you should do a reading for me?" I none-too-gingerly prompted.

She hesitated, but "OK," she finally said.

On the day we'd selected the following week, Katarina's manner was almost embarrassed as she settled into my threadbare armchair. With a notebook and pen—self-conscious as she was about it, Katarina had preferred I not record the session—I sat across from her on my small, mauve-colored loveseat.

"I'd like to start with my friend Everett," I said. A charming, highly talented, and handsome young art student when we'd met—like Maurice, he was an usher at the Public Theater where we all worked—Everett had also adored music and dancing. I had a stack of mix tapes he'd made me: Joni Mitchell, Chet Baker, Everything but the Girl. A total romantic, Everett had always been in love with love, constantly regaling me with stories of the latest object of his affections, and there were many—that is, until he met Jack, fell in love for real, and moved in with him.

Tragically, Everett was stricken with AIDS soon after, in the very early days of the epidemic. As Jack had nursed him through his brief, horrific illness, Everett, I felt, had learned what love really was.

Katarina knew nothing about Everett; he'd died years before I met her, and I'd never spoken of him to her. Now I told her nothing but his name. It took her some time. She had told me that when she got information, it was "like catching a glimpse of something out of the corner of her eye"; if she tried too hard to see it, it would elude her.

"I'm getting something in the blood," she finally said.

That made sense.

"It's hard to connect with him. Did you know he played the piano?" she asked. "He's playing it over there."

"No," I admitted. If Everett had played, I hadn't been aware of it. Most New Yorkers don't have room for pianos; Everett was from Michigan, so perhaps he'd played growing up. He *had* loved music, though, I said.

"He's telling me he's writing a book," she said.

"About what?" I asked.

"Love," she said, quickly and easily this time.

I felt a little *ping* in my heart hearing it. It rang so true to who he'd been.

Katarina seemed to be losing the connection, and was exhausted, so we took a break. Then I asked her about another friend, G.G., giving nothing but the initials my friend had always used.

G.G. had been a brilliant young woman. She, my dear friend David, and I were three New York City fish-out-of-water at UVA. I'd met David first—he played in the school's orchestra with G.G. and had introduced the two of us. G.G. could be blunt, argumentative, and headstrong, but she had a soft side too and was often sweet, and funny. I'd been shocked and terribly saddened some years before to learn that she'd been fatally hit by a truck one snowy day, while crossing a Manhattan street.

"She's really angry that she died," Katarina said. "She had so much more she wanted to do, and she's pissed off."

I was struck by the description; it was, I thought, exactly how G.G.—the human part of her, at least—would feel. And while it made me laugh a little—the phrase "pissed off" just fit!—my heart went out to her too.

Katarina picked up a few other images I couldn't verify, and seemed frustrated. Apparently, as with Everett, she had to struggle to pull in G.G., and the information was hazy.

It seemed, however, that someone else was very determined to come through. "I keep getting an older woman: white hair, in a bun. She has a special connection to you."

I told her I'd known only one woman, ever, with white hair in a bun: my paternal grandmother, named Anne too. She'd died when I was five.

Katarina seemed pleased. "She has an accent. It sounds German," she said.

"Yes!" My grandmother, born in Germany, had a thick accent. I doubted Katarina could have gleaned that from my surname. Even if she *had* been guessing, it would have been a leap to assume that my grandmother had been born abroad; my maternal grandmother, for example, whose family was of Sicilian descent, had been born in Pittsburgh.

"Can you tell what she died of?"

"Stomach cancer," Katarina said.

Bingo! On the first try! I was elated for her, and told her so.

"She's saying she wants you to find a good man, and she's going to help. She's telling me she's one of your guides," she said.

Oh my gosh! I was truly touched. I hadn't known Grandma Anne well. My memories of her were more from photos I'd seen since childhood than from actual experiences. But I loved the idea that she wanted to help with my very earthly man problems from wherever she now was—*if* she still was. Because again, I had to wonder: Was this really coming from my grandmother? Or could Katarina be picking it all up from *me*?

Impressed with Katarina's reading, nonetheless, I suggested she read for my writer friend Rick. Rick and Katarina knew each other a little, but she certainly knew no personal details about his life.

"She told me my Irish grandmother was acting as a guardian angel for my family," Rick said afterward. "I thought it was the other grandmother at first, but she corrected me: 'She says she's from the *green country*.' She also accurately described a dress my Irish grandmother wore. She said most people have a guardian angel or two, but I have a lot of them. We were in my empty apartment, and she said, 'This room is *full* of people.'"

The most dramatic reading Katarina did, though, was for my now ex-boyfriend Leo. He and I had settled into a friendship—just as Patricia had said. Patricia had picked up in that first reading that Leo had a lot of anger. I'd always felt this was due to his relationship with his father, and the fact that he'd never told Leo that he loved him. I didn't share this with Katarina, though, and she and Leo had never met.

Katarina said that Leo's father was present days before the reading, vividly popping into her head. Leo later told me that Katarina had described his father's cancer; what he'd been wearing when he died; and a watch he'd given Leo. She said his father was sorry for how he'd behaved, and wanted to tell Leo he loved him. The effect of this on him was profound.

Had Leo's father known how important it was for his son to hear this? Was that why he'd been so eager to come through? Or had Leo's father needed to do this for his own soul's progress? Was it like some kind of big twelve-step meeting on the Other Side, where one needed to make amends?

"Now I can see why I have this ability. I see the need for it," Katarina said.

Throughout the next year or so, I excitedly watched my friend develop her gift. She was reluctant to talk much about it, so I mentally muzzled myself. It wasn't easy. Paul told me Katarina was proving to have a varied set of psychic skills. She was able to replicate drawings he did while he was seated in one room, and she in another. When he took in their mail each day, he'd keep it hidden while she tried to "see" it—a phenomenon called "remote viewing." Again, she was very accurate. "She predicts the plays before they happen when we watch football on TV," he proudly said.

After knowing Katarina and Paul for a while, I invited them to join an investment club that Maurice had started. Katarina, who'd known little about stock trading, had taken a real shine to it. Not surprising to me, she was very good at picking stocks. Soon, she'd set out day-trading on her own, doing remarkably well. At tax time, she confessed that she'd made more money trading that year than Paul had as a lawyer!

Not long after that, I heard that Katarina and Paul were giving up their Battery Park City apartment, mere blocks from Ground Zero, and moving elsewhere in Manhattan—and later, to Florida—shortly before September 11, 2001. Looking back, I couldn't help but feel that Katarina's gift had played a major part in their decision to get the hell out of Dodge precisely when they had.

After their move to Florida, Katarina and I kept in touch. I phoned her one day, stretched out on my futon bed, to tell her about Ammon, a divorcé with whom I'd been "fixed up" by a mutual friend. An Egyptian civil engineer who wrote poetry, Ammon had three young daughters. When we spoke by phone, he made me laugh, always key to engaging my heart. After two lovely dates, he told me he was smitten, and I was edging on smitten myself. On our third date, he drove me to his town in Connecticut, took me to a picturesque lake, then cooked me a delicious shrimp scampi dinner, which we washed down with champagne before a roaring fire on his massive, luxurious couch.

As a divorcé, I thought, Ammon offered proof that he could commit—more than I could say about most of the men with whom I'd tangled. (Then again, he *had* gotten divorced, Reader, so perhaps my logic was a wee bit askew.)

As I started to tell Katarina all this, though, she interrupted me. "Anne, I can *see* you! You're wearing something around your neck. It's green and round, with a hole in it, like a doughnut!"

The hairs on my arms actually went up. I was wearing a pendant made of sea-foam-green turquoise, in precisely that shape. I hadn't ever worn it in front of Katarina; it was a fairly recent street-fair buy, and I hadn't seen her for more than a year.

"I'm getting some stuff about your date, too," she said. I hadn't told her anything thus far except that we'd gone out three times, and that it was going very well.

"I'm not sure of the name," Katarina began. "But I'm getting a letter *T*."

Well, his last name did begin with a *T*.

"What about his first name?" I asked.

She was stymied. "Maybe an *M*?"

There *was* a prominent *M* sound in his first name, of course, though it didn't *begin* with one. "Anything else?" I asked.

"I'm seeing that you went out of the city," she said.

True, and highly unusual for me on a date. I was impressed.

"You went to another state."

"Yes."

"And you went to a body of water."

"Yes!"

"He cooked for you. And, wait . . . He used a lot of olive oil. I'm seeing a pan that's really *swimming* in it."

Ammon's garlicky shrimp scampi *had* been swimming in olive oil. "*Yes and yes!*" I congratulated her effusively. Truly, I couldn't have been more excited if I'd done it myself.

Katarina, though pleased to have performed so well, seemed a bit freaked out. *I*, on the other hand, was off and running. I didn't just want to hear about a shrimp dinner; I wanted to know if Ammon was "the one"—or at least someone with whom I might manage to have more than a few dates.

A quick catch-up for you, Reader: It had been several years now since my first reading with Patricia, and she'd been right about my meeting a lot of men. Most of them had rapidly come and gone, but there was one who'd lasted a while, a cute, witty animator named Marty, whom I'd met doing volunteer work. He had asked a mutual friend for my number, and phoned me out of the blue for a date, which was a first for me, and I gave him credit for his *chutzpah*, as we New Yorkers say. Marty and I had dated happily for several months—I'd even met several members of his family—before he did a sudden and complete about-face, making it clear that he was through. "I'm sorry. I just went cold," he said.

I was crushed. Though I hadn't been in love with Marty, I'd enjoyed my time with him immensely. Whereas with Leo, things were always somewhat "fraught," due to his depressive nature and lack of self-esteem, with Marty it felt like "normal," light-hearted dating—what I'd imagined "normal" people did, but had never quite attained myself.

I should have realized that his extremely recent breakup with his live-in girlfriend was a red flag; that there was bound to be a rebound woman; and that the rebound woman would be *me*. But I never thought it through. Nor would it likely have stopped me if I had.

All of this had left me with more of a heartfelt yearning than ever to experience a real, long-term relationship. Given that I'd now developed some rapidly growing feelings for him, I was hoping that someone was Ammon.

"What do you see happening with us?" I asked.

Katarina stammered a bit, finally saying she thought it would "work out."

Looking back, I wondered if she hadn't wanted to tell me what she'd really seen. Because after a few more fantastic dates—including a hugely romantic birthday dinner he'd surprised me with at an elegant and historic Village restaurant—things had abruptly changed course. He told me that he needed to find someone younger, because he wanted more kids; that though I was still of child-bearing age, the odds of my conceiving were not good. And that even if I did manage to conceive, the odds of birth defects at my age were extremely high. Then he definitively broke things off.

"You said you thought it would 'work out' with us," I reminded Katarina, my disappointment, hurt, and anger at Ammon coolly lacing my voice, when next we spoke. Poor Katarina; if she *had* seen the true outcome for Ammon and me, back when I was full of hope and excitement, it would have been very hard for her to say it.

A lot of us envy those who are psychic, never thinking about the difficulty in having to tell people things that they might not want to hear, or their own anxiety over possibly being wrong about it. Katarina had said it herself: It was a lot of responsibility.

Around this time, she told me she'd been persuaded to do a reading for some clients of Patricia's who'd lost a family member. Though she'd gotten some things right, she'd gotten other things wrong, and it had left her feeling bad.

Soon, I could see that Katarina was rejecting her "calling." But that didn't stop me from trying. I'd slip in a question or two when we spoke, but she'd say she couldn't tell, or change the subject. I kept hoping she'd change her mind. Her gift was so rare; it seemed a crime not to embrace it. But I felt her pulling away, and could do nothing to stop it.

I finally asked Paul about it, when he picked up the phone one day and told me she wasn't in. "She's afraid if she keeps trying to develop it, it's going to take over her life. She doesn't want that to happen."

Well, disappointed as I was, and hurt on a certain level too, I could understand that. And I had to respect it.

I saw Patricia a few months later for a reading, and asked her about it. "She's one of the best mediums I've met," she admitted, "but it's too overwhelming; her system can't take it. Also, she wants to please the person she's reading for. She shouldn't think that way, but it's how she feels."

It felt like an unbearable tease to know someone who had such an astonishing ability, yet seemed to wish she'd never become aware of it at all. Then again, *I* had now become aware of all those downsides to her gift. Much as I might envy it, I had no idea how it would feel to have it myself.

THERE WAS ONE notable deviation from Katarina's increasing disinterest in using her gift, and I'm forever grateful to her for it. It happened when I lost my father.

My father, Albert, or "Bud," as we called him, was a brainy, brilliant man. A talented writer—as a young man, he'd sold two poems to *The New Yorker*—he'd worked as an editor and director of communications for a large accounting firm through midlife. At that point, he'd started a business, dealing in rare books. The house I grew up in was overrun by books—and magazines, too. I got wonderful books every birthday and Christmas, lovingly and humorously inscribed in my father's neat, artistic print, and I know that my desire to write was born from the love of reading that he passed on to me.

My father wasn't like most fathers I knew or saw on TV. He was a real gourmet and a terrific cook; a lover not just of literature, but of movies, music, and art. He professed no belief in God or the afterlife, and my fascination with the "paranormal" wasn't something we shared. He often teased my mother and me for our avid interest in watching medium John Edward when his TV show, *Crossing Over*, debuted, calling us "true believers" with an indulgent chuckle.

My father could be sweet, and I never questioned that he loved me—but he had his demons, and they were fierce. He struggled with anger and depression to the point of being emotionally absent as I grew older. Even in my childhood years, he often drank too much. I remember his fits of rage; more than once, I ran from the dinner table up to my room in tears. But I remember his sweet side too—and the apologetic "morning after" notes he'd leave, telling me that he was sorry, and that he'd try to do better.

And in some ways he did. He eventually quit drinking and worked around the clock as a rare book dealer, but struggled with heavy debt. By the time I met Katarina, he'd become seriously reclusive, rarely going out of the house he shared with my mother. There, surrounded by his piles of collectible books, bins of vintage movie posters, and shelves displaying old tin toys, he argued with the political pundits on TV and cooked up gourmet treats like chicken livers for their shih tzu, Chippy, who, he once told me only half jokingly, he considered his only real friend.

Then, at the age of seventy-four, my father was diagnosed with lung cancer. He was treated at a Manhattan hospital, and I helped alongside my mother and sister as he braved his way through chemo and radiation. Oddly, this time was something of a blessing for me. Though I was close in some ways with my father, I often felt his emotional detachment. While he would occasionally ask about my work or my writing, and more often recommended books and movies he thought I'd like, the fact that he never asked what was going on with me personally—with men, dating, and the trouble I perpetually had with both—hurt. His seeming lack of concern about that had bothered me my whole life. During this period, I finally told him so.

It was hard to express it to him, but I wasn't sure how much time we'd have, and I didn't want to carry around that hurt for the rest of my life. He listened. And to my surprise, he actually did change. He pointedly began to ask me about the men I was meeting, and to *comment* on them too—not always in the way that I hoped! *"Just walk away!"* I remember him saying, in a tone of utter disgust, as he reclined on my futon after one of his treatment sessions, upon hearing me tell my mother about the bizarre, dysfunctional behavior of the latest guy on whom I'd set my sights. *Annie,* I thought, *be careful what you wish for.* Still, he was arguably right in his advice, and his sincere effort to do what I'd asked touched me.

Eventually, his treatment, which culminated in surgery, was pronounced a success, and he was sent home to recover. We could barely believe the good news. He'd lost much of his sense of taste prior to the surgery, a common side effect, I learned, of radiation. Weeks after, he still barely ate. I kept running platefuls of goodies up the stairs and into his bedroom on Thanksgiving—the ultimate holiday for a foodie like my dad, who'd always done the cooking, and so impressively!—trying to tempt him to try just a little. Sadly, he couldn't.

A few days later, he collapsed on the bathroom floor. My mother and sister, the only ones home at the time, called 911, and the EMT guys came and shocked him with those paddles I've seen only in TV dramas. But they couldn't bring him back.

The days seemed to blur, as my family and I collectively passed from our short-lived elation to shock and finally to grief. Though my father hadn't been an easy person to live with, we'd loved him a lot. My insomnia, which had long since improved, returned in full force, and my grief seemed to be a one-way road to depressing thoughts of all kinds. It was as if, in the wake of his death, I'd realized how fleeting life could be and, fearing I might never attain love, happiness, or success with my writing, I was grieving, in a way, for myself.

Surreal as it was to lose a parent, time eventually marched along again in a shockingly normal fashion. Soon it was nearly Christmas. I loved the holiday, but knew it would be tough to get through it this year. My father had always spent a day or two food-shopping, and another day or two preparing the sumptuous meal. This year, my sister and I were pooling our efforts for the dinner—definitely a modest affair—and I hoped my family could summon up a modicum of cheer, despite our collective sadness.

To that end, I'd gone to a Soho gardening store, Smith & Hawken, looking for presents. I was even shorter on money than usual, as I'd taken time off from work to accompany my parents to my dad's appointments and sessions. I knew I shouldn't be racking up debt on gifts, but I wanted to buy something for my mother. She was so sad. I wanted to get her something special, beautiful . . . something that might make her happy whenever she looked at it, and, if only for a moment, make her see life as something that wasn't just shitty and unfair.

Patricia Masters had once told me that when I was depressed, I should seek out beauty: that it would always buoy my spirits. And she'd been right. As I wandered around that day, taking in the delicate pink of potted orchids and the snowy whiteness of narcissus plants, I felt the dark clouds lift. Then my eyes lit on some hanging crystal stars. They were meant to be suspended on evergreen boughs, but my mother, an artist with a love of color, was in the habit of hanging all kinds of things around the house—strings of lights, colorful beads, blown-out Easter eggs we'd painted as kids, slices of dried, preserved oranges—and I knew she'd add these enchanting little stars to the ongoing still life that was the backdrop to her life.

As I headed to the counter to pay for the crystals, I noticed a salmon-red amaryllis in radiant bloom perched on a tabletop. I had once, briefly, owned one of these lush, dramatic plants, in the very same shade—a gift from a friend. It had in one swoop rendered my little apartment more chic than shabby, and I'd been heartbroken when, apparently because I'd overwatered it, it met with sudden demise.

There in the store, I longed to have that amaryllis—*yearned* for it. It was rare for me to covet material things that way, but yearn I did. I was already splurging on the crystals; my boots were splitting, my gloves were hole-y, and my coat had two missing snaps. So I stood and truly *feasted* my eyes on its beauty, soaking it into my hungry soul, then paid by credit and left the store.

When I got home, I found a package outside my door, and I settled into my threadbare armchair to open it. I'd recently finished the research and writing portion of a pop-up book, created by artist Chuck Fischer, entitled *Christmas in New York*. In thanks, the publisher, Bulfinch, had sent me, I was dumbfounded to discover, a salmon-red amaryllis. I stared at the gorgeous specimen, vivid and elegant as the one I'd once loved and lost, and I cried. Then I telephoned my sister. "The funniest thing happened," I said, and told her the story. "I feel like Dad sent it."

After we hung up, I looked again at the amaryllis. It had two thick "parental" stalks, each with three buds—like the six kids in our family, I thought. And *buds*—there, too, was a poetic echo of my father's nickname, *Bud*.

I called Chuck and asked him if he'd received an amaryllis too, but he said no, he'd gotten a lovely basket of fruit. Somehow, I found that satisfying—as if my father *had* somehow guided the gift-givers to that particular option for me, and me alone.

It had of course occurred to me that Katarina might be able to connect me with my father. But I'd become resigned to not bringing up such things with her. So I was particularly surprised when, about a month later, in the midst of one of our now-rare phone conversations, she said out of the blue and with no hesitation that she might be able to contact him.

Given my friend's desire to avoid her gift, I found this truly selfless, and was moved by her words. I realized I'd been feeling cranky about Katarina cutting me off like a wino at a bar. Much as I knew she had every right and reason to, there was a part of me that, like a baby crying for its binky, just wanted what it wanted. And what I wanted was *knowledge*. And not just knowledge of my own future, romantic or otherwise—but knowledge of this gift she had; knowledge of the survival of consciousness; of realms in other dimensions; of the answers to Life's Big Questions.

Not that Katarina had it all at her fingertips. But it seemed to me she had an open porthole—or at least a peephole—to the Great Beyond. To get so close to it, only to have it shut so swiftly and so firmly, had been massively frustrating in a way that was hard to express.

Before I could tell her how grateful I was, though, my father blew in. Like a gust of wind slamming open a door, he was by all appearances there. Now, Katarina, while my friend for several years, knew next to nothing about my father. Perhaps because she was not in regular touch with her own mother, back in Poland, family was just not something we'd ever talked much about.

"'You're so sad,' that's what he's saying," she began, in her lovely accented voice. "All your sadness, it's holding him back." My sadness, *our* sadness, she said, was preventing him from moving on. And for me, she continued, the sadness wasn't even entirely about *him*. Not that I wasn't grieving. But there were other things, she said—men, and money—that I was upset about, and I was bundling it all together. My grief wasn't just about him; it was about *me*, too.

It was true! Her words, pinpointing what I'd told no one, caught the emotion in my throat.

She went on. There was no reason to be sad about him, he was saying. He was *fine*. Then she asked me if I'd been having trouble sleeping lately, and I said that I had. "He's been trying to come to you in your dreams," she said. "But your sleep is so troubled, he can't get through."

Then, suddenly, "Anne, I can *see* him!" she exclaimed. She told me he was saying that he was in a place "between here and there," and that they were "taking excellent care of him." He was surrounded by books and magazines, she said.

Reader, I beamed. Odd as it may sound, I'd actually never discussed my father's love of books, or his rare book business, with

Katarina. Again, it was just not an element that came up in my friendship, centered around the writing group, and then later around the investment club, with her and Paul. Also, the phrase *between here and there* was quintessentially my dad. What does that even *mean*, "*between here and there*"? The wordplay reminded me of one of those poems he'd gotten published as a young man, which were highly playful in tone, and also of the light-verse poetry of Edward Lear and Ogden Nash, which he loved. He'd taken a small volume of their poems to the hospital with him when he was having surgery. Katarina never used that sort of wordplay herself.

Then she asked me if crystals had any special meaning for me.

I told her not that I could think of.

"He's saying there are crystals everywhere, and that it's 'beautiful beyond belief.' '*Bliss*,' he says. 'It's that good.' He can't wait for you all to get there and see it too."

I was getting a little teary now—despite the fact that he'd essentially just said he couldn't wait for us to die, which made me laugh a little too. That love of beauty was also very much my father. And how many people could say the same about theirs? It made what she was saying ring true.

"He's in an armchair, with a blanket on his lap. He says he feels younger and better than he has in twenty years. It's very warm and cozy." She said that he was drinking coffee, which *had* been his habit, and eating something that looked like a cookie, crumbly and dark. "He's saying, 'Look! I can eat this now!'"

Hearing that gave me a full-body rush. She had no idea about his difficulty eating on Thanksgiving, or how bad I'd felt about that.

"He's saying he missed the food at Christmastime." She paused. "He's a *good* person. I can feel it. He's sweet. But he's saying, 'I made some mistakes.' He was well prepared for what happened. His life had gotten very hard."

All true. And again, nothing we'd ever discussed.

"He's pointing now, to a big red flower. It's a poppy—no. I'm getting it wrong." English not being her native language, Katarina sometimes had trouble summoning the proper word. "It's an *amaryllis*," she corrected herself.

Shazam!

It was then, Reader, that I realized: *Crystals!* The crystal star ornaments I'd bought for my mother at Smith & Hawken. They *did* have a special meaning, and had been completely tied in with my father's death.

I told her my amaryllis story, explaining about the crystals, too. It was the cherry on top of the sundae, the last piece of the jigsaw puzzle locking into place. It was Bud. My dad. *Daddy*. No question about it.

"That's amazing," she said, as I shared this feeling with her, her voice now fairly crinkling with happiness. "He's saying every time you look at the amaryllis, he's sending you a kiss."

Well, that started up my tears again.

"He's telling you not to overwater it!"

Ha! Was he making a joke about my crying? Or did he somehow now know—were spirits omniscient?—that I'd overwatered the amaryllis my friend had sent me years before?

"Can I ask him one thing?" I said, wiping my eyes, the watered-down mascara inky on my fingertips, and likely on my cheeks as well. Could Daddy see he'd reduced me to a tear-stained raccoon? "He didn't believe in an afterlife. He used to make fun of my mother and me for our interest in psychics and mediums . . ."

"He couldn't *let* himself believe. It was like, he *so much* wanted it to be true, he wouldn't let himself," she said.

Huh. That had never occurred to me. If it was true, it gave me a whole new insight into my father.

Katarina and I spoke a bit more that day. I told my father, somewhere in there, that I loved him. But then, he already knew that.

It was the sweetest Christmas present.

✳

THAT WAS THE LAST TIME Katarina shared a reading with me. Disappointed as I was that she had rejected what I saw as her "calling," I've come to understand her decision. And I'm so grateful for what she did share.

Katarina helped me heal, far more quickly than I might have, my grief over losing my father. The experience gave me, if not rock-solid belief, at least some pretty convincing grounds for hope that he was, somehow, still "there"; and that it was a place of indescribable beauty, where I, and all my loved ones, would eventually join him.

Knowing Katarina opened up for me, a tiny bit wider, that crack through which we sometimes glimpse what lies "between here and there"... and beyond.

3

LAUNCHING A
NEW ADVENTURE
✳ OR ✳

Psychic Friends

HAVE YOU EVER HEARD THE EXPRESSION *DARK NIGHT OF THE soul*? It's a poetic phrase, and pleasing to invoke—and many of us writerly types have certainly invoked it, sometimes with our tongue planted firmly in our cheek. But if you've ever *lived* a true dark night of the soul—and believe me, you'll know it if you have—you'll probably agree that there's nothing pleasing about it. Or at least, nothing you can find while you're in it. Looking back on it can be a whole other story.

After my experiences with Katarina, which helped me through the loss of my father, I felt, for a time, that I was striding pleasantly and confidently along on a sunny, well-lit path. I had stepped into adulthood in a way that, as I'd observed in many of my friends, often happened when one lost a parent. While I felt more persuaded toward the idea of the soul's continued existence after death, I also felt much more aware of my own mortality, of how few years I might have left in this life—and more driven than ever to pursue what I considered one of the supreme markers of happiness in life: a successful long-term relationship. For me, a total romantic since childhood—my favorite books had been *Wuthering Heights* and *Jane Eyre*, God help me, with their tortured depictions of love—waiting to find "true love" felt like waiting for my life to begin. And by my late forties, I felt like I'd been wait-ing forever. And so I joined several online dating services, and met a passel of men. Though none of them "stuck"—truth be told, very few even made it beyond a first date—I felt I was finally "putting myself out there" in the way my girlfriends had long urged me to do.

It was just at that time that I received an email, out of the blue, from a friend I had worked with a while back in the field of children's new media. She had since moved to Oregon and, I knew mostly from her Facebook posts, was now married and the mother of a lovely baby girl. "I know this sounds strange, Anne," I read, "given that you two are an entire country apart, but I have a friend out here I feel *com-pelled* to introduce you to." This man—his name was Mike—and I reminded her of each other, my friend said: We were the two people "most attuned to other people's emotions" that she'd ever met. Well, *compelled* was a strong word, and I tended to put stock in people's intu-ition, so I was intrigued. I gave her the green light to give him my number—or actually, it was my email address, my friend and I being "new media" types.

I got to know Mike via email and over the phone before he finally came East about a month later, to visit with his family in New England, and then travel to Upstate New York, where I'd be visiting a friend, to meet me. By that point we had been, without fail, talking and tex-ting daily. It was a feeling I'd never had, even with Leo: a feeling of someone, some *man*, actually thinking of me as the singular person he wanted to talk to before he went to sleep, each and every night.

A computer-tech guy with the soul of a social worker/monk, Mike shared my interests in psychology, neuroscience, mind-body medi-cine, and spirituality. He was a bit older, with gray in his otherwise chestnut hair and beard, but like me, had never been married, and had no kids. Mike was semiretired due to some money he'd inherited and some good investments he'd made, and I was doing various types of freelance editing and writing from home, so after our initial visit—we had an undeniable rapport—it was easy for us to visit back and forth, and we took a few road trips together. We traveled easily and well, road-tripping up and down the East Coast and the West; I'd always heard that was sort of a "litmus test" for marriage. I met his family, and he met mine.

My family members seemed elated that I had an actual boyfriend. I hadn't brought home a man since Leo, and I think they were starting to wonder if I'd end up as one of those New York City women in a tiny apartment with fifteen cats. Mike and I even discussed my moving out West.

The problem wasn't the distance, though. The problem was, while Mike often said he loved me, and demonstrated it in many ways—he was kind, caring, generous, emotionally supportive, interested in my thoughts and ideas, and seemed to truly enjoy spending time with me—once we became close, he wasn't sure he was still *attracted* to me. He was . . . but then he wasn't. He wasn't . . . but then he was. As he put it, he was "confused."

Well, so was I! Especially because, despite this fact, he'd suggested we try to have a child together. He told me he thought I'd be a fantastic mother, and that he really wanted kids. Coming on top of his physical rejection of me, which, for someone who had struggled with her weight and self-image all her life, was like a punch in the gut, it was almost too much to process.

I had always loved kids, and assumed I'd have them at some point, but I'd never felt quite ready to give up my freedom. I'd helped raise my siblings, and babysat and nannied a lot of other people's kids, so I had at least an inkling of what taking care of kids required. And there was so much else I wanted to do, I'd never felt sure I could make the required sacrifices. And then, I'd never met the right guy.

I'd come close with Mike, so close it was tempting to go for it. At forty-eight, my biological clock had certainly wound down, if it was even still ticking. And I did feel real love for him, despite the painful feelings his "confusion" had caused me. Luckily, though, I'd had enough smarts to know that having a baby with him would be a recipe for disaster.

Reader, Mike wasn't a jerk. He had confided in me that he'd experienced sexual abuse as a child, and I came to understand, through our conversations and some research I did into the subject, that it had messed him up about combining love and sex. Though he'd had some very long and apparently "functional" relationships with other women, he'd never told them about the abuse. Because he felt close enough to me to share those traumatic experiences and emotions—and they broke my heart—he apparently could no longer feel sexually attracted or comfortable with me that way.

I tried, for a year and a half, to help Mike process his feelings and his trauma—for his sake, and for mine. I so very much wanted us to work out as a couple, aside from the whole baby thing. And he *did* try. But we parted ways one chilly March day after my forty-eighth birthday. It was wrenching for us both, though maybe less so for him since, a mere month later, he began seriously dating someone else—someone much younger. As I watched the crocuses and daffodils spring up, and the hyacinths bloom, the thought that April was, to quote T. S. Eliot, "the cruelest month," was frequently in my head.

Spring warmed into summer. While I was still nursing my wounds about Mike, palpably missing his daily calls, and heartsick at the thought of him spending that time with someone else, the truly unthinkable occurred: My dear friend David was diagnosed with a very virulent form of leukemia and, with devastating swiftness, died. He was forty-six years old.

David had been one of my closest buddies since we'd met at the University of Virginia through a mutual friend. David was outgoing, curious, and funny, and our conversation always just flowed. Meeting him, a fellow New Yorker who likewise missed bagels and lox, really good pizza, and the particular brand of "crazy" we both knew so well, had made me feel at home in a place that, while undeniably beautiful, felt, culturally, like a different country.

Both writers and editors, once we headed back North and managed to snag rent-stabilized Manhattan apartments (*Yes!!!*), we'd worked several jobs together, and come to share a wide circle of friends. David was constantly rallying us all to see Shakespeare or opera in Central Park, Broadway shows, and the far more eclectic pop-cultural entertainment he had a knack for ferreting out. He loved sharing the things he found exceptional in life—things uniquely beautiful, humorous, original, or bizarre—and would crinkle up his eyes and flash his infectious, hundred-watt smile when he saw that we loved his curated cultural "must-do's" as much as he did.

David had been my quirky and beloved pal through my entire post-college life. He was always just a phone call away, eager to talk, to listen, and to see, if not the sunny, at least the funny side of things, with his characteristic giggle.

David had spent the past few years helping his mother to care for his father, who had Alzheimer's—an incredibly difficult time for him—while I'd been busy zipping around the country in rental cars with Mike, so we hadn't seen much of each other, something I'd been feeling regretful about. When I heard that he'd been hospitalized, I went, along with a number of his other friends, to visit him, but he was already in a coma-like state, his body shutting down. It was truly hard to fathom.

Very swiftly thereafter, I got news from one of our mutual friends that David had died. Reader, I was numb. I simply couldn't imagine him gone—nor could I imagine my own life without him.

THAT FALL WAS A BLUR, but I somehow made it through to the final weeks of a year that had brought me to my knees. Before I'd realized it was even December, it seemed, it was nearly Christmas. Christmas season was, I always thought, Greenwich Village at its best, and I'd loved walking through its narrow, twisty streets after nightfall, reveling in the colored lights, fragrant wreaths, and graceful garlands adorning the old brick townhouses, and peering into the glowing windows of bars and cafés literally overflowing with good cheer.

This year, though, as when I'd lost my father five years before, I found myself thrown into a period of darkness and doubt, unable to connect with the joy I usually took in the season. I wasn't quite muttering "Bah-humbug," but almost. I felt trapped in a whirlpool of emotion, the flotsam and jetsam of the past year's events swirling around me. And I couldn't get past the pain.

My family wasn't big on New Year's Eve celebrations, and I usually opted for a quiet dinner with friends. But that had been getting harder and harder to arrange, as more and more friends coupled off, had kids, and moved out of the city. This year, I hadn't had the will to attempt plans of any kind, nor had anyone invited me to help them ring in the New Year. And so December 31 found me alone on the living room couch in my childhood home, now populated solely by my mother, who was upstairs cuddling with her remote, in bed. Swaddled in my threadbare granny nightgown, covered with a slightly pilling multi-colored afghan my Grandma Jennie had helped the adolescent me to crochet, I half-watched the hoopla in Times Square on the rather dated television, trying not to be depressed. I'd never been big on resolutions, but with the loss of Mike and David, I felt called to examine my life—to examine myself.

Mike's departure had brought home my painful, still apparently unbreakable pattern of loving men who couldn't fully love me back. Thanks to Patricia Masters, I'd come to better understand my father's part in that, but neither understanding it nor actually *losing* my father had changed it, and I had no idea what would or could. David's passing, on the other hand, was a wake-up call, an ushering toward a door to . . . somewhere different from where I'd been. It reminded me again how brief our stint on Earth could be, and how important it was to discover what we had to contribute, and make the most of the time we had. David, I reflected, had not found a life partner during his time here as David. Perhaps I wouldn't either. But if so, did that mean I was incapable of having a full and meaningful life?

As the ball dropped and the confetti flew, I knew I had to make a radical change. And more than just a new nightgown, I surmised as I looked down at the holes in the one I'd owned since, oh, the bicentennial. I needed to let go of the hurt, the grief, the loss, the disappointments . . . and find joy, somehow, again. I needed to find my way back to myself.

The mysteries of life, death, and the invisible world were, from the start, what I'd always been most passionate and curious about. But even after Patricia's prediction that I'd write about people who did what she did, and Katarina's astounding connection with my father, I'd never really "leaned in" to that wonder-lust again. Somehow, in the intervening years, life had always gotten in the way. There had been the need to support myself; the drive to achieve with my writing; and of course, the constant search for romantic love.

And sometimes, too, the *visible* world had proved to be more than I could handle. There was the time surrounding 9/11, when I saw just how *fragile* I really was. For many months afterward, I couldn't hear a plane without cowering or an ambulance without cringing; I couldn't watch the news at all. I would, literally, flee from the room if footage of the falling towers or talk about terrorism was airing, which was only about 99 percent of the time.

Following that, there had been years of panic attacks and insomnia, years I now thought of as "the lost years," where getting healthy and normal again had required most of my time and attention. Throughout those years, that childhood Anne, with all her passion and curiosity about the whys and wherefores of existence, had walked through my days with me like a shadow, catching my notice now and again in sunnier moments, but disappearing in the long stretches when things grew dark.

Now, though, in the wake of David's death, I found myself wondering daily: Did David's consciousness live on? Could he communicate with me? Where was he, and what was he doing? And what, really, was more important than trying to find out the truth about that?

I looked in the medicine cabinet mirror that night—or in the first minutes, really, of the nascent year—as I brushed my teeth. "The truth is out there," I said to my reflection, wiping a bit of minty-fresh aqua gel off my cheek. I'd been reduced to quoting TV characters now—*The X Files'* Fox Mulder, in this case—instead of modern English poets. But I was serious nonetheless. There in the home of my youth, where I'd played with the Ouija board and tested myself with my ESP cards, I had finally reconnected with my inner child, and she needed some real answers. I had no idea how I'd find them, but I knew one thing for sure: This time, I wasn't going to let her down.

A FEW MONTHS LATER, I lay on the couch across from Melinda, my longtime therapist, wondering if I'd heard her right. It had sounded like she'd said I was "done."

"I didn't think therapists *ever* thought *anyone* was *done*. Done as in *finished*? *Fixed*? *Fully cooked*?" I ran my hands along the familiar tweedy fabric of the couch's cushions, thinking how strange it would be not to do this on a weekly, or sometimes *twice* weekly, basis.

She laughed. "I think you're in a good place to try things on your own," she said.

It wasn't as if it had come entirely out of the blue. It had been nearly a year since Mike had broken up with me. And I'd spent many weeks now talking through my feelings about David's death, and had come to a place if not of happiness, at least of acceptance. I was, once again, very short on cash, having lost my well-paying kids' media job when the Internet bubble burst. And my therapy wasn't covered at all by insurance. So I'd tossed out the idea of taking a break to Melinda, expecting her to protest.

"I don't want you to stop, though, without a *project* to work on," she said. I suppose she wanted to make sure that, cut loose from her long-time support, I wouldn't drift like an unmoored boat on the familiar high seas of anxiety or depression.

Taking the "1" train home from my session that day, I sat in that crowded subway car, pressed in on all sides by the "huddled masses," and took in my new, sans-therapist self, still a bit disbelieving. And then I pondered what my project might be. I thought back to my Fox Mulder moment in front of the mirror, my desire to find the "truth." Despite those early experiences I'd had with Patricia Masters, and with my friend Katarina, and how convincing and moving I'd found them at the time, now, many years later, there was still something in me that wasn't totally convinced of their veracity. Though I couldn't come up with any way to explain my experiences with Patricia or Katarina that *didn't* involve "supernatural" or "paranormal" abilities, I wasn't 100 percent without doubt. It wasn't that I felt I'd been purposely duped. In the case of Katarina, she'd not only been my friend before realiz-ing these abilities, she had taken no money, and was reluctant even to embrace those abilities she appeared to have! But had I been, somehow, too *biased* from the outset, too much of a believer already because of my childhood sense of there being "more"—or too emotionally involved to clearly assess what was occurring?

It was time for me to find out the truth—*my* truth, at least—and not just about life after death, and abilities like Patricia's and Katarina's, but about *all* of what Patricia had referred to as "the invisible realms." About past lives . . . and spirit guides . . . angels . . . and ghosts . . . and whatever I could learn about this thing we called "the soul."

I got off the train a stop early and visited a nearby stationery store, where I bought a portable plastic file bin and a set of hanging folders, which I began labeling, once home, with the names of topics I wanted to explore. I would read books and take classes, seeking out more practitioners in the areas that intrigued me, and deep-dive into it all in a way I'd never done before. I would ask Griffin to be my unofficial mentor—he'd been off and running on such research and study for years now, and I knew that he would guide me, and be a sounding board, as I carried out my explorations.

As I went about hanging the empty folders in alphabetical order, I felt the most peculiar sense of rightness about what I was doing; a *fatedness* almost. A sense of finally doing the task that I was here to do—though I wasn't even sure what that meant.

Folders completed, at least for now, I was ready to get started, so I sat in my threadbare armchair to ponder my next move. The invisible world loomed large and unwieldy—well, it *was* a *world*, after all! How and where would I begin?

I could feel a part of me looking over my own shoulder—a little Jiminy Cricket in a lab coat, if you will—whose high little voice was the voice of reason, of logic, of that rigorous early training I'd had at my math-and-science high school. *Could I somehow conduct an experiment?* the voice asked. *And how would that work?*

I remembered a book I'd read as a kid, purchased at the Waldenbooks at our local mall: *Psychic Discoveries Behind the Iron Curtain.* I was probably ten or eleven, and barely knew what the Iron Curtain was, but any book about psychics was a rare find in those days, at least in the mall, and excited me, so I nabbed it. Sure enough, the book's content was well over my head, and though it sat on the radiator in our family bathroom for a good many months, its pages curling up from the perpetual steam (eight people, one bathroom!), I don't think I ever read more than a few snippets here and there. Now I wondered: *Had anyone in that book conducted true scientific experiments?* If so, I hadn't heard about them. Then again, the Iron Curtain was still hanging fully intact at that point in my young life.

No matter. I knew that I couldn't possibly, as a lab team of one—or one and a half, if you counted Jiminy—"prove" that the abilities I was exploring were real, that is, using the scientific method. But then, I wasn't really out to convince anyone else. What I wanted was to see if I could truly convince *myself.*

I'd taken many writing classes over the years, and while the project at hand was not writing-related, but rather experiential, I recalled the old adage often quoted to me by teachers: *Write what you know.* Well, what did I know so far of the invisible world? What had I experienced? Psychics—and some who were mediums, as well—was the clear answer.

And thus, Reader, I decided to begin my project by launching an informal "experiment": If I had readings with, say, ten psychics and mediums every six months or so, over several years, would they come up with any of the same information? By information I meant not only predictions, but the sort of advice and guidance that such practitioners frequently gave—often, ostensibly, with the aid of entities in other realms. If so, I'd also have good reason to put my trust in the guidance I would be receiving, *and* to be more convinced that it was all "real."

I'd have to see how long I—and my wallet—could manage it. And I'd have to wait—perhaps as long as a year or two—to see the results. (Meantime, of course, I had a file bin full of other topics to pursue.)

To me, it was a thoroughly intriguing idea.

Plus, now I'd actually *have* to have readings—loads of 'em! They would be necessary research! *Woo-hoo!*

I couldn't wait to start.

I KNEW I'D HAVE TO DO some searching to fill out my "Dream Team," as I came to think of the psychics and mediums I would include in my experiment. In the years since my readings with Patricia, I'd dabbled a bit, and while I'd found some readers disappointing or even blatantly unconvincing—one who pored over tea leaves in a multilevel Upper East Side "warehouse" of intuitives, one at a house party where the hostess had hired a psychic to give brief readings to her guests— I did have a few good, and varied, candidates on tap. Settling into my threadbare armchair, I grabbed a spiral notebook and a pen. Then, casting my mind back in time, I started a list.

EDWARD RAGOSTA

In my early thirties, I'd heard about a psychic who read cards in a dimly lit local Village café. A raven-haired fellow about my own age, dressed in a T-shirt and jeans, Edward Ragosta set up shop with his well-thumbed tarot deck on the second floor, among the artfully mismatched antique tables and chairs. Though he worked with cards, he also claimed to channel information from a group of angels and guides he usually referred to collectively as "Spirit." Edward had a friendly but no-nonsense air and a blatant, endearing New Jersey accent: "Cut the right whitcha right, and the left whitcha left," he'd say, pointing to the two card piles after I'd shuffled and cut.

Naturally, in my first reading, I had asked about men. As usual, I was feeling sad about my lack of a love life, and sorry for myself. Not that I did much to improve things. I never used personal ads or matchmaking services, or went anywhere very likely to elicit a date.

I knew that, much as I *wanted* to find love, I did have a tendency to keep men at arm's length—as if I'd dug a moat around myself, letting very few across the drawbridge. The ones for whom I *did* lower the bridge were, inevitably, not interested in me romantically or unable to commit. Living in the Village and working in theater and publishing, where eleven out of ten men were gay, hadn't helped. Not that I hadn't fallen for a few of *them*, too. (Reader, I know you saw that coming.) But I didn't tell Edward any of that.

"You don't have to put love on hold, or slo-mo, to pursue your career," he began.

"I'm not!" I protested.

"I'm sorry, but you are. It doesn't count if you comb your hair, but then you put a hat on. You're primping, but you're *hiding*. You're not a prude, but you're used to Victorian times. You had a life back then."

Huh! Was that why I'd always been so attracted to Victorian styles? I'd owned several pairs of old-fashioned, lace-up boots before they were in fashion; wore only long, Victorian-style nightgowns; and adored Victorian houses with "gingerbread" trim. Not to mention my fondness for Victorian novels, whose authors often used the literary device of directly addressing their readers—a device I was prone to using myself (as you, Reader, may have noticed).

"You still have this strict moral code. Do you wear lace-up shoes, high ones? You like that crisscross style, yes? Like a corset?"

Gak! In addition to the boots, I owned two tunics and a shoulder bag with crisscross lacing too. Note: I wasn't wearing any of them at the time.

"Now, have you been socializing? *No!* Because you've been looking at it as being about as friendly as a bikini-waxing! You need to leave your suit of armor at home.

"Of course, you're not gonna do this without a corset in the shape of a chastity belt, but you need a good old-fashioned love affair. Because you're rusty!" He flipped a few more cards. "You will put energy into forming friendships," he said. "And obviously, the suitors will be the ones that aren't *gay!*"

I busted out laughing; he'd nailed it.

"There *is* someone coming up who'll make you accessorize more than usual," Edward continued. "I see you wearing red more. *Scarlet*, perhaps."

"As long as it's not the Scarlet Letter," I said.

"Don't take this disrespectfully, but you have to *sin* before you get to wear the Scarlet Letter," he said, chuckling.

Edward saw me with a cat—not a live one, but "a form of a cat, or a cut-out cat" that he said I'd received as a present. Well, I had a cat-shaped mouse-pad, I said. "No, no," he insisted, "this is *three-dimensional. It stands up.*"

I was impressed that he wasn't willing to take the "hit" I'd offered.

Edward called this cut-out creature my "familiar"—referring to the animal spirit-companions that witches were thought to have. I had no idea what he was seeing. But about a year later, my older brother's girlfriend, an artist, gave me a three-dimensional, origami paper rabbit she'd made, with prominent, catlike whiskers. For years, I kept it perched on my desktop computer, thinking of it as my "avatar"—when I was blocked with my writing or feeling down, I'd pick it up and whiz it through the air, willing *myself* to "take off" and fly high, in my work and life, in a similar manner. (Reader, it's odd, but it's what I did.) Almost two decades later, I was listening to a recording of Edward's reading and realized that this rabbit was—but for the longer ears and shorter tail—the "cat" he'd seen, whiskers and all.

I'd had a few more readings with Edward over the years. Though he'd moved to California before ultimately returning East, his phone readings had proven just as good. No question—I wanted to include him in my experiment.

JEFFREY WANDS

When I was a little shy of forty, I met Jeffrey Wands, an acclaimed Long Island medium well before Theresa Caputo, *THE* "Long Island Medium." My youngest brother's wife, Dana, lovely and much adored, had passed away suddenly at thirty-four, leaving my brother, her family, and all of us who knew and loved her shocked and devastated. After her death, Dana's mother had booked sessions with several mediums. In a session with Jeffrey, who had a weekly call-in radio show and had published several books, Dana had come through like gangbusters, thanking her parents for a tree-planting and tennis tournament they'd held in her memory—both right on target.

In a reading his mother-in-law had booked for my brother, Jeffrey had said Dana was commenting on the tiny size of his current apartment, and his idea of moving to Hoboken, both correct. Jeffrey said Dana was teasing my brother about shopping for couches when he didn't need a couch; in fact, I learned, he'd been trolling furniture stores, helping our sister-in-law pick out a couch the week before!

Some years later, just after my father's diagnosis of lung cancer, Dana's mother had booked another session for my brother. "I hadn't said anything about Dad," he emailed me afterward, "but Jeffrey got it exactly right. 'Worried about your dad's chest. Getting a *C* for cancer. Right lung worse than left.'" Which, Dear Reader, *was* the case.

Finally, Dana's mother had booked a third session for my brother. When a time conflict with his job arose, he'd offered me his spot. I was delighted to accept.

Seated behind a desk in his small office when I entered, Jeffrey wore a button-down shirt and had his dark hair combed back off his open, pleasant face. He had a relaxed manner and a quick smile. Outwardly, there was nothing remotely "spiritual" about him: He could easily have passed for a lawyer or financial advisor.

Jeffrey started by mentioning my brother, saying Dana was happy he'd found a new apartment—which he recently had. *Off to a flying start!*

Then Jeffrey said he had a "dad figure" there who wanted me to know he'd "found his peace . . . though he vacillates a bit with the craziness of the family." My father had died six months earlier, some time after my brother's last reading.

"Ask him if he thinks I should move back to Staten Island," I said. I'd been concerned about my mother living alone, and feeling slightly guilty.

"No, he likes you where you are," he said. "He doesn't worry about your safety. So please tell your mom you're safe. He says, 'Every time she hears about a fire in Manhattan, she assumes it's your building.'"

Ha! My mother to a tee.

"He wants you to start focusing more on your personal life," he said.

Oh my gosh! I was touched, remembering that conversation my father and I had had about that very thing, a little before he died. Was he remembering it too?

"He's saying you have to let the person in. His concern with you is the whole element of being able to get somebody across the barbed wire and the alligators."

Ha! It was true: I still hadn't managed to change much in that regard. So my dad knew that about me now? I was sure he hadn't known it in life.

"And there's another Anne or Anna . . . I thought a grandmother. She's honored you have that name. *She* was very beautiful too—according to her."

"That *is* my grandmother! My father's mother. And she *was* very beautiful!"

"And then there's a Jack or a John."

"That was her husband, Jack! Short for Jacob," I said. "Does he have other family members there?"

Actually, Jeffrey said, there were several from my *mother's* side present. That didn't surprise me; I'd grown up surrounded by them. I didn't tell that to Jeffrey.

"He's saying he can't get away from your mother's family, even over there!" He laughed, and I joined him. "He's got a dog there too."

"Which dog?" I asked. We'd had two. But it was the second—the shih tzu, Chippy, the one he'd spoiled with cooked chicken livers and such—who'd been my dad's little buddy. Chippy had been black, with white on his face and chest.

"It's the little black one, with the white over here," Jeffrey said, touching his own chest area.

Holy canine! "The dog wasn't stupid. When your dad went to the refrigerator, *he* got a snack too. According to your dad, the dog was the only one who'd listen to him!"

Swish! Jeffrey had sunk it.

"I like that he was eccentric, and crusty in his way," he said. "And his whole alcohol vibe. I can smell the gin."

Right again. My father *had* imbibed many a martini in the years when he worked in Manhattan.

"How do you get all this, Jeffrey?" I asked, my head swimming. So much had come in, so fast. "Do you see symbols, hear words, feel sensations?"

"All of the above," he said.

I asked, then, if he dealt with higher spiritual beings, as well as spirits of the dead. "I don't know," he answered. "There is definitely a higher presence. It's just how you interpret it . . . But you *are* meant to be happily in love," he continued. "Your dad seems to think you *haven't* been."

Again, quite a hit for Jeffrey, considering that I was now in my mid-forties.

"He says you babysat the men in your last two relationships. No offense, but he isn't high on what you picked so far! And then you just try to *fix* them . . ."

OMG! While I'd tried to stop doing it since Patricia had pointed out the downside of this, I'd gotten Mike into therapy, as I had Leo, and a few others too.

"There *is* one coming up—a man, that is—who you don't have to fix. You *are* capable of finding a non-screwed-up individual."

Easy for him *to say*, I'd thought at the time.

And while that had not yet come to pass, it was easy for *me* to tap Jeffrey: I wanted him on my Team.

JENNIFER HICKS

About a year after my father's death, a friend recommended a psychic medium named Jennifer Hicks. Jennifer, a Brooklynite, conducted my reading by phone. The first thing she said was that she was hearing the song "Chim Chim Cher-ee," from *Mary Poppins*, in her head. I was dumbfounded. I'd seen the Broadway show the day before, and this was well before I was on Facebook or any other social media. The song had been playing in *my* head all morning long.

Apparently, Jennifer heard things psychically, a phenomenon called "*clairaudience*" or "clear hearing." But she got most of her information in images, which were often metaphors or symbols. She'd developed a vocabulary of meaning as she figured out, over time, what the images meant. "It's like playing charades," she said. Sometimes she got names, too; sometimes just initials.

That day, Jennifer picked up mostly on "dead people." She told me she was getting a female with the initial *D*. "Who went to a Catholic school? Something like Mt. Holyoke." That sounded like my sister-in-law Dana, who'd attended the Catholic Marist College, I said. Jennifer affirmed this. Dana was taking her to the 92nd Street Y, she continued. "What did you see there?" In fact, I'd recently been there for the first time, to see the comedian/actor Robert Klein, who'd read from his charming autobiography, *The Amorous Busboy of Decatur Avenue*, and later asked me to lunch, a highly memorable experience—one I'd definitely have shared with Dana. But it seemed she knew all about it.

Then she said Dana was taking her "to the Woodstock area: Dutchess County, or Greene County . . ." Sure enough, one of my best friends had a house in Greene County, and I'd recently visited her there. Apparently, Dana had too.

Jennifer said Dana was now bringing other people in. She saw a pressed flower, but felt it was a name: Rose. My great-aunt Rose *had* recently passed; she and Dana had been very fond of each other.

"Did Rose play Scrabble, or Monopoly? Or *cards*?"

"Yes!" I exclaimed. She and her sister, Sarah, had been avid Scrabble players. If I'd been asked, beforehand, for my top three symbols that would identify Aunt Rose, Scrabble would have been one of them.

Jennifer was also getting a Ginnie. I told her that *Jennie* was my maternal grandmother—sister-in-law to Sarah and Rose. Dana used to joke that, while dating my brother, she'd fallen in love with Grandma Jennie first.

Then Jennifer told me she felt a man coming through: my father, she thought. I hadn't even told her he was dead. "I'm getting *bones*," she said. "An X-ray sort of thing."

"He *was* an X-ray technician, in the Army," I said.

"Was there a Jerry, or Jeremy, or Jeremiah, related to his Army experience?" she asked. "He's saying he was a good pal."

"He *did* have a good friend named Jerry! I'm not sure if he was his Army buddy, though. He came from quite a distance to attend Dad's wake." I checked with my mother later and found that indeed Jerry and Dad had met in their Army days.

"He's also showing me the Liberty Bell, my symbol for Philadelphia. Does he have family there?"

"Yes, one of his sisters, and his nephew and *his* family too!"

"He's talking about 'the twins' now. Girls. Are there twins, or two girls close in age?"

My two oldest nieces were close in age, plus very *close*, as twins often are. Both were very bright, but the younger one was proving to be quite the whiz kid.

"He's referring to one of them as 'the genius.' He's saying, 'She takes after me!'"

I had to laugh. But it was all true!

Having made an impressive sweep of my deceased family members, Jennifer moved on to friends. She mentioned a *Christopher*, someone in spirit. "I'm seeing frogs or, no, *turtles*," she said.

The only Christopher I knew who'd passed was my mother's best friend Jeanne's son. His sister, Jamie, had a turtle pond in her yard, so that did make sense. I made a note to share this with my mom. Jeanne was still, I knew, deeply grieving, and I wasn't sure how open she was to this sort of thing.

"Who was killed by a moving vehicle?" Jennifer asked then. She was getting "a gigantic letter *G*," someone who'd "crossed over a while ago."

That must have been my friend G.G., I said. Though we'd met in college, G.G. and I had really bonded when I'd visited her later in Switzerland, where she'd worked for several years after graduating.

"She's showing me a cuckoo clock," Jennifer said—a very viable symbol of Switzerland. "She went by a nickname, I feel. The name on her birth certificate was not what she was called." *Yes and yes!* G.G. stood for her first and second given names, and she always went by that.

Jennifer described her as "very no-nonsense, very cut-to-the-chase," which was G.G. to the max. "She's saying, '*G.G.*, as in Greta Garbo.'" That was very cool, I thought, because, just hearing the name, one would likely assume that it was *G-i-g-i*, like the Fifties film starring Leslie Caron. But G.G. spelled it as Jennifer was indicating, with just the two initials.

I sent a mental thank you to G.G. Perhaps because I'd called upon her in my reading with Katarina, she'd popped in again now to say hi. *Was that how it worked with spirits?* I wondered. Once they knew you were open to their presence, and had found a way to connect, would they show up again and again, if their celestial calendars allowed?

Along with all her info about dead people, Jennifer picked up a few things about me. Mediums, after all, are psychics, too, as Patricia Masters had long ago pointed out. It was possible for me to consider a different line of work, she said, mentioning my "healing vibe," which I could put to use doing some type of energy work. Alternatively, I could focus on creative writing, she said. I hadn't told Jennifer what my present work—copyediting and proofreading—was, or the fact that creative writing had long been what I hoped to do.

Looking back on my reading with Jennifer, I was impressed all over again. She was definitely draft-pick number three for my growing Team.

✳

ASIDE FROM PATRICIA MASTERS and my friend Katarina, these were the psychics and mediums I'd met who'd made the cut thus far. I planned to include Patricia on my Dream Team as well—while she was no longer around, I'd had many fantastic readings with her over many years, and I'd recorded them all. But I wanted at least a few more practitioners to add to my roster.

I began contacting all my woo-woo-curious friends, telling them that I was looking for really good psychics and mediums. One quickly got back to me with the name of a psychic she very much liked.

MAGGIE MOISE

Maggie, who referred to herself as an "intuitive counselor," coincidentally lived in my native Staten Island, though she later moved to New Jersey. She conducted our reading by phone. Friendly and straightforward, she had a calm, self-assured voice that belied the fact that she was just twenty-one.

Maggie used tarot cards. She didn't really need them, she said; she could see symbolic pictures, or "visions," without them. But it could be intimidating, and the cards served as a bit of a "crutch." They would "speak" to her, though it wasn't what people called "clairaudience," she said. "You don't hear it in your ears. It's telepathic, more of an *understanding.*"

Now that I was embarking on my experiment, I was determined to keep an eye out for the technique known as "cold reading"—which had been explained to me by two wonderful magician friends I'd met via my friend Frankie, Matt and Prakash, who included feats of mentalism in their highly clever and engaging stage performances. Cold reading, they told me, was a method by which the reader elicited information from the "sitter"—the person receiving the reading—by asking questions and employing observation, probability, and association, all while making it seem as if the information was being obtained through "supernatural" means.

To me, where Maggie was concerned, cold reading seemed highly unlikely: The reading was by phone, so she couldn't see me, and she very rarely asked questions—nor did I volunteer any information.

I asked first about my health. At the time, I had painful plantar fasciitis in my left heel, and a nagging ache in my right shoulder. Maggie told me that I was in very good health, but that she felt pain in her right shoulder and left heel when we spoke! Both, she said, would diminish, not worsen, moving forward—and she was right.

Next, I asked about love.

"As far as love, it's a learning process you're in," she began. "This feeling you have that nobody wants you, of being rejected, is actually creating that situation."

She told me that I was going to be experiencing a "man-storm": "When one man leaves, another will come. It'll be a recurring thing." I was a bit incredulous. As I told her, I hadn't had anything remotely resembling a man-storm in at least ten years. I didn't often meet men with whom I felt a spark, and lately it had been four or five years between each.

"You will," she insisted. "You're manifesting it, because you need to get yourself into a better mindset, to remind yourself that you are a wonderful, beautiful woman."

I thanked her for that.

Maggie said the man-storm was also about learning to spot "red flags" with men, which I'd ignored way too many times. That was true too. It was just what Patricia Masters had said, though she'd used the word *alarms*. I'd had entanglements with men with low self-esteem and depression, needy men rebounding from ex-wives and ex-girlfriends, men who had daddy issues, mommy issues, and daddy-wants-to-be-mommy issues. The phrase "Just say no" was not in my romantic vocabulary.

As part of the "storm," Maggie saw me meeting "a young *boy*, maybe thirty-two or so." She pulled two cards, the Hanged Man and the Knight of Swords. This indicated "conflicting behaviors," she said, periods where he'd be charging forward, full of enthusiasm, mixed with those of great stagnancy. "He's not emotionally . . . *ripe*, yet. But he's going to make you feel *really good* about yourself."

Next, she turned to my father. Like many, but not all, who call themselves "intuitives," Maggie was adept with mediumship as well. Though it had been quite a few years since his death, and while I was no longer grieving, he was of course still on my mind. "He died with a lot of guilt. He keeps saying, 'I'm sorry, I'm sorry,' especially to your mom. He realizes that he made her suffer."

Well, that was true, the suffering part, though I knew they had loved each other. Ironically, now that my father was gone, my mother couldn't have missed him more. She was constantly looking for signs from him, and was obsessed with some flickering in various light fixtures in her house, because spirits, we'd heard, could energetically affect electricity. It had become a bit of a joke in my mostly skeptical family; my brother-in-law had once gone so far as to flick the dining room lights on and off when my mother's back was turned, just to yank her chain. She hadn't appreciated his brand of humor.

"He's learned how his behavior affected the family," she said, "and now he's progressed." She paused. "He *is* screwing around with the lights. It *is* him!"

Now, *that* was pretty wild. Maggie had said this with no hint from me about the flickering lights. But more impressive was the *way* she'd said it, which assumed that someone had been discussing, or wondering, whether it really *was* my father playing around with them. As of course, Reader, we had.

She said I was going to be "staying in someone else's house" starting in February, in New Jersey, in a "very, very laid-back neighborhood." She described the lone tall tree in front of the house, and how many bedrooms it had. As it happened, one of my brothers and his wife had just asked me to house-sit, part-time, at their summer home on the Jersey Shore while renovations took place. The neighborhood *was* totally laid back, there *was* a lone tall tree in front, and she'd aced the number of bedrooms. And the work—and my stay—were set precisely for February!

Finally, she asked if I was doing a project on psychics. I hadn't told her anything about it, and I checked later with the friend who'd recommended her, who swore she hadn't said a word.

I couldn't yet vouch for the man-storm—I'd believe it when it blew in—but no question about it: Maggie had made the grade.

FRANK ANDREWS

The friend who recommended Maggie also told me she'd just read a book she thought I would enjoy: Terry Iacuzzo's *Small Mediums at Large*. It was an engaging account of growing up in a family of psychics—including her famous brother Frank, who used the surname Andrews. I'd once read about him in *New York* magazine, a 2003 issue with a cover bearing the banner "Psychic New York" that also happened to include Patricia Masters, and I'd been intrigued. As I had started to build my Dream Team, I'd actually thought of Frank Andrews, and had been wondering if he was still in town. Before I even tried to find out, though, I happened to mention to my comedy-writer friend Frankie—yes, I was even canvassing the hardened skeptics!—that I was looking for psychics.

"Oh, *Jake* has a psychic for you," he said, referring to a friend, a highly successful sitcom writer. "Jake says he doesn't believe in psychics . . . but he says *this* guy is for real. Personally, I think you're both madder than a donkey on a trike."

"It isn't *Frank Andrews*, is it?" I asked.

"Yes!" he said, looking slightly stunned. "How'd you know?"

"Just *psychic*, I guess," I deadpanned.

"Well, you have the first five letters right, anyway." He snickered.

Apparently, many years before, when Jake was pursuing acting, Andrews, *the* go-to New York psychic of top-ranking artists and enter-tainers at the time, had told him to drop acting and take up writing. Jake had followed his advice and become a writer for several hit TV sitcoms—no easy feat, as anyone who's tried can attest.

That was enough for me. I booked a session.

Frank Andrews, I found, worked exclusively in person, at his Mulberry Street townhouse. On its shiny red door was a plaque: "Pretending to be a normal person day after day is exhausting," it read.

An animated man with big, lively brown eyes and a mop of gray hair, Frank used a deck of cards so worn that some of them were held together with tape.

"You seem like a very happy person," he began. "But not when it comes to men. Men make you cry. That's your problem. It's up and down, up and down, when it comes to love." He paused. "What can I tell you? Put on blue eye shadow, act real dumb, and maybe you'll meet the right guy!" He laughed.

"Oh, Frank!" I said, laughing too. "You've gotta give me more hope than that."

He shook his head. "You can figure them out! *That's* why guys are afraid of you." He flipped a card. "Especially if you get one who's inse-cure. They're not gonna stay, because you're a lot stronger than they are." He paused. "Be careful of a Richard."

"There *is* a Richard!" I exclaimed. Richard was a professor I'd met via my spate of online dating following my father's death. We'd gone out to eat, had some good fun, and planned another date, but he hadn't shown up, calling later with a rather lame excuse. I'd recently bumped into him, though, and he wanted to meet up again.

Frank made a dubious sound. "I don't like anybody around you. I feel like I should travel with you. Like, I'll hide behind a screen: 'No! No! Not *that* one!' You know, if I had, say, *ten* men here, they're all eligible, nobody's married, some are making money, but one's a nutcase . . . *'Anne?* Why are you sitting next to *that* one?'"

OMG. Frank was funny. Well, according to his sister's book, he'd originally been pursuing a career in show business. When I asked him about it, he added that while he had not appeared in the show himself, one of the characters in the long-running Broadway smash *A Chorus Line*—a favorite musical of mine, originally produced by the Public Theater, where I'd worked—had actually been based on him. (The one from Buffalo who gets many of the show's laughs—for you musical theater nerds trying to figure it out!)

Frank went on about me and men: I got them all fixed up, he said, got them into therapy—as Jeffrey Wands, too, had pointed out—and made them very good husbands . . . for someone else! Precisely the case with Leo, who'd ended up marrying the bridesmaid, and a few other exes who'd married the woman they'd dated directly after me.

Then Frank pulled out a huge magnifying glass and pored over my palms, studying the creases and lines. Among other things, he announced that I'd never die in a plane crash!

What? Really? It was music to my ears, as I loved to travel, but had always felt extremely anxious in flight.

He told me he'd accurately predicted several plane crashes, including one for the late fashion designer Perry Ellis. "I told him it was a ride coming up soon in a small plane. He was scheduled to go to either Fire Island or Shelter Island, I can't recall which. So he cancelled his flight. And the plane crashed. It's in his biography," he said. (I later checked out *Perry Ellis: A Biography* by Jonathan Moor, and was elated to find that this was true.) If Frank had been right about

Perry's potential crash, I surmised, it gave me reason to put stock in his prediction about my own safety while flying!

"How could you tell that by looking at my *hands*?" I asked, enormously intrigued. Palmistry was a subject I knew nothing at all about.

He wouldn't say. "If I show you, you'll start doing it and you'll freak out all your friends. And if you do see a crash, you might not be able to tell them how to avoid it!"

True. But I'm still dying to know.

Finally I asked Frank about his abilities. Sometimes he heard things; sometimes he saw symbols or written words, he said.

"So you would be considered a clairaudient and clairvoyant?"

"I don't even use those terms," he said. "I've always stayed away from other psychics and mediums. I didn't want to be influenced by them. I mean, some people have to have a certain kind of thing, with candles and black drapes . . . I've read for people in restrooms, on a train, on a bus, backstage. And you know, people say, 'Do you really believe in all that stuff?' And I go, 'Well, I don't know, but it works.'"

Frank gave me a tour of his home—the highlight of which was a portrait of him painted by Andy Warhol, who'd been an acquaintance—before I bid him good-bye.

And then there were six.

DANA MARIE

Dana Marie came not through a referral, but a gut response; I'd seen her recommended on a mailing list I'd joined, and something told me I should check her out. I contacted her via her Web site—where she used the title "clairvoyant and tarot intuitive"—and told her I lived in Manhattan. But when I called for my reading from my cell phone, which had a New York area code, she asked if I was calling from New Jersey, and if I was near the beach, which, in fact, I was. *Score!*

Dana Marie, who lived in the South Bronx, had asked for my birth date before the reading, and any questions I might have, but nothing more. She had a big, booming voice and a warm, down-to-earth manner.

Dana Marie, too, used tarot cards, as her title implied. "I use them, but I don't *interpret* them. Basically, I just glance at the images—the colors, shapes, numbers—and that triggers my clairvoyance, even clairaudience at times. It makes the clairvoyance more distinct, plus it helps me receive more information from Spirit, from Source, from the Universe, from God . . . whatever you want to call it.

"You have a very caring way about you. You're a nurturer, like a natural-born caretaker," she began, before I'd said anything that could have clued her in. "You have this healing aura about you, and sometimes, when it comes to relationships, you attract the *walking wounded*: guys that have all kinds of problems. I was gonna ask you if you were in the medical field or if you did any kind of nursing, because you're kind of like a *triage* for the emotionally battered; they come to you for help."

Ha! That was a new way of putting it. But of course, all true.

"Looking at your numerology, you are a 'six' life path. So am I. We're the mother hens."

Numerology, I noted. I knew next to nothing about that, though it was on my growing list, along with palmistry and the tarot, too, to investigate one day.

"Whether we have kids, pets, or wounded boyfriends, we go to great lengths to make sure they're OK. And you know, with that healing quality of yours, you could do very well in some type of holistic energy work."

Hmm . . . Just as Jennifer Hicks had said.

"You have healing hands," Dana Marie went on. "You have energy coming out of the palms. Do they get *warm* from time to time, even *hot?*"

"When I meditate, I *do* feel energy coming out of them. They'll start to open, and if I have them face down in my lap, they'll want to turn over, palms up," I said.

She suggested I try doing energy work such as reiki, particularly with kids. I'd not only find it extremely fulfilling, she said, but because I'd be feeling so fulfilled, I "wouldn't want to be with somebody with all sorts of emotional baggage"; rather, I'd attract a man who'd already done the healing work himself.

"You know, you've always been quite intuitive," she continued. "I believe you're very clairsentient, meaning *clear-sensing* or *clear-feeling*, as well as very clairvoyant, *clear-seeing*. You've always had this psychic seed in you. Consider your body the earth. You've been giving it nutrients, with meditation, spiritual work—I see you doing more and more of that. And at last, the seed is starting to grow. And this is opening up a lot of hidden secrets," she said, "about how the metaphysical and spiritual actually work."

That part about me being intuitive was exciting to hear! But I wasn't sure I could believe it. OK, maybe the *clairsentient* part. I did, at times, accurately *feel* certain things. And I'd had a few intuitive hits of that type over the years, but I hadn't had them often, so I pretty much regarded them as flukes. But I never really intuited things *visually* . . .

"This process of opening up your inner wisdom is also helping purge old stuff you no longer need. And I feel there's some resistance, which is manifesting into a bit of worry and anxiety. Are you not sleeping well?"

I told her my old nemesis insomnia had recently been back.

"Yeah, even though we're spiritual beings, sometimes the Earth body resists that opening up of the spiritual; as the spirit body ascends—elevates—it waits for the physical body, which is more dense, to catch up."

I'd heard talk about the idea of an *ascension*—some called it an "awakening"—that many felt was beginning to take place on the planet. I didn't know much about it, but from what I gathered, for some at least, the physical body was moving, albeit slowly, toward a connection with the spirit, or what was often referred to as the "higher self."

"And you know, the Earth body doesn't really *want* to catch up," she continued. "It's like, 'Why do I need to align with the spiritual body? I'm fine as I am in my dense, heavier self.'"

I had to laugh at her imagery. After years of punishing my body with rigid weight-loss diets till I'd finally learned to appreciate it—*most* of the time—for what it was . . . *now* it had to comply with the pressures of my free-floating, über-skinny *spiritual* self?

Dana Marie had been right on many levels. She might have been a fellow Life Path Six, but for me, she was Lucky Seven.

NOT LONG AFTER THAT, I met three more gifted intuitives, whose stories require chapters of their own to tell—and my Team grew to ten, which seemed like a goodly number. As I booked and experienced readings with this gifted group over the next few years—readings much like those described here, so I'll spare you the recounting of each, and eventually deliver just the experiment's results—I never revealed to any of them what I was attempting to do. In fact, I tried as much as possible not to reveal any information to them at all. Whether they would pick up on my project was something I was curious to find out.

As I continued with my research and investigation of other subjects, it became clear to me that my exploratory project—the ever-expanding file folders full of notes, the Ziplock bags full of cassette and microcassette tapes, and the experiences filling my head—were morphing into a book. I was, after all, a writer, and a habitual chronicler of my daily adventures through diaries and journals, so it was second nature for me to record my metaphysical adventures too.

As the months passed, I couldn't help thinking back to something Dana Marie had said in my first reading with her: To me, this period *did* feel like an *awakening* . . . or perhaps even a *remembering*, to hark back to what Patricia Masters, many years earlier, had said. I had actually come across that idea in the years since: that we humans exist in a sort

of "sleep" state; that we know much, on a soul level, that we have somehow "forgotten." *If so*, I wondered, *why?* Was it because, as "spiritual
beings having a human experience," as Pierre Teilhard de Chardin (the
French philosopher, scientist, and priest) had famously put it, we somehow needed to forget our true natures and origins? Had we—as *souls*,
that is—divinely arranged it thusly before embarking on our human
lives? Or had we, as a race, become largely detached from such knowledge through our own doing, through our shifts in values and practices,
over the course of the centuries? Or was it something else entirely?
However it had happened, the question, at least to me, was this: Was
there any way to reconnect? To fully and completely awaken to the
memory of who and what we were? I couldn't speak for the whole of the
human race . . . but for my own part, I was determined to try.

AT ABOUT THIS TIME, Griffin and I took the first of several "middle-
aged road trips," as we came to refer to them. As we motored down
I-64, Carly Simon's "Anticipation" pouring from the dashboard, and
my trusty microcassette recorder humming along on the seat beside
me, I asked my unofficial mentor on all things metaphysical about this
notion of humans being "asleep."

"Well," he said, "full waking awareness is the most valuable thing
at this level of reality. We think we're awake when we're in what science calls 'the normal waking state.' It's actually more like a dreaming
state—literally, a sort of sleepwalking."

"OK," I said, dialing down the radio and rolling up my window to
better focus on his words.

"Most people don't know this. They occasionally get jolts . . . in
danger or crisis moments, maybe, or peak experiences where they
accidentally wake up for a few seconds, or maybe half a minute. These
'unusual' experiences are what really being *awake* is like. Some people
travel to new places a lot, because breaking the routine of your familiar,

outer reality can jolt you into being semi-awake for a while. These experiences only seem like odd, 'peak' things because most of our life is spent in the walking-talking dream state."

I took in what he said, thinking back to my first European trip, which I'd taken, solo, in my twenties. I'd experienced that sort of heightened awareness then. Returning home, I'd felt the loss of it, big time. I wondered if I, too, was walking through life in this somnambulistic manner.

"All sorts of things are possible in the so-called 'waking state,'" he said, "which is really a form of dreaming. We can read, write, form and run institutions, governments, universities, build cities, cultures, empires . . . We're conduits of such powerful creative energy that we can seemingly 'do' a lot without even waking up. The creativity is passing through us, yet we don't know where it comes from or *what we really are* because we're ninety-nine-point-nine percent *asleep*."

By "what we really are," he meant, I knew, that idea that we were eternal souls, and that this human experience was just a tiny part of who we were. "So you're saying it's kind of like we're all the walking dead?" I asked, chuckling.

"The phenomenon of the sleepwalking human race isn't original to *me*. I mean, most systems of 'spiritual' this or 'spiritual' that touch on it in different ways."

"I wonder if that's why there are so many zombie books and movies around now," I mused. "Maybe people are becoming, even subconsciously, more aware of that."

He chuckled now too. "You could be right."

We seemed to have hit a lull in our talk, so I switched off my recorder, cranked the volume on the radio back up, and rolled down the window again, listening to Carly end her song, remembering how it had once been used as an anthem to ketchup. As we merged into the traffic on our next south-going route, Cat Stevens's throaty voice floated in.

"There's so much left to know . . . and I'm on the road to find out . . ."

"It's funny," I said, enjoying the cool rush of the wind pouring against my face as Griffin picked up speed. "This song is really a promo for the Bible. But Cat converted to Islam not long after that." It was interesting to me that he could have had such a radical shift in what he'd once so ardently embraced as "the way" to . . . whatever it was he was seeking.

And would I, I wondered, *get the answers I was seeking?* Where would *my* "road to find out" lead?

I had no idea.

But if it proved to be anything like I hoped, it might, at the very least, keep me "semi-awake" at the wheel.

4

ADVENTURES IN
SYCHRONICITY

✳ OR ✳

Forever Jung

MOST OF US HAVE EXPERIENCED SOMETHING INCREDIBLY coincidental, something that felt so improbable it seemed to completely defy the odds. You might have called it "*serendipity*" or, if you knew the term, "*synchronicity*." Whatever you called it, it probably left you with the opening theme of *The Twilight Zone* echoing in your head.

In my late twenties, I started noticing a preponderance of these uncanny coincidences cropping up in my life—often in batches flowing thick and fast as a sockeye salmon run. I'd be reading a novel and come across a name I'd never heard of—say, the artist Artemisia Gentileschi. That night, I'd be clicking around with the TV remote, and her name would pop up again on PBS, in no way related to the novel I'd been reading. A few days later, I'd be paging through a mildewed magazine while cleaning out my mother's jam-packed basement, and *zoinks!*— a feature story about this artist I'd never heard of till a week before would rear its head. Or, my mother would mention an actor—say, Peter O'Toole—wondering aloud what had become of him. An hour later, I'd see an ad for a new movie, featuring O'Toole. That night, I'd run across an old journal entry from back when I'd worked at the Public Theater, saying Peter O'Toole had come in to see *Coriolanus,* and my coworker had sold him a chicken sandwich—an incident I'd completely forgotten. Minutes later, the phone would ring, and *gadzooks!*—it would be that very coworker, to whom I'd not spoken in years.

I was telling a friend one day about such occurrences, and she brought up the term *synchronicity.* "It means *meaningful coincidence,*" she explained; the famous Swiss psychiatrist Carl Jung had coined the term. While my own coincidences didn't seem to be particularly *meaningful,* they were happening so often, I wondered if that had some meaning in and of itself.

After our discussion, I searched online and found an essay by Jung called "On Synchronicity,"written in 1951. In it, he linked up synchronicity with *precognition* (another term for clairvoyance or intuition) and *telepathy* (communication directly from one mind to another), which piqued my interest. But whether it was his complex writing style or the translation I was reading—Jung had written in his native German—I found the essay difficult to comprehend. Besides, it never really addressed the question I was seeking to answer: *What did synchronicity mean?*

Over the years, I'd remained curious about—if not slightly obsessed with—the idea of synchronicity. Patricia Masters had been right about its increasing presence in my life. Incidents of it excited me no end, even when they weren't my own.

My comedy-writer friend Frankie once told me a story about a woman on whom he'd had a long-time unrequited crush. He was walking down a Manhattan street with a friend, he said, telling him about this woman, when his friend said, "I picture her as being kind of like that girl over there." The friend pointed at a young woman in a catering outfit, holding a tray of drinks behind a large glass window. As he did, the woman turned. It was the very woman Frankie had been talking about. As far as Frankie knew, she wasn't even living in New York at the time, but on the West Coast. He was floored.

"That's some fantastic synchronicity!" I exclaimed, floored by the story myself.

"Good album," Frankie mused. "Probably The Police's best."

I flashed him a look.

"Isn't it just a *coincidence?*" he asked.

"Well, yes, it *is* a *coincidence*. But a *meaningful* coincidence."

"OK, I'll bite. So what's it supposed to *mean?*"

"I don't know," I admitted. "I think, that you're sort of . . . *in the zone* when it happens. "

"In the *zone?*" he echoed. "Isn't that some kind of diet?"

"You know, like, in the flow. On the right path."

Frankie smirked. He pointed out that nothing romantic had ever happened between this woman and himself—even after this remarkable incident. So how could he have been "on the right path" with his feelings for her?

Well, I knew what he meant; I'd had a similar experience myself.

In my mid-to-late twenties, before my dalliances with Leo and Ammon, I found myself falling for Drew, a whip-smart, hilarious red-headed theater-coworker and friend. Drew and I would talk for hours: about books he was reading—on history, religion, art, and philosophy —and plays and movies we'd seen. Drew hailed from Indiana, and his voice had a cute, slightly nasal twang. We shared an obvious affection, but shy and inexperienced with men as I was, I was never able to tell him, over several years' time, how I felt. An avid traveler, Drew existed on bologna sandwiches and ramen noodles until he could save up enough for his next far-flung jaunt. I, on the other hand, had never left the country. Inspired by his example and encouragement, I began saving up for my first European voyage.

Note: This was back in those pre-Euro glory days when one could save enough, relatively quickly, to do Europe on the cheap for several months. And so, Reader, before I knew it, it was time to embark. I would fly to Brussels, where a Belgian friend of Drew's would put me up. From there, I'd follow my nose, with a *Let's Go Europe* book, his budget-travel bible of choice, to guide me.

Drew was bound for points further north, visiting a Norwegian journalist he'd met the year before in Paris. She was blond and gorgeous—at least, in my mind: a spectacular combination of Julie Christie in *Dr. Zhivago* and waifish model Kate Moss, who was an icon at the time. Drew had discovered Air-Hitch, a cheap way to fly for those who could be flexible and adaptable: You'd tell the folks at Air-Hitch your destination, and they'd phone you when an inexpensive flight landing somewhere in that vicinity turned up. From there, you'd train, bus, or otherwise "hitch" to your destination . . . in Drew's case, somewhere in Norway, and the irresistible J-Mo.

The day before my departure, while he was still awaiting his hitch, I confessed my unspoken feelings. He responded, awkwardly, as I feared he would. "I care about you, Anne . . . but *as a friend.*" Much as I'd expected those words, I was still devastated. My chest actually ached. And I was embarrassed, too, and worried that I'd wrecked our friendship—which saddened me even more. Still, my adventure beckoned, so I dried my tears and focused on packing.

And the next day, I was off. After a week traveling around Belgium with Drew's lovely Belgian friend—*Ah, Brussels! Ah, beautiful Bruges!*—I headed to Amsterdam for the first solo leg of my voyage. Arriving in that breezy city bursting with bicycles and canals, I excitedly headed to the Rijksmuseum. I was particularly eager to see its van Goghs; Drew and I had recently attended a fantastic van Gogh exhibit together in New York, at the Met. And so it was all the more astounding when, there in Amsterdam, in front of van Gogh's *The Potato Eaters*, I saw from behind that familiar red head and Kelly-green T-shirt, emblazoned with the logo of our mutual place of work.

No, I thought. What were the chances? Honestly, as I stared at the back of that red head, I was not only dumbfounded, I was truly struck dumb! What if he thought I was stalking him, like that woman in *Fatal Attraction* who boiled the bunny? I was afraid to make a sound.

I thought of just walking away, but that seemed too sad for words. And possibly too silly.

Finally, I uttered his name, and he spun around, his backpack almost *thwacking* me in the head. For seconds, he just stared. My heart was thumping in my ears. Then he grinned and pulled me into a hug.

Drew and I spent a few fantastically fun days together, tooling around Amsterdam, until he caught his bus to the land of the fjords, and J-Mo's waiting arms. And it did hurt, a little. But not like before. I wasn't the same person. Seeing Europe for the first time was like being born again: It felt that expansive. After we parted, I stopped in a café and struck up a conversation with a young Dutch woman . . . and was off and running on my own Big Adventure again.

That night, I wrote in my journal: "The world is so huge, so full of possibility. *I will never get so upset about any man ever again.*" And in the moment, Reader, I believed it.

That fleeting epiphany notwithstanding, what, if anything, had our incredible encounter meant? Just as Frankie had never gotten together with his longtime crush, I'd never gotten together, romantically, with Drew either. If, as Jung believed, there was significance in such coincidences, *what was the significance?*

MANY YEARS LATER, having officially begun my explorations, I was on the phone with my writer friend Rick, who was now living in California. It was shortly before Thanksgiving. As we chatted about my attempts to assemble my Dream Team, he told me about a woman he'd met at a Thanksgiving dinner he'd attended with his boyfriend the year before.

"So I was sitting next to Christina—that's her name, Christina Wright—and I found out she's a psychic. She calls herself *the Psychic Viking*—she's Swedish, I think. And it turns out that she channels Carl Jung."

"Carl Jung?" I asked, my invisible antenna shooting out from the top of my head. "She channels *Carl Jung*?" By this point, I'd read Jung's intriguing memoir, *Memories, Dreams, Reflections*, but I still hadn't answered that long-standing question of mine.

"Yes, and she said that Dr. Jung had told her she'd meet someone at dinner that night who would guide her to *someone else*, who needed to talk with him. I told her *I* was interested in Jung, but she was adamant that it wasn't me, but *someone I knew*. And, funny enough, my friend Linda has recently gotten into Jung! I mean, she's kind of *obsessed* with him. So Linda had a session, and was quite impressed with Christina's abilities—"

"Hey!" I interjected. "*I've* been 'kind of obsessed,' for probably twenty-five years, with Jung's idea of synchronicity! Maybe the person she was talking about was *me*!"

"Could be!" he said. I pictured him grinning as he stroked his trim, reddish-gold beard in his sunny West Hollywood kitchen. "John and I are having Thanksgiving there again this year. If Christina's there too, I'll ask."

Thanksgiving came and went. About a week after, when I'd finished digesting, I received a call from Rick. "Good news!" he said. "Christina was there. I told her about you, and she said she'd love to speak to you. That 'Dr. Jung was highly in favor of it.'"

Well! After I hung up, I sat in my threadbare armchair, chewing on the synchronicity of this woman, Christina, popping up this way. In the years since that improbable meet-up with Drew, I'd had more and more synchronicities occurring in my life. And yet, more and more, it had also appeared that the Universe, God, or whoever was running the show was having a laugh at my expense. Because even my most profound synchronicities never to seemed to lead where they were pointing.

*

MOST OFTEN, these flights of synchronicity showed up in my so-called love life. About a year after West Coast Mike had broken up with me, and soon after Maggie Moise had predicted the man-storm, I'd been fixed up by a mutual friend with a divorced stage manager named George. George had phoned me, and I'd flat-out loved his growly voice and his quirky sense of humor. He suggested we meet for "tea and crumpets," which I found hilarious and delightful. Our call was followed by a mad bout of emailing, flirtatious and fun, before we finally met for breakfast at one of my favorite Village diners. With shaggy hair and wire-rimmed glasses, George had an absent-minded-professor look. When I saw him, waiting for me on a bench in the small square outside my apartment, I couldn't help smiling; it felt like seeing an old friend. Indeed, over bacon and eggs, we talked like old friends—old friends with some pretty zippy chemistry going on.

He asked me to dinner, and again, we had a ball. I was smitten . . . and how.

That night we parted in the rain. I was hoping he would kiss me, but in my uncertainty and nervousness—I liked him *so* much, my butterflies had butterflies!—I reached up prematurely to kiss his cheek instead. Due to his height and my timing—or lack thereof—my kiss landed on his neck, and felt strangely erotic. It seemed he felt it too, as he emailed me later that I could kiss his neck anytime, and promptly asked me out again.

Third date: George cooked me an elegant lunch—*he could cook, too?*—then we strolled through the park, talking for hours. As we rested on a bench, I wondered: *Was this the moment he'd finally kiss me?* But just as he seemed about to lean in . . . he suddenly up and ran. Literally. He looked at his watch, apologized, and simply disappeared.

I was stunned; it was just so *odd*. After a few days' silence, a heavy-breaking wave of sadness, confusion, and deep disappointment rolled over me. I left him a voicemail, in case he was away on business, or in a body cast, but no response. A few more days, and I called our mutual friend, the fixer-upper. George had spoken about me and our most recent date, she said, in *glowing terms*, so she was as perplexed as I was. However, where she now assumed I'd write George off, whatever his reasons or excuses, I once again was unable to let go.

It wasn't the first time a man had disappeared just when everything seemed copacetic. Marty, the animator, who'd "gone cold," had been just one. This time, though, I started seeing his name constantly: *George* on signs, *George* in books—*George, George, George*, everywhere I looked. One might say that I was supersensitive to the name, which had been all around me all along but now held a special meaning that made me notice it more—and one might well be right. But a few days later, at a local ATM, a twenty-dollar bill slipped out of the dispenser and into my palm with the combined words *wheresgeorge* hand-lettered in blue ink.

What??! I snatched up the bill for a closer look: www.wheresgeorge .com, not only the name, but actually the *question*—well, minus the question mark. For a moment, everything stood still. Then I hightailed it to the Web to see what the heck was going on.

Wheresgeorge.com proved to be the home of a currency-tracking project. Users could type in a bill's serial number, along with their own zip code, then print the URL on it and spend it. Future recipients, like me, could thus type in a bill's serial number and latest location, and track its path.

My bill hadn't been a George but an Andrew, and I typed in the number and marveled at its checkered past. But I felt as if I'd been punked by the Universe. I could picture a new constellation forming overhead, the bright stars I'd often gazed at in such wonderment lining up to spell a big, fat *GOTCHA!*

✳

THE GODS OF SYNCHRONICITY had had fun with my work life, too. Case in point my attempt to become a soap opera writer. Writing for soaps had never been my dream, but in my forties, having been laid off from my latest kids' media writing job, I learned about an ABC program to develop writers for daytime TV. It was tough to get in to; I knew talented writers who'd tried and failed. Still, soap writing paid richly, and I was fairly broke, so I applied, and was jubilant when I got in.

My contact person in the program was an affable young man named Marcus who, I learned, would put me through a training period via email and phone. I'd then write two sample scripts for *All My Children*, which would be evaluated by the story editor and, I assumed, if all went well, lead to a job.

Well, you know what they say about assuming.

Since my layoff, I'd been freelancing as a copy editor on projects ranging from cookbooks to celebrity bios to semi-pornographic westerns (which, I learned upon asking the production editor, "Who actually *reads* these things?", were enjoyed mostly by men in prison. As you can imagine, Reader, I was less concerned about errant serial commas thereafter). Once I'd been accepted into the ABC program, I heard through the grapevine that an editor named Justin, at a publishing company called Hyperion, was looking for part-time freelance help, copyediting and proofreading "in house." I contacted him and ultimately was hired. However, I warned him, I'd been accepted into this ABC program, and might imminently be whisked away for a full-time soap-writing job.

Justin nodded and asked if I knew that Hyperion was actually located *in the ABC building*—Marcus's very building!

What? No! If my eyebrows had jolted up any higher, they would've likely taken flight.

ABC/Disney, Justin explained, was Hyperion's parent company!

Crikey!

And so I didn't have far to go when I stopped by Marcus's office, a few months later, to deliver my first sample script. To make things stranger, *One Life to Live*, the other currently running ABC soap, taped across the street; I'd often see the actors in my own building. There was reigning matriarch Dorian Lord, in slippers and curlers, at the cafeteria salad bar. There was hunky Antonio in the lobby, with his equally hunky brother, Christian. And, *ooh*, there was bad-boy Rex Balsam, in the revolving door. It felt like life mirroring art, if one could venture to call soap operas "art," or like my brain had flipped inside out: my outer world mirroring my inner—in this case, my mental focus on the world of ABC soaps.

Meantime, months were passing. "How's it going with the soap writing?" Justin amiably asked.

"Well, Marcus finally read my first script. He was very encouraging," I said. But now I had to write a second, and wait to have *it* read and, I hoped, passed on to the story editor for his critical response.

All this time, synchronicities were piling on top of synchronicities. I'd had the pleasure of meeting comedian and actor Robert Klein at the Y, had lunched with him and visited his apartment (*literally across the street from the ABC building*) and was now enjoying reading his delightful memoir. Who should turn out to have been one of his acting-school classmates, as noted in the book? None other than Robin Strasser— Dorian Lord! Spurred on by this, I approached her when next I saw her in the cafeteria, curlers and all, but in the moment was too timid to mention Robert or ask for her help.

Then, lunching one day at a Chinese restaurant in the area, I'd begun chatting with a lovely woman sitting at the table next to me who, she told me, *directed* ABC soaps. "Email me. I'll get you onto the set!" she said when she heard my story, giving me her card. I did, twice—but never heard back.

Eventually, Marcus approved my second script and passed it on to the story editor. More months passed. "I heard back from the story editor," he finally wrote. "He said your script was good, but 'didn't exceed expectation.'"

What?! "What does that mean?" I typed back, restraining myself from adding several more question marks.

"Well, I think he wanted it to blow him away. And it didn't blow him away."

"So NOW what?" I typed, mentally "blowing away" the story editor, whom I pictured as cranky old Mr. Potter in *It's a Wonderful Life*, with my cocked index finger and thumb.

"Well," came the response, as I fanned away a lingering puff of smoke, "now you wait for a spot to open. But I've got to warn you, you'll be competing against seasoned career soap writers."

Ack! I knew I should probably call it a day. After all, did I, deep down, really *long* to write for soaps? *No.* But the money was so good! And I'd come so far! I couldn't give up now.

Marcus suggested I keep on top of *both* ABC shows, so I did the math: Five one-hour soaps a week, times two, was ten hours of soap viewing a week. And I was to do this *indefinitely?*

I gritted my teeth and I did it.

Six months later, I attended a soap-writing panel discussion a friend had told me about. It included the story editor for *One Life to Live*, a woman named Madeleine, who told an intriguing tale. Initially an actor, she'd done a bit part on *All My Children* as Erica Kane's prison guard—a stint she'd parlayed into her own theatrical show. The *AMC* people got wind of it, so she invited them to come. They ended up offering her entrance into the writer development program! There, she related, she wrote some *AMC* scripts but never got hired. Some time later, though, she got a call from *OLTL*. They'd found her *AMC* scripts in a drawer. Cut to the chase: She'd been hired to write for *OLTL*, working her way up to her current position of power!

Afterward, I approached Madeleine. She was friendly and open, so I told her my tale. "You're writing for the wrong ABC soap!" she said. "Tell them to let you write a script for *me*!"

I couldn't believe this reversal of fortune, or that someone who'd never met me before would be so kind. With Marcus's support, I shifted back to training mode, then took off a week from my freelance work (without pay, let it be noted), and wrote what I felt was a bang-up script. I sent it to Marcus, who'd offered to deliver it to Madeleine. After a few days of holding my breath, I received the following:

> Anne,
> Thanks for the script. Some recent developments:
> Madeleine is no longer with OLTL. However,
> I will read your script and take it into consideration
> should any opportunities arise—just as would be
> the case if Madeleine was still here.
> Marcus

"What?? When did she leave???" Censoring no question marks this time, I pounded the keys like I was putting out a fire.

"The day you delivered the script."

As Charlie Brown used to say when Lucy pulled away the football, *"AGGGH!!!"*

After picking it up off my keyboard, I shook my head in disbelief. I felt deflated, defeated . . . depressed. And mad! All this had taken nearly two years of my life, years during which the Universe seemed to be giving me signals, holding out a carrot, leading me along.

Was Frankie right, after all? I wondered. Were all my coincidences purely coincidences, odd blips of "against the odds" activity with no meaning whatsoever? Or was the Universe actually punking me once more, having what felt like a bit of cruel fun at my expense?

All this is to say . . . I had a bone to pick with Dr. Jung.

✳

FACED WITH THE PROSPECT of meeting the good doctor, or at least speaking, via Christina Wright, to a spirit she felt was his, I educated myself further on the man and his work.

Carl Gustav Jung, born in Switzerland in 1875, I learned, is considered one of the founding fathers of psychology. The idea he's probably best known for is that of the *collective unconscious*, an inherited part of the unconscious mind, he believed, shared by all humanity. Jung also popularized the concept of *archetypes* (symbols, themes, or motifs shared by all people and cultures), and of course, that of *synchronicity*. He'd coined the term in the twenties for the phenomenon of "meaningful coincidence," which he'd observed in his own life and in the lives of patients and friends. Jung saw in such phenomena a link between the individual's internal, unconscious world and the external, physical one. He believed that synchronistic events suggested that the two were, in a very real sense, one.

Though a medical doctor and a psychiatrist, Jung had been not only open to but highly intrigued by the spiritual and the occult. He'd had a cousin who was a medium and held séances, which Jung had attended, and he'd claimed to have witnessed several paranormal events himself.

The man had been a brilliant, innovative thinker. I was certainly excited to "meet" him . . . if indeed I would. Open-minded as I was about talking to dead people, even *I* had to admit that talking to dead *celebrities* was a little hard to swallow.

On the other hand, why not? If I could accept that mediums contacted the dead, why not the *famous* dead? *Were* icons like Socrates, Shakespeare, and Elvis even *famous* after death? Or was the human life in which they'd gained that fame of so little importance after death as to be inconsequential? If there *was* some sort of class system or power structure on the Other Side, I reasoned, it might well be based on something bearing no relation to *our* idea of importance at all. Perhaps, for example, spirits were ranked based on *service*! I thought back to

It's a Wonderful Life again, and how Clarence the angel was trying to help George Bailey—played so memorably by Jimmy Stewart—in order to earn his wings. Might the spirit of Carl Jung, too, be helping us hapless humans in order to attain some sort of advancement or greater soul status? Perhaps not wings but . . . a celestial degree? Say, an MCSW—Master of Celestial Social Work?

I pondered all this as I drank my Starbucks French Roast. (I couldn't help recalling that it had been Disappearing George who'd turned me on to what was now my beloved daily brew. Ah, well, I thought, we didn't have Paris, but we'd always have that.)

The fact was, I had no idea if I'd actually be meeting the famous doctor—that is, in spirit. But I decided to keep my mind open to the possibility that I might . . . just to see what would happen. Because how could one learn anything, I thought, if one didn't *attempt* things . . . do one's level best to *test things out*? While my attempts might not be scientific, wasn't that, *in essence*, what scientific inquiry was all about?

And then of course, I still wanted to know: *What did synchronicity really mean?*

AFTER READING UP on Jung, I searched out some books on synchronicity written by people *besides* Jung. Surely others had wondered about its meaning and reached some conclusions of their own.

I saw it first right in the title of a book that popped up on Amazon: *Synchronicity: Through the Eyes of Science, Myth, and Trickster*, by Allan Combs and Mark Holland. Synchronicity as *Trickster*? How, in all my years of yammering on about synchronicity, had I never gleaned so much as an inkling that these two concepts were related? I ordered the book, and jumped on it like a stray mutt on a Liv-a-Snap when it arrived.

Combs and Holland started out with a section on "Synchronicity and Science," followed by one on "Synchronicity and Myth," which included a discussion of the Trickster. Though I'd often been one to eat my dessert before dinner—and sometimes again after it—I'd always felt compelled to start a book from its beginning and proceed on obediently to the end. So I set out to make my way through the "Science" section like a child accepting her plate of peas and roast beef, with visions of the mythical Trickster, like the promised chocolate pudding, dancing in my head.

"Science," however, proved so interesting I completely forgot about the Trickster—at least for a while. From Victorian-era biologist Paul Kammerer's obsessive investigation of repetitive events, to modern-day physics' *quantum synchronicity*; David Bohm's view of *cosmos as hologram*; Rupert Sheldrake's *morphic fields*; Pierre Teilhard de Chardin's *noosphere*, and more, the authors provided a brisk, fascinating tour of Western science's explorations into *universal interconnectedness*, of which Jung believed synchronicity was merely "the surface effect."

While I couldn't follow all the science, much less try to explain it here (I strongly urge you to explore this intriguing book for yourself!), I loved that there were acclaimed modern-day scientists taking synchronicity seriously enough to study and weigh in on it.

So there, Frankie!

Mind fully boggled by even my brief survey of "Science," I turned to "Myth." In a chapter called "Hermes the Trickster," the authors pointed out that synchronistic experiences shared the trait of being startling and unexpected, outside of the cause-and-effect framework of things. "In the mythologies of many people," they wrote, "the mythic figure who is the embodiment of the unexpected is the Trickster . . ."

Now that I knew what to look for, Reader, I found that this idea was ubiquitous. "Synchronicities are the jokers in nature's pack of cards," I read in *Synchronicity, the Bridge Between Matter and Mind*, by F. David Peat. In *Synchronicity: The Promise of Coincidence*, the author, Dieke Begg, references the notion of "the universe flirting with people": "'To flirt' in its original sense means 'to give a light blow' and 'to jerk away.'

How apt this is for synchronicities that give us a light blow—sometimes not so light—and a jerk."

I'd surely met up with a few such synchronicities. But what did that *mean?* Combs and Holland had this to say: "The Trickster's play frequently gives opportunities, usually unwelcome, for personal growth, by flaunting our most private secrets for the whole world to see . . . These instances offer the opportunity to recognize our faults and, by owning them, to take away their sting, and in the bargain render ourselves more whole."

Aha! Now we were getting somewhere!

Dr. Allan G. Hunter, in *The Pathway of Synchronicity*, proposed that synchronicity works by *testing* us: "An event happens, it coincides with another event, and at that point we have a choice: we can either discount both events, or we can see that perhaps there is a pattern emerging."

Recognizing our faults, noticing patterns . . . Looking back on my synchronistic experiences with my theater friend Drew, and with Disappearing George, I could see that both these men *had* offered me opportunities for learning. How many times had I held in my feelings for a guy for fear of losing him, when I'd never had him to begin with, or hung in there when there were red flags flashing like stoplights? These had been my patterns, painful ones.

And what about my pursuit of soap writing? Was it, as mythologist Joseph Campbell put it, "following my bliss"? No. It was about being tired of being poor. Had I *gotten* a soap job, I realized, I never would have found my way to the explorations, and the writing, I was doing now, work I truly loved; I would have been far too busy to investigate "weird stuff"! And too well paid to ever stop! I'd probably known in my gut that writing soaps was wrong for me all along. Still, I'd twisted myself into garlic knots trying to make it happen. It had taken Madeleine losing her job on the very day I delivered my script to finally make me quit. Perhaps the Universe felt I needed that "light blow"—in this case, upside the head.

I remembered a game my older brother had made up when we were kids. Our playroom had a low radiator at either end. This day, my brother, with his characteristic sense of the macabre, had invented a game he called "Can You Take It?" The object was to see which of us kids, thighs reddening through our dungarees or, in my case, Danskin stretch pants, could sit on the hot radiator the longest.

Can you say, "*masochistic*"?

I don't recall who took the dubious crown that day, but metaphorically, it seemed I was still sitting there trying to, in many areas of my life. Could it be that all this synchronicity was the Universe reflecting back my stubborn, wrong-headed, perhaps even self-punishing ways, so I'd learn to "Just say no"—ditch these disinterested guys, flip off that *AMC* story editor, give Lucy van Pelt a swift kick in the panties, and finally get the HELL off that radiator?

It certainly could.

So perhaps I'd found the answer I was seeking—and thank goodness, because when I finally spoke with Christina Wright, an effervescent woman with traces of a Swedish accent who proved remarkably adept as an intuitive, she said that Dr. Jung *didn't want to discuss synchronicity at all*!

"He says, 'Don't worry about my *old* stuff, it's all about my *new*, improved stuff,'" she explained from her Torrance, California, home—the stuff he was working on now, in the "inner planes." "He wants it to come out to the public. He says they don't measure time where he is now, but he's worked on it long enough! He says, 'The old stuff . . . it has to do with what was going on in those days. It was a different awareness, a different understanding.' He knows many people are still reading it, but he feels it confuses some of them."

He's got that right, I thought.

"He says, 'From where I am today, how I've learned and evolved on the Other Side, there's so much more wisdom. Because life is an evolution. For everybody,'" she said.

Well! Having learned about the Trickster, it shouldn't have surprised me that the good doctor had moved on now past his own idea of synchronicity. Still, no way was I going to let this bird-in-the-hand off that easily.

"I kept thinking that when synchronicity occurred, it meant I was on the right path," I emailed Christina. "But often I was NOT—for example, trying to get a soap-writing job I never got. So I concluded that the synchronicities were NOT a signal of that at all. But a lot of people interpret them that way. Is that wrong?"

"The plan for you all along was to get the job you *got* . . . the editing job. You WERE on the right path," Dr. Jung/Christina replied.

Huh. They were saying I'd been on the right path working at my *copyediting and proofreading* job with Justin. Well, now that I thought about it, I *had* gotten my first book-writing contract when an editor there needed a writer for a movie tie-in book about Jane Austen. The job had also supplied me with a steady paycheck, so I could pursue projects in which I *did* "follow my bliss"—including what I was doing now.

"Things that happen, by choice or destiny, are sometimes signaled by the Universe and/or the individuals' guides, to put it rather simply. These things are difficult to explain; they just ARE. How do you explain sight to a blind person?" Dr. Jung/Christina wrote.

Synchronicity, then, as simply a response, *a* signal, *from the Universe and/or our spirit guides?* I cast my mind back to Jung's idea of synchronicity as a reflection of the interconnectedness of all things, of the outer world mirroring the inner, of the two actually being one. Perhaps, like looking for the meaning of gravity, I'd been looking for the *meaning* of a phenomenon that was simply Universal *law.* Perhaps, I thought, it was up to each of us to *pay attention* to the Universe's signals, and to *use* them to see our patterns, for our own learning and growth . . . if we were "awake" enough to notice.

I WAS SEATED in my threadbare armchair, typing away on my trusty Mac one evening not long after that. I was doing some especially tedious copyediting, longing to get it done so I could continue with research for my explorations. It had been a while since I'd found time to focus on them. There were so many bills to pay, so many obligations to fulfill, so much family—as we New Yorkers often put it—*mishigas*.

"Will the day ever come," I muttered, "when I have the freedom to do just the work I *want* to do?"

No one answered—which was likely a good thing, as I was alone in my apartment. So I got up to brew some French Roast.

I'd had my desktop background set, since buying my laptop, to one of its image-bank photos: a close-up of a dandelion gone to seed— a milky-white, wispy globe—against a background of soft yet vibrant yellow-green. I'd chosen it because it was soothing, and about as non-technological an image as you could get. When I returned to my laptop, though, gone was the dandelion, replaced by a deep-blue galaxy lit with twinkling stars and sweeping bands of golden starlight.

I stared at the screen, awestruck. I hadn't touched a thing. Then I emailed my brother-in-law, my go-to guy for all things Mac, asking if he knew any way such a thing could have happened. He responded that he did not, seeming perplexed himself.

I stood marveling at the synchronicity of this particular image popping up this way. There were so many pictures in that image bank: elephants and lions; wild poppies; wind-swept deserts and ocean waves . . . I might not have a *man* in my life, I mused, but the *Universe* was definitely flirting with me. Was it the outer world mirroring the inner—my longing to have time to pursue my metaphysical, "otherworldly" explorations? Or had the Universe and/or my guides felt

I needed a reminder to "just say no" more often to my perceived obligations, and make my own needs and wishes a priority.

"I'm trying," I said to the cosmos, staring at the image.

But how hard, exactly, *was* I?

It was impossible, I realized, to bullshit the cosmos.

I needed to stop making excuses. If I wanted to make changes in my life, to have that freedom I craved to do what I felt I was here to do, I needed to get back to work—on my exploratory project, but also on myself. It was seeming clearer and clearer to me that the two *were* parts of a single whole; that the Universe was teaching me what I most needed to learn, and attempting—as Patricia Masters and her "invisible friends" had done—to keep me aligned with "my purpose."

Back in my college days, in an art history class, we'd studied a haunting painting by Gauguin depicting several nude and semi-nude figures, animals, and a statue, set against mountains and sea, the title of which had stayed with me: *Where Do We Come From? What Are We? Where Are We Going?* When people asked, and they *did*—often with great surprise, as they considered me "intelligent"—why I was so curious about things "spiritual," "supernatural" or "paranormal," I often referenced the questions in that painting's title. Because they were damn good questions . . . and they were *my* questions too.

Whether or not someone could predict the future, see events from the past, or reach out and touch someone who'd shed their earthly body had never really been what fueled my curiosity. Though those were things I'd been curious about since childhood, they'd never been at the heart of what I was seeking. And though my search for love and partnership had spurred my initial adventures with psychics, it wasn't earthly love I'd been looking for when I'd finally launched myself full-scale into my investigations.

What I'd always wanted was simply *to understand*: where we humans came from, what we were, and yes, where we were going . . . and what, if anything, it all *meant*. I knew millions before me had pondered these questions, including, apparently, Gauguin. Yet it shocked me how few people I knew were even curious about them. For me, attempting to answer those questions was utterly basic to living life—not to mention possibly *improving* life, for myself, others, and still others yet to come on the planet.

Where *did* we come from? What *were* we? And where *were* we going? Reader, while I might never find definitive answers, I could no longer picture my life without the search.

Nor, apparently, could the Universe.

I put aside my copyediting job, deadline be damned—I'd find a way to hit it, I always did—and pulled out a book about out-of-body experiences that I'd recently received from Griffin, eager to delve in.

I was grateful that the Universe had my back, I thought, as I switched off my MacBook Pro and bid it, for now, good night.

5

ADVENTURES IN
PAST LIVES

✴ OR ✴

And Then There Were Nuns

HAVE YOU EVER HAD THE FEELING YOU'VE "BEEN THERE, done that" before . . . but not in this lifetime? Maybe you visited Moscow for the first time and were shocked to feel a profound connection with the city and its people—though you had no genetic link to the place. Or you arrived at college and met your roommate, only to feel an uncanny sense that she was an old friend. Perhaps it was your inexplicable drive to dress in Renaissance attire, panic attacks triggered by African drumming, or an obsession with German submarines: If you're even the least bit woo-woo–curious, it might have made you wonder about the idea of past lives.

I didn't grow up in a family that believed in reincarnation; it wasn't part of the Catholic Church's doctrine with which I'd been, more or less, raised. But for some reason, I'd always had a youthful predisposition toward the idea. Then, in my late twenties and early thirties, I'd had some experiences that had left me with the palpable sensation that I'd already shuffled off a few mortal coils, or maybe more than a few.

The first was at the Convent of San Marco, in Florence, on my maiden European voyage. The Convent was now a serene museum, housing frescoes by the Early Renaissance painter Fra Angelico. As

I visited the tiny, bare, whitewashed rooms where monks had once lived, I felt both comfort and longing. It felt like *home*, a place with which I was intimately familiar, and to which some part of me—my soul?—wistfully, almost *nostalgically*, longed to return.

It happened again on a trip through Pennsylvania Dutch country. I'd toured the grounds of a former religious community where cloistered, celibate sisters and brothers had lived. The rooms were barely larger than broom closets—just big enough to house a desk, stool, and sleeping bench, complete with wooden head-block. Entering them, I had that same visceral response: *I know this. I lived like this.*

"Because you *did*! You lived in *Manhattan*—still do!" my friend Frankie hooted when I told him about it. I'd often joked with Frankie, whose Italian surname meant *Holy Father*, that we'd had a past life together in which I was a nun on one side of the wall and he was a priest on the other, and that we'd had an illicit affair—which was why we'd felt such an immediate kinship upon meeting in *this* life. While we'd never really dated, there'd always been some sort of emotional chemistry between us, and we shared a sisterly-brotherly bond that I knew would never break. He was the yin to my yang, or maybe vice versa. Frankie's humor always brought me down to Earth when I had my head a little too far out there in other dimensions.

"Mock me if you must," I said to him now, "but I think *you* were there too."

"Really? Was I the Scarecrow, the Lion, or the Tin Man?" he asked.

"You know what I mean," I said.

But I knew he thought I was wack-a-doo, so I changed the subject.

Frankie was only one of my many friends and family members who found the idea of reincarnation laughable, or at least highly implausible. But much of the world, I knew, believed in it: Hindus and Buddhists alone accounted for millions, if not billions, of believers. On a personal level, the idea that I'd lived before as a nun or a monk or both made a certain sense. When I was a child, my father had owned a record album called *The Singing Nun*, featuring a Belgian, guitar-playing sister who sang folk songs at least partially in French, which I obsessively asked him to play. I was a huge fan too of *The Sound of Music*—another nun, another guitar—as well as an admittedly bizarre TV show called *The Flying Nun*, featuring Sally Field as a young sister prone to taking flight, powered by her white "winged" headgear.

Later, I'd fallen for a number of "men of the cloth"—and one or two who had considered the calling. There'd been a charismatic young priest at our local parish on whom I'd had my first girlhood crush; an attraction, in my college years, to a man who'd once been a seminarian; and another, in my twenties, to an ordained minister who worked as a cinema usher and disco-danced at night.

And—though not romantically—I'd been drawn to real-life sisters too. In Venice, I'd sought out lodging at a convent that housed travelers, listed in my *Let's Go* guide. Later, I'd "adopted" an elderly retired nun, donating toward her living expenses and writing her letters. Moreover, from childhood, I'd often been told that *I should be a nun*. My *biological* sister sometimes teased me by calling me "the nun" and "the saint," and my family still joked about the time, as a child, that I'd stolen an extra chewable vitamin (they were surprisingly tasty!)—one of the few instances on record back then when I'd done something "bad."

And then there was the fact that I'd been such a late-bloomer with men . . .

In a reading I had once with Patricia Masters in which I'd asked her about said biological sister, Patricia had mentioned that she and I would write a children's book together, and that we'd work well as a team. "That's because you two have a long history of lifetimes together," she explained.

"So, people in my life who are close to me . . . does that usually mean we've had other lives together?" I asked. I hadn't planned to question her about reincarnation. At that point, I hadn't expected it would come up in a reading with a psychic at all.

"Absolutely," she said. "You've had many, many lifetimes where you've lived in religious communities, and at least one in which you lived in a cloistered setting."

Holy head-in-a-wimple, Batman! I'd never told Patricia about the feelings I'd had when I visited those tiny, bare rooms in Florence and Pennsylvania. I was astonished to hear her voice something I'd felt so strongly myself.

"Those lives in religious orders, they're partly why, in this life, you took your time with men."

"I always thought I was just really repressed!" I said.

"It was not repression. It was just . . . something you'd not seen in a long time."

Well, if that was true, it was a relief to hear it. I'd spent years in therapy trying to understand why romantic relationships were so painful and difficult. Might this also be why, despite my many friends, I could be downright reclusive, often needing long periods of solitude and silence in order to feel centered and happy?

Patricia was only the first of several psychics to talk about my past lives in religious orders. Christina Wright, with no knowledge of me beyond a few pleasantries over the phone, had said the same, describing a life in which she and I had been sisters together, specifically *Cathars*—members of a Christian order that had sprung up between the twelfth and fourteen centuries in Southern Europe who'd renounced Catholicism and been persecuted as heretics. We had, she reported, "been burned."

Rather than feeling horrified by her statement, I felt oddly gleeful. I loved it when my intuitive friends picked up similar things, and gave me unsolicited information that validated something I'd felt powerfully myself.

Christina had gone on: She and I had been sisters together *again*, in a convent in the South of France—a place, as it happened, I'd always longed to visit. "We were normal people, just put in a miserable lifestyle. We went around with that *thing* on our heads, and everything was so barren, and we had to sit there and pray all day!" Plus, she said, "We always got into trouble for having fun." There was an apple tree just beyond our convent wall, she said, the branches of which overhung our yard, and we sisters would sneak out at night to pick the apples, gorging ourselves and laughing our wimples off.

Two of her other clients, she added, had been nuns with us too. With these former sisters, she said, there was always a connection, in their present life, with apples. One decorated her Christmas tree solely with apples; another sold homemade apple pies—that kind of thing.

"And you, *you* live in the *Big Apple*!" she said.

Well, that felt like a bit of a stretch. But for many years I *had* kept a postcard on my windowsill, a black-and-white photo of a tree branch thick with apples. I'd probably received hundreds of cards in my life, but this was the one I'd chosen to display where I could see it upon waking each morning; it gave me joy. I'd also kept on display, for decades, a set of apple-shaped candles, none of which I'd ever actually burned because I liked them so much.

And then there had been Patricia Bechdolt, an "evolutionary astrologer" who will trace your soul's history through past lives. In a reading, she told me with no prompting that I'd not only had many lives in religious communities, but had often been a *heretic*, and that I taught other people in the community ideas that went against those of the reigning faith.

"And you're still doing that," she said, "with your book. You weren't raised with these ideas. Yet you've not only come to them yourself, you're teaching them to others."

Let me clarify, here, that I *had* told Patricia Bechdolt about my metaphysical explorations. Christina Wright knew about them too.

Could it be that, having heard about my interest in these topics, the two of them had extrapolated from that?

Truth be told, despite all these experiences, and much as I'd felt in my gut since childhood that reincarnation was likely real, my skeptical, math-and-science-trained brain *still* wasn't fully convinced.

✳

ONCE I'D LAUNCHED INTO my explorations, I began considering a "past-life regression." This involved being hypnotized and recalling—and to some extent *reliving*, as I understood it—some of one's past lives. My ex-boyfriend Leo, who was highly open to metaphysical ideas and quite intuitive himself, had once told me about a scenario, a medieval village under attack, that he'd vividly experienced during a past-life regression, and it had made me highly curious. Still, I was a little scared of being "regressed." And it wasn't just the possibility of reliving a scene out of *Conan the Barbarian*. I was as curious about hypnosis as I was about past lives, but I was reluctant to let just anyone hypnotize me. After all, who knew what odd notion some stranger might insert into my open and receptive subconscious? I might find myself, days hence, buying bubble-gum flavored Go-Gurt, participating in Ponzi schemes, or watching episodes of *Judge Judy* over and over in an endless loop.

I'd once seen a stage hypnotist perform at my Southern university. He'd asked for volunteers and had them, via hypnotic suggestion, perform some highly entertaining acts. I remember one student quacking like a duck. My favorite was a young woman who'd been regressed to childhood. Taking her to the age of five, the hypnotist had directed her to write her name on a chalkboard, which she did in shaky, block letters; fast-forwarding her to seven, he'd asked her what she wanted for Christmas. "A Barbie Dream House," she said, in a convincingly childlike tone.

The hypnotist had later stated that a person couldn't be forced to do anything they didn't want to do while under hypnosis—pointing out that the show's participants had all been willing volunteers—and clarified that subjects were never "out" or unconscious. Even so, it was something, like flossing my teeth or skinny-dipping, that I didn't want to do with a total stranger.

My first past-life regression came about almost by accident. In my late forties, feeling burnt out on copyediting and proofreading, I'd thought about finding more stimulating work. I pulled out a spiral notebook and pen, and attempted to inventory my talents.

There was writing—but it was hard to make a living at that; the kids' media field I'd once done so well in had largely dried up. I'd tried the soaps, to no avail, and had attempted to break into advertising, but my age seemed a barrier to even the lowliest of jobs.

And then there was art. I seemed to possess some ability, and had been told by art teachers that I had an excellent eye for color; I certainly loved it! I had a shelf full of oil paints waiting for me to find time to use them. But I'd never been formally trained, and I knew it was equally hard to make a living at that.

My Team had picked up on my rapport with and love for children. I'd babysat and nannied, and had briefly worked in an experimental elementary school program. But I didn't want to be a teacher or a social worker, much as I'd been told I'd be good at both.

My father had once memorably remarked, "It's too bad there's no such thing as a 'professional friend,' because that's really your greatest talent." Griffin still teased me about that line. But, especially as a single person, I'd always found friendships hugely important and rewarding, and I'd cultivated and maintained many. Dad had been right: It *was* too bad I couldn't make a living at that!

I thought I'd do well in sales or promotion—I was good at raising money for causes, talking to people, and finding work for friends. Shy as I'd once been, I'd striven to overcome it. But the idea of business school gave me hives.

Ditto any career involving math or science, though I'd done very well in school at both.

The only real *physical* talent I possessed was good aim. I could shoot baskets, and once in my youth I'd won a water-pistol carnival game against five grown men, a feat of which I was, at the time, inordinately proud. More recently, on a sunset sail, I'd had the wheel of an antique schooner thrust into my hands by the ship's captain. He'd pointed to a buoy floating off in the distance and told me to steer toward it while he tended to a passenger.

What, me? Captain a huge ship?! I couldn't even *drive*! But as I did it, I found I was loving it. When the captain returned, he praised me: "You're very good at that!"

Still, that and a Metro Card would get me a ride on the subway.

Having exhausted even the most absurd of possibilities, I tossed the notebook aside. Months later, though, I heard about a new-fangled career called "life coaching," and was considering pursuing it.

"*Uhhhh* . . . doesn't that mean that you have to have a *life?*" my older brother asked. *Touché*, I thought. My life didn't include most of the traditional trappings of "success." Aside from the lack of a career or a partner, I had little in the way of savings, nor did I own a home, a car, or even—if you didn't count the occasional small-scale rodent—a pet. Still, strangers were constantly telling me their problems—on planes, trains, and ferries, in cafés, and even one poor soul in our therapists' shared waiting room who apparently couldn't wait. I was always trying to tap the untapped potential of others—and not just the men I dated.

I mentioned my interest to a friend, who put me in touch with a friend of *his*, a life coach named Marianna Lead. Marianna, who told me she was an MCC (a Master Certified Coach with the International Coach Federation, to be precise) was friendly and helpful, and taught a training course for coaches, which I considered taking—though in the end I decided against it, to pursue my writing instead. In speaking with Marianna, though, I learned that she was also a hypnotist! When I found out that she used hypnosis to conduct *past-life regressions,* Reader, I set up a session.

✳

I arrived at Marianna's Brooklyn apartment, adrenaline pumping. Would I truly find out things I'd experienced in other times and places? Would doors of understanding about my present life be unlocked? Would I gain a greater understanding of who I really was?

A vivacious brunette with an open face and intelligent eyes, Marianna had me lie on her comfy couch—after so many years on Melinda's, it felt like coming home!—then spoke in a soothing, singsong voice as she led me through a series of visualizations. She had me mentally create a magic carpet, which I could slow down or speed up at will, and stop if I felt unsafe. Then she slowly counted out numbers, each of which was supposed to take me into a more deeply relaxed state.

She instructed me to tell her when to stop counting—in other words, *I* was supposed to know when I'd gone deep enough. Or, I gathered, my *subconscious mind* was. But *conscious* me wasn't so sure. In fact, neurotic that I was, I began to worry about it. How deep was "deep enough"? Could one go *too* deep? And how deep could I *get, anyway,* if I had to be worrying about *that*? And so, possibly sooner than I should have, and not feeling particularly hypnotized—*Were some people more hypnotizable than others?*—I told her that she could stop.

Next, Marianna had me mentally arrive at various doors opening onto past lives. "Your subconscious will guide you," she said, "to those that will teach you what you most need to know." I arrived at a door marked "1798." She told me to step through and look down at my feet. I saw small, bare toes; then, moving my gaze upward, a long black skirt made of a rough material, and a rope belt. I was female, about eighteen, with fair hair—not my present-day color—wandering around an empty house.

Beyond that, though, the images didn't flow easily. Eventually, as Marianna prompted me with questions, I came to feel that I'd worked in this house, as a tutor or governess to two flaxen-haired children, whom I loved. The family was gone, and I'd come back to visit this lonely place. Listening to a recording of the session later, I had no idea why my subconscious would have taken me there. It felt likely my brain had concocted this morose tale from elements of my own life, *Jane Eyre*, and, yes, *The Sound of Music* (case in point, those flaxen-haired kids). After all, I'd once worked as a nanny, and had never had kids of my own—well, with all those lives as a celibate religious type, who could blame me?

"Now, move forward to the moment of your death," Marianna said. I did, and felt I was an old woman who'd never married and spent my years going from family to family, caring for other people's children. I'd died alone, and empty . . . as empty as that bare husk of a house.

"Were you *never* with a *man*?" Marianna asked, sounding incredulous.

"No," I said. The words just seemed to pop into my head.

"So . . . what are you supposed to take away from this?"

I had no idea.

She told me, then, to go out of my body and ask the "wise men" whom we consulted between lives. Words and images were coming more easily now. The wise men were saying it was about a *choice* . . . That *I* felt I had to repeat this scenario—taking care of other people's children; hiding myself away, like a recluse. But they were telling me that no, I had a choice.

"Huh!" she said, surprised. Outwardly, I knew, I appeared to be a very social person, and I did have that side to me. But I was in many ways a loner. Now in my late forties, not only had I never married, I'd never even lived with a partner. I'd once told a friend that if I ever did marry, my husband would have to have his own house, and I, mine—so much did I value my alone time and my independence.

"What else are they saying?" Marianna asked.

Now they were saying something about *cruelty*, I said. I saw myself as a little girl in that lifetime, locked in my room by a woman who wasn't my mother. When my father had discovered it, he'd been furious. He loved me, but I'd run away. I'd spent my life waiting for him to find me, but he never had. He'd been too weak.

She asked me to describe this father, and I did: a dark beard and hair, blue eyes.

"Put your hand on his heart," she said. "Who is he, if anyone, in your life now?"

"I'm not sure if it's just because it's a *father*," I said, "and it's not him *physically*, but it *feels* like my present-life father," I said. "He died about six years ago."

"You can hug him if you want," she said.

I envisioned this, and got so choked up I could barely speak. She asked if I could forgive *both* fathers—and inwardly, I did, feeling something in me lighten.

Then she had me go to the wise men again and ask what I was to learn from this. An answer came clearly: *"Let go!"* I needed to *let go* of waiting for men who weren't there for me.

Then Marianna had me ask the wise men if there were other lives I needed to see.

"It's weird," I said. "I'm seeing, really clearly, a *pirate flag*. I'm on a big ship. And . . . *I'm a pirate!*" I laughed. "I can see the dirt under my fingernails. And I have on these ragged, filthy clothes!" Oddly, this life felt far more convincing than the first; the images flooded in effortlessly. Also, the pirate bore much less resemblance to present-day me than the governess—except maybe on a bad PMS day.

"Again, it's seventeen hundred something. Spain, I think," I said, when she asked me where I was.

This time, Mariana had me go directly to my death.

"It was cholera," I said. "There's a lot of guilt. I stole from people. I died with a lot of money, but a lot of regret." The initial humor I'd felt in connecting with my pirate self had completely disappeared now, and I found myself, rather, quite somber.

"And what are you supposed to learn from this?"

"That that's why I don't have money. I feel guilty for having it. When I do, I feel I should give it away." The details were still coming fast. But was I unconsciously concocting this life *because* of my money issues? Unlike being a nun or a monk, I'd never had any conscious sense of having been a *pirate*. Yes, I'd found Johnny Depp as Jack Sparrow hilarious, but according to box-office figures, most of the free world had.

Soon, Marianna brought the session to a close. I sat up, feeling as if very little time had passed. I'd never felt "out" or "under," but listening to the recording of my session later, which was much longer than I expected, I realized that my sense of time while working with Marianna had clearly been distorted.

As I listened to the bit about the pirate, I flashed back to my real-life incident on the schooner, how oddly comfortable I'd felt at the wheel. I also recalled that I had, in my present-day bedroom, a large antique steamer trunk, with a domed top and metal trim, which I'd been captivated by at a flea market. As I'd lugged it home, a woman had shouted, "Yo ho ho!" and a man, "Nice booty!" I also, I realized, owned a small painting of an old sailing ship, purchased on Nantucket—an odd choice for me, as I went in more for Matisse prints and colorful Impressionist works, but I'd been drawn to it.

Was I half off my nut to be considering that the pirate life might have been real?

My regression had been intriguing, and had definitely pushed some emotional buttons. But I still wasn't convinced that I hadn't on some level been making it all up.

✳

ABOUT A YEAR LATER, I decided to try another regression. I wanted to see if I could experience something my critical, analytical mind would find more convincing. I asked my intuitive friend Maggie Moise if she could pick up past lives.

"Sometimes," she said. "But I know somebody who's very good at it: Reverend Kev O'Kane. He told me stuff I'd actually dreamed about. The things that he sees, about your past lives, show how you've developed to be who you are now."

That sounded exciting, and potentially enlightening, so I gave him a call.

"Rev. Kev," as he called himself, turned out to be a Spiritualist minister and clinical hypnotist, as well as an intuitive counselor and medium. We set up a reading—note: not a *regression*, but a *past-life reading*—to be done over the phone. I told him nothing about myself, and I'd made sure that Maggie hadn't either.

"You don't need to *regress* a person to get their past lives?" I asked Rev. Kev, a chatty fellow who was also a "recovering attorney," as he jocularly put it.

"No," he said. "The source of it all, for me, is the Akashic Records. The records of your soul's journey since it was created . . . of all the growth, thoughts, deeds, and feelings you've ever had or done. Sometimes I get the info directly from them, and at other times, more often, I get it from the Masters—the highest beings. I don't control how it comes, but accept it when it arrives."

"If that's so easy to do, why do other people do regressions?" I asked.

"Doing any reading, has, I think, a lot to do with what you believe you can do," he said. "I tried to do a past-life reading and found I could do it as easily as any other. It's about getting my consciousness out of the way and opening myself to receive. Let me just clarify, though. Having a past-life *reading* generally doesn't create change in this life, but having a past-life *regression*, which I also provide for clients, wherein you *relive* the experience, often causes one's subconscious and conscious minds to desire and create the changes needed. Also, in a regression session, we can apply therapies to alleviate the hold the past life may have on this one."

Huh. Had my subconscious created any changes after Marianna's regression? I did feel a change in regard to my father. Forgiving him had seemed to ease something in me. But was it more powerful because I'd done it during a regression? I couldn't say.

Kev gave a long, loud exhale, then began. "You had a lot of lives as a male warrior. In one, I'm seeing you as being extremely large. Almost like the Hulk."

I nearly spit out my mouthful of French Roast.

"I mean, you were *huge*! Your shoulders were bigger than my waist! Each shoulder! Now, this was back when Nephilim were walking the Earth."

"*Nephilim?*" I asked.

"Basically, angels that were mixing with humans. Some people believe they were descendants directly from Atlantis. They were giants—ten, twelve, eighteen feet tall. You were huge also in muscular body build. You were incredible! And incredibly scary."

Me, scary? I apologized to the roaches in my kitchen before I went in for the kill.

"So you became a warrior, because it was the easiest thing for you," he continued. "Besides, you loved committing carnage! Now, we're talking way before the birth of Christ. It feels like you were in the armies of Joshua, that part of the world. You were sort of like his secret weapon. But it wasn't a secret, because you were so huge!"

We laughed. "Were they just as visible as humans, or more invisible?" Hard as all this was to believe—and it *was* hard!—I wanted to see where it went.

"Some were more ethereal than others. *You* were grossly physical, *that* end of the spectrum. Now, women were much smaller than you, so most of them were afraid of you, but there *was* one you married. You loved each other tremendously. She helped you understand more about the love of God, and that whatever you do to another, you do to yourself. She was also the first person that didn't judge you on your appearance."

"Sounds like *Beauty and the Beast*," I said. I had seen the Broadway show *twice*, and cried both times—at a *Disney musical*! I had to admit, it was a story that resonated emotionally with me.

"You gained in that life quite a bit by moving from loving to create carnage to learning what love *is*. Today, you don't judge others on their looks."

That was true, I thought.

"And you've become more loving in each lifetime since. OK . . . This next life is much later," he continued. "But you have to realize, since *there's really no such thing as time*, lives are not continuous. You could have a life in Old Testament times, and one in the eighteen hundreds, following each other. Because when we get up there, we can choose to be born anytime, anywhere. If what you have to learn is best learned in the year zero in Jerusalem, you'll go there."

I'd heard that before, about time not existing in other realms. "Time is a series of dimensions," I later heard Rev. Kev explain in an online radio interview on *The Bob Charles Show*. "It is not a *thing*. When we go to the 'past,' or the 'future,' we go to other dimensions. It's a change of *consciousness*."

Rev. Kev went on to tell me about other lives: a Boston housewife in the early 1800s; a businessman in Ancient Rome, who dealt in pottery; and a reclusive German-American salesman in 1930s Milwaukee, retired—highly decorated—from the military.

As the Boston housewife, he said, I'd raised five rambunctious boys to be polite and loving. "You taught your boys to love themselves, and helped them learn how to love others. So today, because of that, your rapport with children is one of your biggest strengths; you can get children to see the light inside of themselves. It doesn't feel like you're using that so much right now, but you *can choose* to—and the Universe will turn whichever way it has to, to make that happen."

Well, it was certainly true that I had a rapport with children. "Do you feel that's a path I'm supposed to be on?" I asked.

"I do." Kev told me, in fact, that I hadn't had kids in this lifetime because I'd planned it that way, to focus on this "assignment": to open children up.

I took a moment to absorb that. Much as I'd felt a loss when my child-bearing window had definitively shut, a few years after West Coast Mike and I had parted, I'd largely made my peace with it, knowing that I had my four nieces, and that I could always do volunteer work with kids in need. Hearing this made me want to get to it. And while I couldn't know for sure that Kev was right, even contemplating the idea that I'd *planned* not to have kids—that I hadn't failed, been denied, or just somehow missed the boat—had a healing, and a freeing, effect.

Regarding the Roman businessman, Rev. Kev said I still had good sales and negotiation skills from that lifetime. "And this might surprise you, but you also have a gift for math."

"No surprise. I *was* very good at it!" I said.

As for the retired soldier–turned-salesman . . . it was intriguing to me that I'd apparently had a number of lives that involved war. Was that why I had those nightmares with soldiers climbing over my windowsill? And why I owned two shoulder bags that were military in style, two army-green duffel bags, army-type boots, a camouflage-print scarf, and a camouflage-print skirt that I wore constantly—despite an animal-lover friend once telling me that I looked like I was dressed to kill baby deer? A cab driver had once asked me if I'd been in the military. "You have a soldier-like gait, and carry your duffel bag in just the way that people in the military do," he said. And a friend who'd been a Marine had said the same thing about the way I walked. Could it be that I carried vestiges of those military lives in me still?

"It's funny, all these warrior and military lives," I told Kev, "because I couldn't be more of a peacenik now."

"That's because you've *had* those lives! The biggest advocates for peace are warriors. Just like the biggest anti-smoking nuts are people who used to smoke!"

I'd never thought of it that way, but it made sense. If we didn't *learn* from our many lives—assuming they were real—what would be the point in having them?

He went on to point out that my talent for sales had also come up with the German-American salesman. "You had the gift of gab, for selling; you were very good at it. You still have that. But you were a loner. Other than sales calls, you were a *recluse*. Now, they're showing me this because that ability is *in* you. So you have to be aware and avoid that. If you don't, you won't move ahead spiritually or help others to open up."

Huh. Reclusiveness had come up in my regression with Marianna, too. I'd thought then that I was making it up, because it was something I knew about myself. But this time it was Rev. Kev bringing it up, not me.

I had to admit, Kev had hit on most of the qualities that I'd noted when I'd inventoried my abilities. And he hadn't brought up a single life that exemplified a quality I didn't now possess! He hadn't, for example, talked about lives where I'd been an athlete or a singer or a dancer, or someone who could build or fix things, or someone good at technological stuff. Indeed, none of those were my strengths. And as he'd never seen me or talked with me before, he couldn't have made any judgments by the way I looked, or anything I might have said.

He asked if I had any questions before we closed.

"Well, I've had a really hard time with romantic relationships . . ." Since my breakup with Mike, and it had been some time now, I hadn't met anyone who even remotely stirred my heart.

"OK," he said, quickly. "Already, a life is coming in. Do you know what 'sacred prostitutes' were? Basically, they were prostitutes for

God. So, Ancient Rome again . . . You were chosen as a young girl, about seven, and taken to live in a house with other young girls. Basically, you were trained as a priestess."

Aha! There was the "religious lives" angle!

"You were trained in how to bring out the light in men—priests and high officials, mostly—through, uh, *loving* them," he said. "The idea was that, through the lower chakra, the sex chakra, you could help raise a man's energy—it was a tool to reach God. It was considered by a lot of women to be a big, big honor. But to you, it was horrible. Mostly, it was about being put into a life where you had no power. Because of the strength you've had in other lives, it was anathema to you. Now, this life bred in you the desire to open people up. And later on, you realized, 'That has to happen when they're *young*.' So this opens *that* up in you, the work with children. But you're still feeling guilt and shame and anger at your parents about that lifetime."

He suggested I write a letter to this girl—*Hypatia* was her name— offering empathy, comfort, forgiveness, and protection. "Write what comes to you. You're very psychic," he said.

Huh! I thought. Dana Marie had said the same thing. But I had yet to really consistently experience it.

Rev. Kev paused, and I jotted down my assignment to write the letter. It seemed a little strange to compose a letter to "myself," back in ancient Rome, to heal a wound that was still festering in me today. But something else I later heard Kev say on Bob Charles's radio show addressed this point. "The past is as mutable as what we call the future," he'd said. "We *can* rewrite the past. Quantum physics tells us we jump between dimensions with each choice we make. When we have orange juice, we jump to a dimension where that's more probable than the one in which we have coffee. So we can change the present by going back to the past!"

Finally, Kev resumed: "So here you have the 'weave' of lifetimes that have brought you to where you are now," he said. "All of these lives taught you something wonderful. Some had very negative things in them. Even as the Boston mother, one of your sons fell in with a bad crowd, became a drug addict, and died. But you learned from that: that a mother's love is *unconditional*. And whether it's your child or *any* child, it's the same."

Well, that was true: I tended to love unconditionally. And not just children, but the "wounded" men in my life . . . for better or worse.

Several days later, I wrote my letter to Hypatia. I told her that I knew the unbearable things that had happened to her, and that she'd done nothing to deserve them. I told her that I'd protect her, and that I loved her more than she could imagine. As I read the letter aloud, then crumpled it up and burned it, as Kev had instructed, I felt my throat grow swollen with emotion. Whether I was connecting with a past life or with my own inner child, I didn't know.

AFTER KEV'S PAST LIVES READING, we'd had a bit of time left, so I had asked him about a present-life matter. I'd recently been offered the opportunity to house-sit, on and off, on the Jersey Shore, where my brother was renovating his summer home—the stint in the "laid-back neighborhood" in New Jersey that Maggie Moise had seen so accurately in her reading. I loved the Victorian seaside town, and its neighboring town, too, with its ghostly vestiges of a once flourishing turn-of-the-century amusement park: the empty shell of the crumbling Beaux-Arts casino; the ancient, ornate carousel house—its candy-colored horses long since auctioned off—gone green in the salty air. I thought it might give me peace and quiet to write. But most of the renovation would take place in winter, when the area emptied out, and I wouldn't know a soul. I wondered if I'd feel isolated and lonely, or depressed.

On the contrary, Kev said, my time by the beach would be good for me; in fact, I'd love it. He saw me making many friends there. He described one, a "loving and giving" woman in whose house I would also eventually stay. Knowing her, he said, would be "like looking in a mirror," except that she was "much more out in the world" than I. She'd show me how, one day, I could be comfortable being out in the world too. He also said she was a very good cook, and that knowing her would be a "culinary treat"; she would teach me to make "a few very simple dishes, involving vegetables, and using only two or three ingredients." He saw a blond woman connected to this, the two of us talking in a small café or ice cream shop.

It was so specific! How amazing, I thought, if all of that came to pass . . .

House-sitting at the Shore turned out to be a wonderful experience, as Kev had foreseen. There, not long after that, I did meet a woman, Deirdre, who had long blond hair and was very loving and giving; and after my brother's renovation was done, she asked me to house-sit for her too. We found we were both from big Sicilian families; had both published books; were both devotees of Jane Austen and the Brontës; and both owned the same unusual pair of funky purple clogs. Deirdre was married to a younger man, and I'd been *seeing* a younger man (and more on that to come). As for her being more "out in the world," she hosted a call-in radio show and had once had a cable TV show too; she had a large fan base—which would have been hard for me, as I valued my privacy and anonymity, but I could see that she enjoyed it, and handled it with aplomb. And yes, Reader, she was an excellent cook, and was thinking of writing a cookbook about vegetable dishes using just *two or three ingredients*—several of which she taught me to prepare. Oh, and while I hadn't met her in a small café, the second time we'd crossed paths had been in one.

In light of Rev. Kev's spot-on accuracy with his intuition, I added him to my Team. While I *still* couldn't say that the critically think-ing part of my brain was totally convinced about reincarnation, Kev's psychic precision slid me a few more notches closer to the belief that those past lives he'd picked up—improbable as some of them seemed—were in fact real.

✳

REV. KEV HAD TOLD ME during our reading that he did group past-life regressions at the midtown Manhattan A.R.E., which I learned, when I Googled it, was the New York branch of Edgar Cayce's original Association for Research and Enlightenment, founded in Virginia Beach in 1931. Of course, I knew of Edgar Cayce, the famed medical intuitive and most documented psychic of the twentieth century. But for all the years I'd lived in New York City, I'd never known the place existed! I looked up when the next group regression was occurring and decided to attend, curious both about group regressions and the A.R.E. itself.

On the evening of the event, I arrived a few minutes early at the A.R.E.'s old, weathered building. As I scanned the directory posted outside its door, a snowy-haired gentleman in a sport coat and turtleneck came out. He glanced at me, then said crisply, "Second floor."

"How do you know where I'm going?" I asked, startled.

"*I know*," he replied. Then he turned and headed off.

Well, he was right. As I climbed the worn flight of stairs, I pondered the gentleman's comment. I didn't look particularly New Age-y: No tie-dye, no crystals; I carried no yoga mat. And there were at least a dozen offices listed on that directory, with occupants ranging from lawyers to designers to consultants of various sorts.

Heading into what looked to be the A.R.E.'s main office, I asked if Rev. Kev was about.

"He's here," a young man holding a file folder replied.

At the far end of a dimly lit room, I could see Kev, recognizing him from Web photos—the cherubic face and head of fair, close-cropped hair. He was seated across from another man, and they seemed to be meditating. I hesitated, but, "Rev. Kev, someone's here to see you!" the young man sang out.

Kev opened his eyes, stood, and looked at me blankly. "Excuse me," he said, in a detached tone. "I just have to get back into my body." Then he quickly sat down again.

Maybe it was that memorable first impression of the place, but the more time I spent at the A.R.E., the more I felt I'd stepped into another world, a world where everyone was engaged in life on an entirely different level. It had nothing to do with the place itself, which needed a good painting and was furnished with couches and chairs that were distinctly second-hand. It was the people scattered about on them, waiting for their sessions—on everything from "the science of light" to "the art of spirit protection"—to begin. They looked to be ordinary individuals of all ages and ethnicities, matter-of-factly going about their lives—lives that just happened to include higher dimensions of consciousness and the beings who dwelt there.

Once recovered, Kev greeted me warmly, and soon the room filled, and the workshop began. Kev started with a counting exercise, as Marianna had done. Then he led us through a past life, starting as she had by having us mentally observe our bodies. Again, I saw bare feet and muscular legs—clearly a male's, this time—and a brown robe, cinched with a leather belt. I mentally touched my face and found a thick, wiry beard and wiry hair. I sensed I was in my twenties, walking in woods on a gravel path, with a backpack full of books. I had two dogs—long-legged and skinny, with pointy noses—not a breed I'd actually seen, outside of pictures, in my present-day life.

Next, Kev took us to a childhood meal. A playful, affectionate old woman in heavy shoes, whom I felt was my grandmother, was cooking. I had a pewter spoon and cup, and a crockery bowl full of stew. The details throughout, I had to admit, were remarkably clear.

"Now, who is this person in your present life?" Kev asked, telling us to look into their eyes. I did, and felt it was my paternal grandmother, Anne.

He took us to several more "significant events" in this lifetime: for me, these proved to be taking vows as a priest or monk, and my grandmother's funeral—the first joyous, the second evoking some true tears. There was a young woman present at both, blond and blue-eyed, with braids. She'd been my childhood friend, and later had wanted to marry me, but I'd chosen to devote myself to God. I knew I'd hurt her, and felt guilty about that. When Kev asked who she was in my life today, I saw my youngest niece, to whom I'm extremely close.

We looked at a few other things in that lifetime, and then were told to experience our death: I was old, walking with a staff, falling with chest pain to a cold stone floor. Then Kev had us go out of our body, to learn from our guides what this particular life had to teach us. I was to learn, my guides explained, that my rejection of the blond young woman had been fine, and in fact, necessary; that it wasn't about rejecting her but about following my own life path. Now, that was interesting. Having been rejected by many men, in my present life, I was now being shown how it felt to be on the other side.

Afterward, we discussed our experiences. One young woman said she'd heard a language she didn't know, maybe Arabic; an older man said he'd been a young girl, in Nebraska, in 1914. A young man said, awkwardly, that he felt he'd made it all up. "I'm a writer," he said. "So, to make up a character, and details . . . it's what I do."

"Well, was everything perfect and wonderful?" Kev asked. "People, when they make things up, don't usually make up things that are boring, or horrible and painful."

The young man disagreed. "I make up tragedies as well as comedies when I write. Sometimes I write stuff that's really boring too. And then I have to rewrite it." He smiled.

I took his point, and said that I, too, had felt I was imagining it, much as I did when I wrote.

"When you make up things, generally you don't have a lot of emotion about it," Kev said. "But when you're reliving an emotional event from the past, you don't just tell somebody about it, you *go* there!"

Well, I *had* experienced emotion during this regression, as I had with Marianna. But didn't I often have that kind of emotion watching a good movie? And wouldn't my imagination pull from highly emotional elements of my present-day life to create the images in my regression? With no disrespect to Rev. Kev, and despite the fluidity of the images this time, I still couldn't say I was convinced I hadn't made it all up.

✳

AS PART OF MY PROJECT, I'd been reading as much as I could about the subjects I was exploring. Seeking more information on past-life work, I turned to the book *Many Lives, Many Masters* by Brian L. Weiss, MD. The groundbreaking bestseller told Weiss's own story: a traditional psychotherapist by way of Columbia University and Yale Medical School, and a skeptic about things like past lives, Weiss often used hypnosis to regress his patients to their childhood, looking for the roots of their trauma. In 1980, while regressing one patient, Catherine, Weiss was startled to find that he'd regressed her back past her childhood and in fact past her birth, and to what appeared to be a past life. Moreover, the past-life traumas she was recalling seemed to be integrally connected to her present-day paralyzing anxiety, phobias, recurrent nightmares, and panic attacks.

Soon Catherine began channeling messages from highly evolved "Master Spirits"—about life, death, and other realms—along with personal details about Dr. Weiss's deceased son that she couldn't possibly have known. After creating a process of past-life therapy for Catherine with which he was, in three and a half months, able to bring about her complete cure, Weiss was forced to reevaluate his skepticism about the afterlife and other such metaphysical matters, changing the way he would conduct his work, and his life, forever.

Well—I loved that Weiss, a man of science, and the product of not one but *two* Ivy League institutions, had not only become convinced of the existence of past lives, but had taken what must have been a very risky leap, for a man in his profession, to put this book, and several others in the same vein, out into the world.

Eager to learn more about him, I Googled Weiss. I found that he was holding a seminar at Manhattan's Javits Center a few months hence, so I signed myself up.

When I arrived at the Javits Center that day, a massive and bustling convention center on Midtown Manhattan's far west side, the huge auditorium was jam-packed. Weiss, a warm, engaging, and articulate man with silver hair brushed back off his face and small wire-rimmed glasses, spoke about his work and his journey from skeptic to confident believer. Among other things, he talked about patients who, through hypnotic regression, had spoken in languages they had no knowledge of in their present lives—a phenomenon known as *xenoglossy*. He also pointed out that a belief in reincarnation was historically a part of the traditions of certain sects within Judaism, Christianity, and Islam. I'd never heard that before. *Did that include*, I wondered, *the heretical sect of Cathars, to which Christina Wright had told me we two had belonged?* He also said many of the world's greatest thinkers, including Pythagoras, Plato, and Socrates, had believed in reincarnation.

Weiss then led us through a past-life regression and an exercise in intuition, in which we partnered with a neighbor—in my case, a young Russian fellow seated to my right named Sasha. During the regression, I received impressions of a life as a male soldier in what looked like rural England or Ireland, living in an "officer's tent," and ultimately being killed by a bayonet, thrust through my heart by another soldier on horseback. It was fairly vivid, but again, I felt like I was imagining it.

As for the intuition exercise, I can't say whether the images I picked up for Sasha materialized in his life, but I was delightfully surprised to find that the single, odd image he had seen when he read for me—the antlered head of a deer, "with no body attached"—appeared to me *the very next day*, in a café I'd never been to before that had a stuffed stag's head mounted above its bar, a rare thing indeed to find in Manhattan!

✳

AFTER MY EXPERIENCES with Brian Weiss and his book, I found myself wondering if there had been any scientific studies on the subject of reincarnation. Weiss's patients' memories might have appeared to cure them of traumas, but one couldn't—at least not yet—travel back in time to verify the truth of what these patients remembered. Even if a person under regression could speak in a language he or she normally didn't know, as Weiss had described (and how cool was that?), it didn't necessarily mean it was because of a past life.

Synchronistically enough, several days later, I got a rare text from my childhood friend Nancy. After a year at Brooklyn College, Nancy had transferred to UVA, my Southern alma mater, where she now worked, providing research software support to various departments there.

"How's it going, Annzo?" she wrote, using a moniker she'd given me somewhere around sixth grade. "How's my oldest and best-est friend?"

"Great," I wrote back. "Busy with my metaphysical explorations. Been looking into past lives."

"Wait," she replied, "do you know about the guys here at the U studying kids who remember past lives? I've worked with them myself."

"NO!!!!" I pounded back. *What?! At my own university?!!*

Nancy sent me a link to the University of Virginia's Division of Perceptual Studies, a research unit within the Department of Psychiatric Medicine, founded in 1967 by the late Dr. Ian Stevenson, with the purpose of investigating "apparent paranormal phenomena." Their home page described a study begun by Stevenson, a former professor at the medical school and chair of the psychiatry department, in the 1960s, involving children with past-life memories! His colleague Jim B. Tucker, MD, a professor of psychology and neurobehavioral sciences, was now serving as the director of the DOPS, and continuing this provocative work.

These children, the page stated, "usually between the ages of 2 and 5, speak about memories of a previous life they claim to have lived. At the same time, they often show behaviors, such as phobias or preferences, that are unusual within the context of their particular family and cannot be explained by any current life events. These memories appear to be concordant with the child's statements about a previous life. In many cases of this type, the child's statements have been shown to correspond accurately to facts in the life and death of a deceased person. Some of the children have birthmarks and birth defects that correspond to wounds or other marks on the deceased person whose life is being remembered by the child. In numerous cases postmortem reports have confirmed these correspondences."

Cowabunga! Had this study really been going on the whole time I'd been there?

I got my hands on Tucker's book *Life Before Life: Children's Memories of Previous Lives* and read it in one shot. The case studies in it were impressive. There were very young children—some mere toddlers—who had memories of lives in cities or countries to which neither they nor their parents had ever been, including specific knowledge of names, ethnicities, occupations, personal possessions, and household objects—all verified through scrupulous research by Tucker and his peers. In the book, Tucker discussed the skeptical point of view, but also pointed out how aspects of contemporary physics might support the possibility of such phenomena.

When I finished the book, I emailed Jim Tucker. When he kindly agreed to answer my questions, I dashed off a list. I asked him what his beliefs about an "afterlife" had been when he'd started this work, and what he believed now. I asked what he thought about past-life regressions—I'd read that he didn't encourage them—and whether he'd ever experienced one himself. Finally, I asked if this work had changed him in any way.

While awaiting Tucker's response, I Googled him. Along with several articles, I found a fascinating episode of a British documentary TV show called *Extraordinary People:* "The Boy Who Lived Before," in which Jim Tucker was featured. It told the story of a five-year-old boy named Cameron who lived in Glasgow, Scotland. Cameron, from the age of two, had described what seemed to be very intense memories of a former life on Barra, a tiny, remote island more than two hundred miles away—which neither he nor his family had ever visited. The boy insisted that he'd lived there, describing his Barra family and home in detail: the white house on the beach, where planes would land, and where he'd play with his siblings—a brother and a sister—and a black-and-white dog, before he "fell through" to his present life. He even claimed to know the name of his "Barra dad," who'd been killed by being "knocked down by a car": Shane Robertson.

As years passed, Cameron became so distressed about missing his "Barra mum," and so desirous to visit this seemingly random island, that his mother, Norma, took him to two psychologists, neither of whom could give her a satisfactory explanation. When one stated that Cameron's "fantasy" didn't fit the profile of most kids' imaginary scenarios, Norma, joined by Jim Tucker, whom she had also contacted for help, traveled with Cameron to Barra. With a local historian, they were finally able to locate the house—indeed rented in summers by a family named "Robertson"—verifying many details the boy had recalled. Cameron, though chatty and excited throughout the trip, became quiet and visibly saddened once inside the house where he claimed to have lived.

Back in Glasgow, Norma was able to contact a member of the Robertson family—Gillian—who substantiated the existence of the black-and-white dog during her summers with her brothers there at the time Cameron's memories seemed to have taken place. According to Gillian, though, there had been a "James Robertson," but no "Shane," nor any family member killed by a car . . .

And so Norma and Jim Tucker were left with a mystery. Had the detailed accuracy of Cameron's story been a huge coincidence? *(Say, what??)* Or had the boy possibly been mixing up memories from *several* past lives? Whatever the case, the trip had markedly changed his behavior. Whereas before, he'd been agitated, unable to stop talking about the loss of his Barra family, he now appeared to have reached a place of emotional calm and peace.

The show touched on another very curious case too, that of a boy named Gus who claimed he'd been *his own grandfather* in a previous life! Gus's father explained how, while changing his son's diapers, the toddler had expressed a memory of changing his *father's* diapers in the past! Gus's belief grew more persistent as he grew older, and his memories more persuasive. When the boy eventually mentioned an incident involving his grandfather's sister, who'd been murdered, a true story his parents had never told him and one that very few people knew, they had to admit there was something unusual going on.

WHILE I WAS STILL WAITING to hear back from Tucker, my friend Jean-Pierre, who was rooming with me for a while, left an issue of *Harper's* magazine lying on my bed. I saw, glancing at the cover, that it contained an article by Leslie Jamison called "Giving Up the Ghost: The Eternal Allure of Life After Death." The story, about a boy in Louisiana named James Leininger, who from the age of two had experienced dramatic—and traumatic—dreams and detailed memories of what appeared to be a past life as a fighter pilot shot down by the Japanese, featured none other than Dr. Jim Tucker.

"Jean-Pierre, did you know this article was in here? Is that why you gave it to me?" I marched into the living room to show him the piece.

"No!" he said, from my threadbare armchair, where he sat eating a bowl of Thai noodles. "I didn't even notice that. I bought it to read on the train," he said, wriggling uncomfortably in his seat. "You know, this chair could really use a new cushion!" He sucked in some noodles and grinned.

I settled onto my bed to read the article, marveling at yet another sparkling gem of synchronicity in my life. It proved as provocative as the show had. Much like Cameron, the toddler James had recalled details about an apparent past life that ultimately checked out—including the name of the boat his plane had taken off from, and the first names of several crewmates who'd been killed in service and been "waiting for him in heaven."

✳

A FEW WEEKS LATER, I heard back from Jim Tucker.

"I would say I was open-minded and inquisitive when I started working with Ian [Stevenson]," he wrote, in response to my question. "I am still that way today. I've become more persuaded that an after-life is possible but also unsure we can ever really understand what it entails. After reviewing all of the cases, I would say that we now have good evidence that some young children have memories of a life from the past."

Well, bravo to him for going out on that limb and saying it!

As for why he didn't favor the idea of past-life regressions, he sent me a link to a piece Stevenson had written entitled "Concerns about Hypnotic Regression," saying that he agreed with the view-point it expressed. Basically, the piece said that the state of a person undergoing hypnotic regression resembled that of a person dreaming, in that the subconscious parts of the mind, freed from inhibitions, often emerged as a new "personality." "If the subject has been instructed by the hypnotist—explicitly or implicitly—to 'go back to another place and time' or given some similar guidance, the new 'personality' may appear to be one of another period of history," Stevenson wrote. He went on to point out that neither a marked emotional experience during a regression nor even a dramatic improvement in some "symptom" constituted valid evidence of a past life. Further, the process of hypnotic regression entailed some risks: In some cases the "previous personality" would linger, leaving the subject in an altered state for days.

Still, Stevenson had this to say: " . . . I will mention that very rarely something of value may emerge . . . Examples occur in instances where the subject proves able to speak a foreign language not normally learned." These types of cases, he wrote, were among those he deemed worthy of continued research. According to Tucker, though, they were "very rare exceptions."

Regarding Tucker's *personal* experience with regressions, "I've participated in a group regression before, which I found mildly interesting," he wrote.

Despite the lack of any personal experience, say, of the sort Brian Weiss had had, Tucker was devoting a good part of his life to researching the topic of past lives. Having watched the "Barra boy" video and read the *Harper's* piece, I could certainly understand why. Still, given that he, too, was a medical doctor with a career and reputation to consider, I applauded his conviction and courage.

Finally, in response to my question as to whether this research had in any way changed him, "I think this work has given me a more hopeful view of life," he wrote, "as it seems there is more to reality than just the difficulties we see in the world."

✳

THE WORK OF Tucker and Stevenson, like that of Brian Weiss, had propelled me a giant step closer to being convinced that reincarnation was real. Still, though, I wished for a more personal experience of my own, something of the type these two men had had. It wouldn't have to be an entire academic study, but I wanted something that resonated; I'd know it when I felt it. I hoped that, once again, the Universe would provide.

Not long after my exchange with Tucker, I took a walk along the Hudson River, pondering. How might a belief in past lives, and future ones, change one's daily life? I remembered an exercise I'd done in a workshop led by Patricia Masters, which I'd attended with a friend. Patricia had broken us into pairs, instructing us to stare at our partner's face for a full ten minutes—no easy feat. As we did, she said, we might see his or her faces from past lives. While I hadn't managed to do so myself, my friend told me, amazed, that she had. She described the parade of faces she'd seen—male and female, dark-skinned and fair—morphing into one another.

A belief in multiple lives, I thought—making my way to the end of a pier that offered a view of the New Jersey skyline, and further south, the Statue of Liberty, holding her torch aloft—would surely put things into a new perspective. If we believed we'd been both men *and* women, it might go a way toward easing the "war between the sexes" and decreasing judgment of those who were transgendered, gay, or bi. If we became convinced that this wasn't our only go-round on this planet, it might add some lightness and relief to our current disappointments and pains. After all, how could we rail at life's unfairness if we had *all* been both rich and poor, sick and healthy, killers and saviors, changing and exchanging roles each time we came back around?

And what of all those experiences, presumably tucked somewhere in our subconscious, from all of those lives? What of those talents, gifts, and lessons learned? What of all the knowledge and wisdom we must have acquired? Would there ever be a way we could connect with, and access, all of that? And was this part of what Patricia had meant when she'd said, long ago, that everything she was going to tell me I already knew, but simply wasn't fully aware of?

Back home, I sank into my armchair, which Jean-Pierre had vacated, presumably for a less butt-punishing perch, and pulled out Jim Tucker's book. "Today, people in the world who believe in reincarnation may outnumber those who do not," I read again, browsing through. Based on recent polling, Tucker wrote, the number of Americans who believed in reincarnation fell "between 20 and 27 percent, depending on the poll," including 21 percent of Christians, according to the 2003 Harris poll results.

My guess was that this belief would only increase as work like Tucker's continued. I imagined what life might be like a hundred years hence, when we, as more evolved beings, might perhaps on a daily basis employ a technique similar to that workshop exercise we'd done. "Ah, good morning" we'd greet our mother/father/boss/teammate/sibling/ lover, as his or her past incarnations flickered holographically before us, reminding us of lives we'd shared. Or perhaps we would reach into an internal database of our own past lives, to pull out abilities, memories, or knowledge from those incarnations that might help us in our present-day lives.

There was so much hopelessness these days about the future of our planet. Most people I knew thought things were doomed to go to hell in a handbasket. I, on the other hand, was feeling more and more hopeful as I pursued my explorations. Because we humans, I had a hunch, might well, as a race, be slowly opening up to a new type of understanding about who and what we really were, about where we'd come from and where we were going, and about our very real and undeniable connection to one another; I could feel it, day by day, within myself. I'd heard talk in New Age circles about "the Shift"—a shift in human consciousness, to a higher level—occurring now on the planet. I had yet to really comprehend what that meant, but it was high on my list of topics to explore. And if we were, globally, opening up to a new sort of understanding—perhaps collectively "awakening," as Griffin and I had once discussed—I couldn't help but think of what positive changes might arise.

I hoped that I'd live—or come back—to see it happen.

6

ADVENTURES WITH
ANGELS
✳ OR ✳

Halo . . . Is It Me You're Looking For?

GROWING UP CATHOLIC, I WAS TAUGHT TO BELIEVE, MORE OR less, in angels. They appeared in the gospel readings we heard at mass and in the hymns we sang. Humans, we were told, occasionally had encounters with angels. The Virgin Mary was visited by one named Gabriel in the New Testament, and Daniel was saved by one in the lion's den in the Old. But if such an encounter were to happen to us, say, on a New York City street, would there be a prayer of a chance that we'd believe we'd actually met an angel?

During my years working at the Public Theater, my friend and coworker Blaine, who normally managed the theater's film program, had been doing his first assistant-stage-managing stint, for a play that had its opening on a Saturday night. The review came out in the next day's *Times*, and members of the cast and crew who hadn't gotten a chance to buy one—this was years before the Internet—naturally wanted a copy. Blaine had promised to buy them some papers, but he'd been unusually busy, and now he was afraid he'd missed the boat; in Manhattan, the Sunday *Times* sold out quickly. He asked me if I could go out on my break and try and track down even a single copy. That way, he could Xerox the review and hand it out. I promised to try.

As Blaine had suspected, every newsstand I tried had sold out. But I was determined not to let him down. I headed farther east to what was back then a somewhat dicier section of the East Village, and spotted a deli. Standing outside it was a tall, thin, raggedly dressed, African American, apparently homeless man. He asked if I could spare some change, and I dug into my purse and handed him a dollar bill.

As he thanked me, I saw that he was holding some newspapers under one arm. He pulled out a few sections and thrust them toward me. "These are for you," he said.

I looked at the sections of the paper he'd given to me. One was the self-same Arts and Leisure section of that day's *Sunday Times* for which I'd been scouring the East Village.

"Thank you . . . *so much!*" I said, dumbfounded.

He nodded his head slightly, with a little bow. He had a grace about him and was not unattractive, despite his unkempt appearance. "My name's Jeremiah. I'm your guardian angel," he said. "I'll be watching you."

I walked away in a bit of a daze. *Was he really my guardian angel?* I wondered, as I headed back to the theater. If so, why was he appearing to me as a homeless man? And of all the things I could have used a guardian angel's help for . . . why *this?* Granted, I was in hot pursuit of that paper in that moment. But if my guardian angel was going to choose a gift with which to reveal himself, why not a winning lottery ticket, or a personal ad leading me to the single, available, not-inordinately-screwed-up man of my dreams? Still, if *not* my guardian angel, how had he produced precisely what I'd been searching for, and as if he'd known I was seeking it?

I'd pondered that odd encounter for days. In the end, I mentally filed it away under the category "Unbelievable." It made a good anecdote that I loved telling, always with a bit of a laugh. I wished I could believe that I had a guardian angel, and that I'd met him that day, but I couldn't quite make the leap. It just seemed too . . . silly.

Many years back, I'd read the huge bestseller *A Book of Angels*, by Sophy Burnham, which recounted stories of people's ostensibly true experiences with these winged creatures here on Earth, and found it quite intriguing, if a little hard to fully believe. It wasn't that I felt the author or any of the people whose stories were told in the book were lying. I simply couldn't take the mental leap into an acceptance that angels were real. More recently, I'd read a book called *Angels in My Hair* by Lorna Byrne. The book was a lovely and moving memoir by an Irish woman who claimed she'd gone through life seeing and conversing with angels. I found it, too, much as I enjoyed it, a bit hard to swallow. I had less trouble accepting the possibility of ghosts, lingering spirits stuck between this world and another, addled by a traumatic death, or perhaps just not wanting to let go. But angels? With wings, and halos? Michael and Raphael, and Gabriel, the one who appeared to Mary to announce the virgin birth, just hanging with this woman, Lorna, sporting fashionably color-coordinated robes? Open-minded as I was, and with no disrespect intended, at the time, I had wondered: Was Lorna "touched by an angel". . . or simply "*touched*"?

I was pondering the question of angels aloud one day with Ethan, the young son—college age, perhaps—of one of the owners of the Loving Cup, my favorite coffee shop down at the Shore.

"Well, angels, unlike ghosts, have been turned into something cutesy by our society," he said. "Like, cupids on Valentine's Day. We're not really presented with angels as *the hammers of God* anymore."

I preferred to think of angels more as *messengers* than blunt instruments; that was, after all, what the word *angel* meant—derived from the Latin male name *Angelus*, I'd learned, when I'd recently looked it up. Still, he had a point; angels had been co-opted by our culture in a way that, with the exception of Caspar the Friendly, ghosts had not.

Some highly intelligent people I knew believed in angels, including Rev. Kev O'Kane. He'd told me about my past life as a *Nephilim*, and had talked about angels and archangels who were helping me with my book. That had sounded completely unbelievable at first, but then he'd also told me that these angels had concerns about my book, and were describing some editorial problems I was struggling with that Kev himself had no way of knowing about. At one point, for instance, he reported that the angels were saying I had so much material, I didn't know what to do with it or how to structure it—which was precisely true. He said they were pointing out a section of text early on in the book that was "like a block of wood"—they were afraid it would confuse people and stop them from reading further. He gave me a range of ten pages where this block occurred, and when I checked my manuscript, it was true. There was a section there that veered off-topic when I'd attempted to present some information about energy and quantum physics that was fairly complicated. Looking it over, I decided the angels were right—it *would* likely put off many readers—and I cut the section out.

I'd heard about angels from others on my Team too. Dana Marie, who'd gotten some impressive hits about me in several readings, had said she'd seen some archangels around me, including Raphael, the healing archangel, whose aura was emerald green. She talked so matter-of-factly about them, as if she were talking about the UPS guy or the woman at the dry cleaner's, that it made me smile. Edward Ragosta, too, claimed to be in touch with angels. "They're called 'the Angels of Theory.' There are eight of them. Their spokesperson is Joy. They've been with me for a while. But they've been waiting for me to be ready for them." He was, he explained, in the process of being spiritually "upgraded."

"Part of my spiritual homework is to sit with them in meditation, to attune with their energy, and so they can attune to mine," he said.

"They're really excited about this interview. They're excited to be making their debut."

It was tempting to file all this under the category of "Unbelievable" too. And yet Edward, like Kev, had been so right-on so many times with his intuitive abilities, it was hard for me to dismiss the things he claimed to be experiencing, incredible as they might seem.

After setting off on my exploratory journey, I found myself wishing for another angel experience of my own. As was so often the case with my explorations, I didn't have to lift a finger; the angels found me.

It happened after Rev. Kev's group past-life regression at the A.R.E. Several of us were standing around discussing our experience. One woman mentioned a few practitioners at the A.R.E. whom she felt were not to be missed, including a man named Roger Ansanelli. "He does sound healing. And he plays these *singing bowls*. He says he's channeling music from the angelic realm. You wouldn't believe the sounds that come out of him. It's otherworldly! And he gives you messages, from the *angels*!" she exclaimed.

Antenna up!

The A.R.E.'s flyer, which I picked up on my way out and read on the subway home, described Roger as a "sound frequency worker," among other things, saying that he directed "dedicated sound frequencies of love" into each of his workshops' participants as they meditated, as well as playing crystal bowls and "being sung by the higher realms." Well, I thought, a little vibrational tune-up could never hurt a gal! Mainly, though, I was now highly curious to meet Roger and the beings that "sang" him for myself.

A FEW WEEKS LATER, I sat in a small room at the A.R.E., along with eight or ten others, waiting for the workshop to begin. Roger proved to be a friendly, highly energetic and highly entertaining sort, casually dressed in a T-shirt, running pants, and sneakers, his fair hair pulled back in a ponytail. Later, he told me that in addition to his healing work, he was a head trainer and rehab specialist at a gym. And yes, he said, the two types of work did at times overlap.

The night's topic was our nature as beings of light. He talked about being large in our thinking and being, and not defining ourselves, which he called "self-limiting." Then he had us do an exercise in which we looked at one another, appreciating the beauty in our neighbors' unique features: eyes, teeth, hands. He said that while we'd been doing that simple act, the vibrational frequency of the room had already been raised.

Roger said that he wasn't here to fix anyone; we were all great and powerful beings of light, and none of us was "broken." Rather, he said, he was assisting us in getting out of our own way and moving to a higher vibration, and that it would be there that we would find the best way to heal ourselves. He had each of us say our name and share what it was that we were here, on the planet, to do. "To love," I said, when it was my turn. It felt a little vague to me, but it was true, and I didn't know what else to say. Some of the others, though, were more specific about it: "I'm here to make music that will help us raise our collective vibration," one man said. I was impressed and a little bit intimidated by the statement, even though I didn't know exactly what it meant.

Next, Roger unzipped a padded bag and removed what looked like an oversized crystal wineglass, minus the base. He ran a cylindrical tool around its rim, creating an unusual sound—a bit, in fact, like the sound made by running a finger around the rim of a wineglass, but stronger and more refined. Then he led us in a beautiful meditation that involved visualizing different colored light, to continue to raise our vibration, he said.

Partway through, he began to sing. But this wasn't like any singing I'd heard before. Though I'd read online that Roger had trained as an opera singer, the sounds he produced—and they were *sounds*, not words, at least not in any language *I* knew of—weren't operatic; truly, they sounded heavenly, celestial. Roger continued this remarkable effusion, a haunting melody, explaining between strains that we were now in the presence of the angelic realm.

I tried to wrap my mind around this. Could it be true? Was there any way to tell?

My eyes were still closed, but I could hear Roger moving around the circle as he sang. Soon I sensed him standing near me, slightly to my right. He stopped singing and spoke.

"You worry about being fearful. But you're more courageous than you think," he said. "It's time for you to join the party. In fact, it's time for you to start your *own* party."

That angelic message didn't sound like it was for me. It might have fit me when I was younger, and very shy, but I was pretty well "in the party," now, and had been for some time. As for "starting my own party," since I'd begun my explorations I felt like I was doing precisely that. So I figured the message was for the woman seated to my right.

I realized I was correct as I felt Roger, moments later, move directly in front of me.

"Are you writing the *book*?" he asked.

"Yes!" I exclaimed, grinning and nearly jumping out of my chair. "I'm in the middle of it right now!"

"Or, I should say, *books*," he clarified.

"Yes, I am! And I've been told by others, too, that there are more than one." At least four members of my Dream Team had told me, with no prompting, that the book I'd begun writing was actually the first in a series of books in the same genre.

"Are you writing the one about *joy*? They want you to write the book about joy."

A book about joy? I *was* planning another book, and it *was* about joy—finding joy in midlife, despite nothing having happened the way I'd hoped or expected. It would be a short book . . . much shorter than this first one about my metaphysical explorations.

"It's a smaller one, they're saying. Shorter. Not a big book. It's like a little gem."

Holy halo, Batman!

Angelic message delivered, Roger moved on. I found myself placing my attention less on my meditation and more on what he was saying. Was he getting as good a hit with all the others as he had with me? He told one young man that he felt himself unlovable, and needed to know how many people loved him. He spoke to a woman about her feeling that she didn't fit in. At some point, I opened my eyes; the writer in me was curious. As Roger stopped in front of each person, he turned the chalice so that the bowl faced him or her and moved it up and down, as if scanning the person's body . . . or sort of energetically hosing it down.

He moved on to a man across from me. I couldn't help but notice him when I'd arrived; there was nothing showy or pretentious about him, but he was, hands-down, one of the most handsome men I'd ever clapped eyes on. The man, whose name was Patrick, had said his "message to the world" was about putting out love, just as I had. Indeed, he seemed as sweet as he was stunning. I'd noticed his kindness toward the elderly woman seated next to him, who, during the exercise, had cried several times.

"Patrick always knew he wasn't like the other guys," Roger said. "Sure, he played sports. But he knew he wasn't like other people. You are a very bright light, Patrick. They're very pleased with you."

Patrick smiled self-effacingly. It seemed that this paragon of the male species was not only spiritually aware and sweet, but humble, too. Whatever planet he was from, I was ready to flag down the mother ship and climb aboard.

As Roger moved on, I realized I'd better close my eyes again; with Patrick in front of me, I'd never be able to keep my focus.

I attempted to get back to my meditation but my mind was processing it all. Most of these messages, I thought as I listened to them, could easily have been concocted by looking at these folks, by extrapolating from information they'd given, or even from their actions. But what about what he'd said to *me*? It wasn't anything my actions could have revealed. And I hadn't signed up for the workshop ahead of time, so Roger couldn't have Googled my name and learned I was a writer.

Next, Roger announced that we would do some "toning"—no, not abs, though I suspected that if I lifted his T-shirt, I'd find a pretty good six-pack there. Each of us was to lead the group by chanting a solo "*om*," the others then joining in. It was a little scary for me; I was terribly inhibited about my singing voice, or lack thereof. I shakily projected my *om* and, once I got past the fear, it felt wonderful. As the others chimed in, several with strong, lovely voices, we created a many-stranded "*joyful noise.*"

The session ended with the whole group of us singing with Roger and the angels, joining in their unearthly chorus. It felt like some sort of universal song—a song, if you will, of the cosmos. With no typical melody, we had to listen as we sang and anticipate where the music was going, or, in a sense, to let the music "sing" us.

I left the session feeling happy and uplifted. While my inner jury was still out on the whole angel angle, and whatever it was that Roger was doing with vibration, I liked it. I wondered if he and the angels could help me become clearer on what I wanted to put out there in the world—on what I was here to do, and how to do it. I booked a session to find out.

I MET ROGER a few months later in his high-ceilinged Hoboken, New Jersey, studio—high enough, I mused, for the angels to have plenty of wing room. It had a massage table, shelves of books, and, along one wall, a row of metallic tuning forks in a rainbow of colors. There were a few pieces of sculpture, too, one of an angel's head and wings.

It wasn't my first time at the studio; I'd begun attending Roger's weekly "sound frequency meditation with the archangels" there.

Several of the attendees from that first session were often present, including the model-esque Patrick, who turned out, not surprisingly, to actually *be* a model, and to have an equally sweet, equally stunning model wife. Still, men like that, Reader . . . they gave a girl hope.

Roger had told me his private sessions varied, depending on the client's needs; he never knew beforehand what he'd do. In my own, it turned out, there was little to do with singing or sound at all. The first thing he did was take away the notebook I'd brought along to jot down notes in about the session. He told me it was well and good that I was writing a book, but of foremost importance on my present journey was *my own evolution.*

"Imbue your book with *freedom, liberation, light, hope,*" he said. "Though this *is* about your own evolution first and foremost, you're using it as a platform for it to be a group evolution." This involved my family and whoever read my book, he said. I was bringing them all along with me, as was my nature. "But the order is '*Being* it, then *feeling* it, then *sharing* it.' You can't feel what you aren't," he said. "And you can't share what you don't *feel.*"

It made sense. I could report on everything I'd witnessed, an impartial observer. But that wasn't the book I was writing—or I should say, the book that was *writing me.* Because, just as Roger was apparently being sung by other realms, I felt that I was being *written.*

Roger paused. Then, "How do you feel about fairies?" he asked, with a smile.

"How do I *feel* about them?"

"Yeah. Just . . . how does the idea of them hit you?"

"I love it!" I said. I'd grown up reading fairy tales, had bought a beautiful vintage book at a flea market once called *The Flower Fairies,* simply because I'd been enchanted by the illustrations, and I'd built many a fairy house with my nieces, using chunks of plushy moss, acorns, seashells, petals, and leaves. But I couldn't say I actually *believed in* fairies. To me, they were even further "out there" on the believability scale than angels. Still, I did love the idea of them. I'd recently read a book called *Ask a Medium,* by Rose Vanden Eynden, a "certified medium and Spiritualist minister." The author believed that fairies were real—part of a group of energies called "elementals," who interacted with humans. It sounded like Roger agreed.

"You are a great soul, as all souls are," Roger continued. "You have a strong connection to the animal kingdom, the plant kingdom . . . and thus the fairy kingdom." He asked if I liked birds, and then horses. Apparently, I had a big connection to horses.

"I don't think they like *me* all that much, though." I told him I'd been thrown by a horse as a kid at a Staten Island day camp, and more recently, kicked in the thigh by one during a workshop at an Arizona spa, which had left me badly bruised and hobbling.

"They were trying to tell you something," he said.

"I've heard about horses sensing your fear . . ."

"It wasn't so much that you were afraid. It was that you didn't have enough of a sense of yourself. Horses can't sense who you are if you don't know who you are yourself," he said.

Ouch! That one hit home. I'd often felt, particularly when I was younger, a bit wishy-washy, especially in my large family of highly opinionated, highly verbal sorts. I hated conflict, and tended to swallow my feelings in the interest of keeping the peace. Griffin had recently referred to me as being something of a *doormat* back when we'd first met in the theater world—a word Roger actually went on to use himself in that same session, referring to how I'd let people walk all over me when I was younger. Though his words touched a nerve about my former self, I felt a lot less mat-like these days; my project had changed me. In helping me reconnect with my childhood passion and curiosity about the invisible world, it had brought me home to myself. Ironically, the more I explored what most people considered *"woo-woo,"* or *"airy-fairy,"* the more grounded I felt in who I was and what I knew from my own experiences. While I might have missed my therapist, Melinda, herself, I didn't miss therapy at all; I no longer felt the need to recite a litany of my troubles, or discuss things about myself I felt were "wrong." And while I was continuing to ask my Team about men, and love, I was no longer pining for it, or waiting for my life to begin. I was truly, for the first time, happy in the moment, excited about all that I was learning and discovering.

"Get up," Roger soon directed me, springing out of his chair in full-on trainer mode. "Wrap your arms around yourself, and feel and sense yourself. *Savor* it. Now feel your head. Wrap your arms around your head. Smaller, right? A lot smaller?"

"Yes."

"The thing is, you're existing about ninety percent in your head. Your body is so much larger; there's so much more of it. But you're only living about ten percent there."

He gave me a daily exercise: I was to make big circles with my arms, gathering energy and light; to roll them up "like a big ball of yarn"; "offer them up" by raising the ball before me; then "take it in"—to literally push it into my solar plexus or heart.

"You have to get comfortable with your size," he said. "Your largeness." And I knew he didn't mean my belly and hips.

"At different points in our life, we gather more of what we are," he said, as I practiced the exercise to make sure I had it right. "Our experiences lived help us to do just that. They make us ready to be more of what we are, and free us from what we are not . . . and what we've outgrown."

He paused. "Good!" he said, when I'd finished the exercise. I had to admit, I did like the feeling of pushing that big ball of light into my stomach. Was I imagining that I could feel it, or was something really happening?

"And that's what *you're* doing too," he said. "With your book, and also in other ways. You free people from what they are not, and encourage them to be more of what it is they are . . . or what gives them joy.

You help them to remember that life is something that's incredible. And that they're not alone, *ever!*"

I took in that compliment. I would indeed be gratified if it were so.

We sat again, and Roger's focus seemed to shift. He asked me my astrological sun sign, and I told him I was a Pisces—symbolized by the two fishes swimming in opposite directions. "Pisces know what to do, and then they do something else," he said.

Ha! That had always been true for me . . . especially regarding men. Well, at least now I could blame it on the planets.

"You have a lot of power, and it frightens you. Instead of driving the bus, you could drive *the rocket,*" he said. "Think about that."

I'd be happy if I could drive a *car,* I thought. I was one of those New Yorkers who'd never owned one, and despite having gotten a license, many years before, I had never really become a driver. In truth, I was terrified of speed. It was partly why I was so afraid to fly. So, *me . . .* driving the *rocket?* It was hard to wrap my mind around that.

"You could really do well with studying some shamanism, too," he said, adding that I'd had a past life as a shaman, and one in the medical field. I still had those abilities in me, he said. "Some days, put down the pen. Talk to the Earth, the fairy kingdom . . . trees, animals, minerals, and crystals . . . and also *listen.* Ask to access their gifts and wisdom."

Then Roger began receiving messages from and about members of my family. *Were they from the angels?* I wasn't sure. "Which one is the gardener?" he asked. That would be my second-oldest brother, a gardener by profession. "Is he a good cook, too?" Yes, he was; he took after my father that way.

"I keep hearing your name as *Annie,*" he said, while talking about my family. Yes, that *was* what they'd always called me. "And who's wanting to have a baby, and what's her connection to Charles?"

That would be my sister, I told him. She very much wanted a second child. Her daughter had been named partially after our beloved

Uncle Charles—a feminized version of the name, of course—who'd been godfather to me and my five siblings.

Always keeping in mind my skeptical friends and the technique of cold reading, I noted that Roger did occasionally ask questions. But even when he did, he never asked anything that wasn't specific and that didn't immediately hit home.

In particular, he picked up on my father. I told Roger nothing, but he got it all: my father's regrets about the difficulties he'd caused our family; his tumultuous relationship with my mother; the mistakes he'd made. Then he mentioned something he said he felt related to my father and me just before he died. "He's not exactly saying that he wished you'd been *closer* . . . It's that he's sorry he didn't inquire more about what was going on with you."

Oh . . . my . . . gosh. It was totally on point, and I got choked up.

"It's not that he didn't care. It's that he felt you were very bright, and he trusted in your wisdom."

Wow. Now, that was something that had never occurred to me. While numerous psychic friends had touched on this issue, none had ever *explained* it. How often had I felt hurt or angry with my father, and others, about things I was totally misinterpreting? Getting these sorts of insights was like therapy with something extra . . . *angel therapy*!

Roger told me my father loved me; that he was proud of me and what I was doing, especially regarding the book I was writing—which made sense, given that he was a writer and editor himself; I hadn't told Roger that. And that he was proud of all of us kids. He said my father now realized that if he'd been responsible for making all of *us*, then, no matter what he'd failed to do, he'd actually done a lot.

"He says there's nothing you can't do!"

It was startling to hear that; my father hadn't been the type of parent who'd said that sort of thing. Perhaps he'd learned the importance of expressing it now.

As we took a break for some water—he led me to a small cooler, handing me a paper cup—I asked Roger where he got his information from. He said he had many sources: his own guides, other people's guides, and other people's loved ones, as well as the angelic and other higher realms.

"So, do you consider yourself a *medium*?" I asked, slipping in a little interview while I had the chance.

"I didn't know I was doing mediumship," he said. "One day, some-one said to me, 'You know, you're doing mediumship.' And I said no. Because I thought of Whoopi Goldberg in *Ghost*, with the crystal ball. To me, it was just like . . . information back and forth. Now, very often, to distinguish when it's angelic presence or a higher-realm being, I'll get this energy that comes in, through me and around me. Much like the show *Touched By an Angel*. When she goes into her angelic self, she starts to glow. That's the experience I have. I *feel* it. I'm not saying I start to glow . . . though, of course, that would be nice."

I laughed. "Roger, you *always* glow!"

So do you!" he said, with a grin. "But when it comes in from a loved one, there's this very specific, different feeling. It's almost like a wind rushes in, they come in really fast, and very specific. Sometimes I get the information word for word. Sometimes I get images, and I have to kind of put this into language. And not just images, but there's a *feeling*, some-times, too. And sometimes I get what I call "*conclusive thought*," where it's as if five or seven or ten really brilliant people have discussed the subject and they've come to a conclusion . . . and now *I* have to explain it. That's where I have a pet peeve. I try my best to be exactly word-for-word on what really is being communicated. Because, a lot of times we don't have, in our language—in *language*—what can communicate it the best. Like, try and communicate to me the color purple! Knock yourself out!"

"Also, I'll get an idea of people's gifts," he continued as I sipped my cup of water. "And I'll get an idea of what they've lived through. I get to know a person's soul expression, and the beauty of that, and how powerful they are. And then I help people reconnect to what they are, and what they came here to the planet to be. Because in being that, they give the planet their gift. *It's the reason they came to the planet! To bring it!*"

He paused, drinking. "And then, I also help them move out of being what they're not. Sometimes it's telling someone they don't want something; you have to tell them to let it go. And when they do"—he paused, and his voice softened—"they feel such ease in being! And then—with hands open—they receive a different life." He smiled. "And *boy*, are they ready for it! And so good at it too!"

As we moved back to our chairs, Roger seemed to be still in receiving mode.

"Each soul is exceptional. No one, no other soul can bring what each soul brings. So to say each soul is precious is an understatement. To say each soul is *Glory* itself, with a capital *G*, or is Glorious, is also an understatement. But one I can live with." He chuckled. "And what we do for each other is help one another remember that Truth! . . . It's helping people play their own beautiful melody."

I told him I loved that.

"Think about it! How can we glorify God if we're not being what we are, which is *Glory*?" he asked, spreading out his hands.

Well, the man had a point, no arguing with that.

Roger told me then that he wanted to see if I had any energy blockages that needed clearing. He pulled out his pendulum, a metal pendant attached to a cord, and followed its motion as he asked various questions—not to me, but perhaps to the angels?—about the chakras, or energy centers, in my body. According to the pendulum, I had nine "blockages": some in the heart, some in the solar plexus, and some in the sacral or sex chakra.

"Do you meditate? Or do yoga?" he asked.

I told him I'd been meditating, and did yoga at times too. He explained that one particular chakra that in most people was blocked, was in my case surprisingly clog-free—and that those practices tended to produce that result.

Next, he had me lie on the massage table. "What one thing would you want in your life, if you could have it?" he asked.

"More love," I said.

"And what would you like to lose, if you could?"

"*Fears,*" I said. "And the feeling that I need to fix everybody all the time."

"You don't need to fix people," Roger said. "You can't expect to get things from people that they don't have yet to give. They haven't gotten there yet themselves." He paused, receiving. "Your simply being present with them is all you need to do."

I felt a weight lifting off me just hearing him say it.

Roger worked over me for a time, murmuring what sounded like a combination of prayers and incantations; I heard the words *shame*, *abandonment, guilt* . . . I wanted to peer up at him to see what was happening, but I resisted.

Sure enough, "I sense you're still 'recording,'" he chided me.

"I can't help it," I said, smiling. I should have known he'd pick that up.

"This isn't about the book. It's about *you*," he reiterated. Yet, apparently there were things he wanted me to remember. "*Come and let's share together all of life!*" he at one point exclaimed, striding over to write it down in my notebook this time, in large block letters. It was obviously important—it was the only thing he'd written in my notebook thus far—so I asked him to explain why that was. It seemed a simple enough idea to me.

"Yes, because *you* know how to *do* that!" he said. "Many people don't. And it's what life is about. Sharing together . . . all of life! All the love, the joy. *You* have a master's in that. But a lot of people, when it comes to that, they're still in kindergarten. That's what you're here to teach them . . . with your book, and with who you are."

Well! I would certainly try.

Finally, still standing over me, he did a bit of that undeniably *glorious* singing—like the angels' closing theme song, I thought, as I let it wash over me—and then he helped me up. He asked me to let him know in the next few days how I was feeling. And then we hugged good-bye. And, Reader, let it be noted: When the man hugged—*Mama mía!*—he *hugged*.

And *still*, he wasn't quite done. "There's someone coming soon . . . meaning a *man* . . . who loves boats and sailing. It's all about water," he said.

That sounded promising! I told him I was going to be spending some time at my brother's summerhouse at the Jersey Shore. He paused. "Mother Mary's here. She's letting you know that she walks beside you. On the beach . . . with dogs."

It was an astonishing thing to be told. I did walk on the beach, I admitted, whenever I was there. "And I do see a lot of dogs," I said. "But I don't walk *with* dogs."

He just smiled.

Let alone Mother Mary, I stopped myself from adding, as I smiled back.

"We are surrounded in love at every moment and every step . . . at every breath, we are embraced and loved," he said, standing in the doorway as I departed. He asked me again to let him know in a few days how I felt.

As I stepped out of the building into the day's light, I thought about that phrase—that we were *surrounded by love*. I did believe that. Sometimes, I thought, it could be hard for us to see it; to feel it. But somehow I did know it. I always had.

Taking the train home, I looked at the words Roger had scribbled in my notebook. *"Come and let's share together, All Of Life!!"* I came to see those words, in the days following my session, as an invitation, and maybe even an affirmation. Sharing what I was experiencing in my explorations *was*, I felt more and more clearly, what I was here to do.

What I began to notice, in the weeks that followed, aside from an increased sense of joy and well being, was that the amount of time I was able to spend meditating lengthened dramatically. Before, I'd had a hard time sitting still for fifteen minutes. Now I went a good half hour, still wanting more. And meditation, I'd come to learn, whether with the archangels or alone in my threadbare armchair, was good for whatever ailed me. Like plugging in to the Source, it recharged me; it helped keep me sane in a world lacking in sanity, and gave me an inner GPS for dealing with life's challenges.

That funny "gathering a ball of energy" exercise seemed to be having an effect too. As I took my daily beach walks, once I'd started house-sitting, my arms would spread out as if embracing the miles of sand to the north and south, the miles of water to the east. Indeed, I *was* getting larger, and more powerful, too, if only in my own imagination. But that, I was learning, was where change always began.

Regarding the angels, on a certain level they still seemed fantastic. But obviously *Roger* believed in them. And, more and more, *I* believed in *Roger*. As with many of the practitioners with whom I'd been working, he was so accurate in what he picked up, it was hard not to give credence, or at least consideration, to all the other things he said.

As for his singing, in subsequent meditation sessions with him, I noticed a discernable difference in his voice when he was singing "as Roger" as compared to when he was doing the angelic channeling. The whole quality of his voice, the *timbre* of it, changed. And the melody . . . it was so lovely, and yes, *otherworldly*. If the angels *were* truly there, I thought, gracing us with their divinely loving presence, how insane would I be to squander it?

✳

ABOUT A YEAR LATER, I was thinking about my session with Roger and was reminded of what he'd said about Mother Mary. Not long before, I'd met my new friend Deirdre, down at the Shore, she of the funky purple clogs whom Rev. Kev had so accurately described. Deirdre and her husband regularly brought two of their four dogs along to their house, and Deirdre sometimes let me take them with me on my walks. Becky, her chocolate Lab, especially loved to join me; she wore a somber expression along with her purple bandanna—except when she hit the beach, where she galloped through the waves, chasing seagulls with joyous abandon. I talked to the Earth—*Gaia*, as Roger called her—and tried to listen for what she might have to tell me; I listened, too, to the roll of the waves and the cries of the gulls, and Becky's delighted barks and yaps.

I couldn't say for sure about Mother Mary walking beside me—though I loved to think it was so, as I'd prayed a "Hail Mary" practically every night of my life, and had a special feeling for Mary. But as for the *dogs*, Roger had been right.

I decided I'd better pay attention to what the angels had to say . . . whether via my intuitive friends, or a homeless man outside a deli. If they were indeed real, I was grateful to be in their presence. And I resolved to call upon them more often, when I was in need of guidance or help, or added blessings in my day-to-day life. And when, Reader, was I not?

Maybe, like Edward Ragosta, I too was being "upgraded" by the angels—having my frequency raised to a higher vibration, as Roger would put it, by their unearthly song—to take on my soul's task at hand.

7

ADVENTURES IN
MEDIUMSHIP
✳ OR ✳

We Have Met the Messenger and She Is Us

THERE'S A TERM THAT'S GETTING A LOT OF PLAY THESE DAYS, *BFF*s: *Best Friends Forever.* "She's my BFF," I've often heard my young nieces say. Those of us who are a tad older know how rare it is when a friendship actually survives the test of time. And though fifty may be the new twenty-five—to quote a newspaper headline tacked up on my fridge—as one passes that midcentury benchmark, one may find oneself pondering the question: *Could* friendships last forever? If we *do* transcend the death of our earthly body, do our *friendships,* too?

My friend David had been a cherished and loyal buddy to me for more than twenty years. He was such an integral part of my life that when he died, my day-to-day existence had been palpably changed. And yet, through my remarkable experiences with mediumship via my friend Katarina, Jennifer Hicks, and Jeffrey Wands, I'd come to feel that David was likely, in some way, still around. Since his death, I'd had a tangible sense several times that he was close by. Once, I'd been watching the movie *Oklahoma!* I'd always loved old musicals, yet had somehow never seen this classic. As I watched, I felt him hovering over my left shoulder, letting out his characteristic giggle—as if he found the show incredibly corny and thus hilarious. The feeling had been so strong that, a few days later, I emailed his sister and told her about it. She asked if I'd known that David had played the trombone in a pit orchestra for a local production of that very show, and said that, indeed, he'd loved making fun of it. I told her I hadn't known it, but that now my experience made total sense: It was just what he would have done if he'd been there in the flesh.

The most notable instance when I'd felt David's presence was at his funeral service in his native Long Island. I'd been asked, along with one other friend, to deliver a eulogy. After the service, we'd all been invited to David's childhood home. At one point, I left the throng and went to a corner of the living room where there was an upright piano. In my visits to this house, I'd never seen the piano actually played; it seemed more a surface to house knick-knacks and such. On top of it was a large headshot of a beaming David. As I stood staring at the familiar face of my beloved friend, I had a vivid, startling sense of him jumping out of the picture at me. I *felt* his presence coming out of it, loving and comforting, as if in waves. I'd never experienced anything like it.

Shortly after David's service, I started to assemble my Dream Team, and had my first reading with Maggie Moise. Though Maggie didn't claim to be a medium, per se, as I'd chatted with her via email afterward, I told her a close friend of mine had died, and asked if she could possibly pick up any information on him. I shared nothing about him but his first name, and then sent her his photo and date of birth at her request. She said she would see what she could do.

A few days later, I heard from Maggie. She described a number of things about David that resonated with me: his sense, now, of utter freedom and release (she said he was showing himself to her naked, but that this was purely symbolic—though I had to laugh because David had been a big fan of nude beaches, often trying to rally his friends to shed our inhibitions and join him); his concern over a boy he had left behind (David had been survived by a nephew who'd lost his father as a baby, and he and David had been very close); his powerful love of music (David had played the trombone, worked in music management when younger, and was passionate about music of all kinds); and the fact that he loved to write (he'd written and edited for most of his career). She told me she was seeing a bear cub, which she thought pertained to the Chicago baseball team, the Cubs (in fact, we had a mutual friend who lived in Chicago, with whom David, a baseball fan, had attended a number of Cubs games). And she described his witty, charming personality to a tee.

Maggie had done very well, I thought—with no last name to go on, she had no ability to Google David and find out such details about his life. Still, I'd been hoping she'd pick up something more personal, something David might reference that only I would know.

A few days later, I got my wish.

"Last night, I was sleeping with David's photo under my pillow, and I got the image of an upright piano," Maggie wrote in an email, "a family piano that is sort of like furniture but is sometimes played at holidays or whatnot." A little *zing* shot through me!

It was possible, of course, that she was psychically picking up on that moment I'd stood gazing at David's portrait. It didn't necessarily prove that *he,* in spirit, had actually been there at the time. Either way, though, it gave me some validation that the moment I'd experienced in front of the piano had been as unique and significant as it felt.

A FEW WEEKS LATER, I got an email about a "message circle" that medium Jennifer Hicks was holding: a group of people gathering, under Jennifer's tutelage, to attempt to collectively receive messages from the dead. My money was even tighter than usual—partly due to all the readings, workshops, and sessions!—and on top of that, a large invoice from one of my freelance clients had gone astray. I'd had to resubmit it, and it was taking a *long* time for my paycheck to arrive. It had become my strict practice to avoid accumulating credit-card debt, since my father had run up a lot of debt before he died, and it was proving stressful to watch every nickel and dime until I got paid. Still, Jennifer apparently didn't hold these circles often; it wasn't really very expensive; and the friend who'd introduced me to her had told me these circles were well worth it. So I signed up to attend.

The next day, at a movie screening with Frankie, I told him about my plans.

"Why are the dead always so chatty and communicative, and at every medium's beck and call?" he asked. "I'm telling you right now— when I'm dead, I plan to make myself unavailable." He paused. "I love ya, Annie, but if I go first, don't contact me unless you have an antidote for whatever it was that killed me. And don't ask me to watch over any- one unless it's a cute brunette who enjoys walking around without her clothes!" He laughed at his own joke, and I chuckled too, as I promised to respect his wishes, mentally noting that if Frankie *had* ever lived a life as a monk, it couldn't have been an order requiring a vow of silence. (Then again, perhaps he was making up for lost time.)

The day before the message circle, I sat in my threadbare armchair, wondering what David would think about my desire to be in touch. He'd been skeptical about phenomena like mediumship, but he'd also been highly curious, someone who liked to push boundaries and test things out. I wondered what he might show me, were he to pop in. I thought of Maine and California, the two places outside the tristate area to which we'd traveled together. I also thought he might show me something to do with music or theater, two of his greatest loves.

But the thing David would most likely use to identify himself, I concluded, was the fact that he had celiac disease, an autoimmune dis- order of the small intestine, which requires the person who suffers from it to maintain a strictly gluten-free diet, or risk destroying part of his or her intestine. David had been diagnosed with celiac later in life, after a long period of feeling ill and not knowing why. Once he knew the cul- prit, he'd gone after it with a vengeance. He'd joined a celiac support group, gone on a passionate crusade to educate restaurants . . . even had T-shirts designed for the cause, which at the time was not nearly as well known as it is now.

David was vigilant about screening what he ate, and missed the foods he'd grown up on, especially baked goods. His mother, since college, had sent him "care packages" of homemade cookies, pastries, and brownies. After his diagnosis, he was constantly scouting out gluten-free bakeries and specialty shops, *much* harder to find in those days. If anything like that came up in a message, I'd be hard-pressed not to believe it was David dropping in.

The event took place in a New Age center that was everything the A.R.E. was not. Interested and open as I was to things metaphysical, places like this, with their pointedly soothing décor, complete with candles, incense, hanging red-silken feng-shui doodads, and miniature plug-in waterfalls, made me cringe. It just felt so clichéd. It was stuff like this, I thought, as I took in the man seated at the reception area, a massive crystal dangling on his open-shirted chest, and his hair slicked back into a tiny man-bun—what my brother-in-law had once called a "dork-knob"—that made the New Age movement so easy to mock. David was probably having a field day, if he was indeed hovering about.

The New Age hipster proved remarkably friendly, leaving me feeling slightly guilty for my less-than-generous thoughts, and directed me toward the proper room with a genuine smile. As I passed by a door with the sign "Clearing in Progress," I thought back to the clearing I'd had with Roger. *So*, I wondered, *could one just walk in and "get cleared" here, the way one could go in for, say, an oil change, or a mani-pedi?*

Finally I arrived and met Jennifer face-to-face. A slim, attractive woman of approximately my own age, with glasses and a head of curly, shoulder-length hair, she greeted me warmly. She clearly remembered me from our phone reading, and invited me to join the eight or ten participants who were already seated in the dimly lit space.

Jennifer explained that we would start off with a guided meditation to "open our channels," and then see what messages we could collectively pull in. She instructed us to be open to what we received, to remove our sensors, and to say whatever came into our head, even if it seemed nonsensical; something that meant nothing to us might well mean something to someone else. She also explained that she'd started to develop her own psychic abilities, many years before, in a circle like this one, and expressed her belief that we all possessed such abilities, to varying degrees. With practice, she said, we could develop them.

I had the vague notion that I'd heard that idea before—perhaps I'd read it—but I'd never quite taken it to heart. Now that I'd been told several times, though, how psychic I was, perhaps it was time for me to get to work testing it out. Perhaps those abilities I'd longed for as a girl, and despaired of having, were there, simply lying in wait for me to put in the time and effort to unleash them. Or maybe they were just not the type that allowed one to pick up symbols on cards. After all, Patricia Masters had said there were many types of psychic abilities.

Jennifer's guided meditation set us off on a walk through the woods and into a pavilion surrounded by flowers. As we entered, she told us to envision a person who'd passed away sitting beside us. We were to ask this person a question and try to receive an answer. I envisioned my maternal grandmother, Jennie, to whom I'd been very close—a head shorter than me, her blue eyes bright, her smile loving. I could *feel* her, so clearly. "Why am I having so much trouble finding a partner, Grandma?" I asked—my perpetual question.

"It's not time yet," she said. "It'll come, but not yet." Had she really said it, or had I simply thought it? It was the same answer my Team had been giving me: that I had a book to write, a "mission" to fulfill, and that a man, unless he was totally helpful and supportive, would be a distraction.

Jennifer told us to pay attention to our dreams; the answers might appear in upcoming weeks, if we hadn't received them now.

Next, we attempted to collectively pick up messages from the departed. Jennifer said a man was coming through for her, with the initial D. "I'm hearing *Dmitri*," she said. "Does that mean anything to anyone?" It didn't, so she moved on.

Her focus shifted, as she asked a woman across from me if she'd had a dog that had died when she'd been a child. She had. It seemed the dog was showing Jennifer a particular corner of the woman's bedroom. "You might see something fall over there," she said. "I'm getting the feeling he's going to make some kind of mischief there, to let you know he's around.

"Yes, animals in spirit do talk," she affirmed, smiling. "What may seem even weirder, they talk in English. At least, they do to me."

Well, I'd heard that from other mediums too, including Christina Wright, who'd described three cats "on the Other Side" in a reading for one of my friends, getting all of their genders, colors, and markings just right. Christina had referred to a cat my friend had once had as being French, with a name like *FiFi*, which my friend admitted was a hit: "I don't know why I always thought of that cat, who was actually named *KiKi*, as being French, but I always did."

Next, Jennifer moved on to another woman and got a few impressive hits on two relatives of hers: both sailors, and with a large difference in height.

"Is anyone else picking up anything?" Jennifer asked.

"I'm getting the name *Beth*," a young man said. "I keep hearing a voice shouting, 'Beth! Beth!'"

"I'm connected to a Beth," a woman said.

"I'm also seeing children splashing in a brook," he said. "But separate from that."

The splashing children didn't make sense to the woman. And the man couldn't get anything else.

"I'm getting that guy again with the *D*," Jennifer said. "He's not going away. Only now he's saying 'Dieter.' Does anyone know anyone with a name like *Dieter*?"

No one did.

Dimitri? Dieter? If it *was* the same man, why would his name change from one thing to another? It sounded like this spirit was playing games, and the humor of it reminded me of David.

"*Dieter*, again, I'm hearing *Dieter!*" Jennifer said.

I giggled. The name *Dieter* made me think of that Mike Meyers character on *Saturday Night Live*, host of the fictional West-German TV talk show *Sprockets*, with his round glasses, slicked-back hair, and black leotards. I loved that skit, and David had too.

Was this David, pulling a prank? It wouldn't have been his first. After I'd graduated from college, a year ahead of David, I'd stayed on in our college town, Charlottesville, for the summer. David had returned there to begin his final year in early September, just as I was moving back home to New York. On the morning of my departure, he offered to drive me to the train station. I was feeling blue about leaving, so David, to make me laugh, had "mooned" my train, providing a memorable parting shot of his round, white butt not only to me, but to many others on the fortuitously named Southern Crescent as well.

"I'm hearing the name *Danny*," a very young woman now said.

"There's the *D* again. Does *anyone* have anyone who might be trying to reach them with a *D*?" Jennifer asked.

"I lost a very close friend named David," I said.

"*David*," she repeated. "That's actually quite close to *Danny*. Five letters, beginning with *D-A*. Sometimes it can be tough for me to distinguish the actual name."

I'd heard this before from mediums too. It was something my friend Frankie loved to mock: "If they're really speaking to the dead, why is it that they always get *initials*? What, the dead can't say their full names?" When I'd mentioned this to my friend Griffin, though, he'd been a bit tweaked: "Why do people think it's so easy for spirits to *do* this stuff? When you think about what they're doing—sending information from one level of consciousness to another—it's amazing they can get anything intelligible through at all!" Higher-level beings, he pointed out, didn't think and talk the way we did, so things like names, words, and sentences, as *we* would construct them, wouldn't likely be *their* easiest method of communication.

"Would you like to try and see if we can contact him?" Jennifer asked next.

"Absolutely!" I said.

Jennifer said he was showing her someplace very cold. "Where people might go skiing. Vermont, or maybe Maine."

"We did travel together to Maine!" I said.

"OK, now another person's here," she said, "someone who got killed by a moving vehicle! But I'm shooing them away! I can't handle more than one at a time!"

Now, that was pretty wild. G.G., one of two other friends who'd been on that trip to Maine, and who had died about ten years before, in her twenties, *had* been struck by a moving vehicle—a truck—while crossing a Manhattan street. G.G. had popped up in my first reading with Jennifer, over the phone. But that had been years before, and at the time, I was sure, I'd never mentioned to Jennifer that I'd met G.G. *through* David—who was, at that point, very much alive. There would have been no reason to do so. I was impressed now at how Jennifer seemed to be bringing in this mutual friend of David's and mine as she brought him in. (Over time, Reader, I came to understand that this was the way mediumship often worked: One spirit brought in others. Sometimes those brought in were connected to that chaperoning spirit, in their human lifetime; other times, not.)

"He's showing me how he died," Jennifer said. "That's one of the first things they usually do, by gesturing. For instance, if they point to the chest area, it usually means lung cancer, or something with the lungs, or if it's a woman, maybe breast cancer." She paused. "It wasn't an accident for this one. It was an illness. Is that right?"

"That's right," I said.

"He's showing me, *like this*," she said, running her finger up and down her arms and legs. "As if it was systemic through the body, then the head. It sounds like something with the nervous system."

"I'm not sure how he literally passed," I said. "But it's accurate, what you're describing." David had had leukemia, the most virulent form. So it was in his blood—the circulatory, not the nervous system. But it would be depicted, if someone were describing it using gestures, in the exact same way.

"Now he's showing me something really odd," she said. "He's taking me into a bakery. He's showing me cupcakes, and things like . . . pastries. Does this make any—"

"*Yes!*" I blurted out, interrupting her. I rushed to explain about his celiac disease, and how much he'd missed his mother's baked goods. "It's the perfect sign from him. Cookies, cupcakes, pastries . . . that, without a doubt, is David's heaven!"

Everyone laughed. But I felt myself tear up a little, through my own laughter. He was here! It was David! To my mind, in at that moment, he had definitively shown up.

"I don't know what you're writing, but he's showing me a book, or actually, *books*." She mimed *volumes* with her hands.

I had told her, via email, that I was doing a writing project some weeks before, but I hadn't told her what it was. It could have been articles, plays, screenplays, poems, comic strips—all of which I'd written at various points in my life—though admittedly none of these would likely be someone's first guess.

"He says you need to stop going over what you're writing . . . to stop going over the same stuff . . . and move ahead."

OMG! All that week, I'd been trying to "add pages" to what I'd written. Instead, I found myself going over and over it, tweaking and tightening. I was annoyed at myself for procrastinating; it wasn't the time for fine-tuning, but hammering out a first draft. It made sense that David, also a writer and editor—we'd worked together twice in the publishing and media fields, and both times, he'd been my boss—would point this out. I mentally thanked him for the caring nudge.

After that, the spirit formerly known as David quieted down. Jennifer said his energy had moved on, so she broke us into pairs; each of us was to see what we could pick up for the other. I worked with the young man who'd gotten *Beth*, whose name was Stanley. I asked him to try and pick up more from David—I wasn't ready to say good-bye. Meanwhile, I'd see whom I might contact for him.

No sooner had I closed my eyes, though, than Stanley broke in. "Did David like Broadway shows?" he asked.

"*Loved* them!" I said.

"Because I immediately saw a street sign with the word *Broadway* on it."

Not all people, and certainly not all *men*—especially *straight* men—loved Broadway shows. Stanley had gone out on a limb, and he was pleased. He closed his eyes, then popped them open again.

"And he was someone who would never move out of the city?"

"True." While in recent years I'd talked about moving, David never would have considered it.

"And he was very into culture . . . the arts. A very learned guy about culture?"

"He actually wrote a blog specifically about cultural things going on in town!"

"And he liked to walk around the city a lot? Especially Central Park?"

This, too, I confirmed. David loved walking in the city—not an unusual trait, if one lived in New York. But I'd never told Stanley that David *lived* in New York. And David did particularly love Central Park—again, not unusual, but it was truly one of his favorite spots.

He'd often gathered friends there for Shakespeare in the Park and pic-nics. And we'd boated there numerous times, always at his suggestion. There was one encounter I particularly remembered when a friend and I had been walking *over* Bow Bridge just as David and a friend were rowing a boat *under* it. He'd shouted up to us, then held on to the side of the bridge to keep the boat in place while we carried on a chat. It was a story he loved to tell.

I praised Stanley, and he beamed. But then he seemed to lose the thread.

My turn was next. It was hard not to feel a tad competitive as I closed my eyes. Quickly, I had two names pop into my head: *Anna* and *Henry*. Stanley said these were the names of two of his cousins, very much alive, on different sides of the family. He thought it was interest-ing that I'd gotten them, Anna in particular, because her sister was get-ting married that weekend, a wedding he'd be attending.

"And, don't laugh, but I'm getting the Incredible Hulk," I said.

"Not bad! I've been trying to get my son to go see the movie *Green Lantern*."

Well, it seemed I'd had a few *possible* psychic hits, if not medium-istic ones. But I was far more impressed with his scorecard that night than mine.

After a bathroom break, Jennifer paired us up again. My partner this time, a sweet-faced young woman named Melissa, told me she'd studied psychic development with Jennifer and was a reiki master too.

I tried reading for Melissa first. I got some hazy images of a woman in a kitchen, with old-fashioned, cat's-eye glasses and curly reddish hair. Melissa said it could be her grandmother, whom she hadn't known well. I got some names and initials, some of which resonated with her, but nothing that impressed me much.

Once again, my partner had it all over me.

Melissa immediately started jotting things on a pad. She said she was getting the letter *G*, a female, felt warmth, and was seeing flowers.

I noticed that her eyes rolled up and back a bit, and that her eyelashes fluttered, as if she were seeing the images above her.

A female G*!* I thought, excited, wondering if it might be G.G. again. I'd purposely never said G.G.'s name aloud when Jennifer had described the person killed by a moving vehicle, so there was no way Melissa could have learned it.

I told her this might be someone I'd known.

"I'm seeing a watering can now," she said. "Did she like to garden?"

"I'm not sure," I admitted. G.G. had lived in the city. If it had been something she'd done elsewhere, maybe Switzerland, I hadn't known.

"I'm seeing a check," she said then.

"A *check?*" I asked.

"Yes, it's actually a big check mark," she said, drawing in the air with her pen. "Does that mean anything?"

"Well," I said, thinking of how Jennifer had said spirits used symbols, "I'm actually very tight on money, and I *have* been dying for a big *check* to arrive." I let out a small laugh.

"OK, yeah," she said, smiling. "She's showing me mail now. I'm seeing stamped letters. And the check. Like, 'The check's in the mail.'"

"*Really?*" I said. That was so funny. "I hope she's right!"

Melissa then told me she was getting the name *Sal*. That excited me. Sal was my maternal grandfather. Growing up, I'd seen him and my grandmother Jennie nearly every day. But in all my readings with mediums, Grandpa Sal had never shown up. Some of his sisters, yes—but never Sal himself, nor his brother, Charles, who'd been my much-adored great-uncle and godfather, and who'd died far too young.

"I'm seeing his hands. Did he have big, very strong hands? I'm feeling muscles, strength. Like he was a big, strong man."

"Yes, he was in good shape, even as an older man, and he *was* strong. He used to flex his arm, when I was little, and make me feel his muscle. I'd joke with him that it was hard as a raw potato!"

Jennifer, who'd been circling the room, came over now to listen.

"She just heard *Sal*, and that's my grandfather," I explained.

"*Sal*," Jennifer repeated. "Yeah, I'm getting his energy too. Did he like to play the horses?"

"*Yes!*" I nearly shouted. "He went to the OTB every afternoon!"

"That's just like *my* grandfather!" Melissa said, laughing.

"Who's *Charlie*?" Jennifer asked. "He's got Charlie with him."

"That's his brother!" I said. "We called him Uncle Charles."

Jennifer smiled and nodded approvingly, then moved on to some of the other pairings.

"I don't know why, but I'm getting cherries," Melissa said next.

"Sal had a cherry tree in his yard," I said. Sicilians seemed to have a thing about fruit trees; he'd had a fig and a mulberry tree too. He'd also grown tomatoes. Maybe the watering can had been him coming in, and not G.G. at all.

"OK, now I'm getting a fisherman, and fishing," Melissa said.

"Sal's father had a fish store, on Staten Island. He grew up working there, going to the Fulton fish market in Manhattan and bringing back fish to sell. Also, when I was a kid, he taught me how to draw this funny symbol, like a logo, with four intertwined fish, that they used for some kind of family partnership they formed.

"But wait," I said. "The fisherman could be someone else, too. My friend David. His last name was *Fischer*, and he joked about that sometimes."

Melissa, pleased, closed her eyes and sat in "receiving" mode again. "I feel funny saying this," she said, almost shyly. "It's really *odd*, what I'm getting now."

"From David?" I asked.

"I think. I'm getting the letters *B-U-T-T. Butt*."

"That's hysterical!" I said.

"Does that mean something?" she asked, surprised.

I told Melissa the story about David "mooning" me on the train. I told her that when he'd died, and I'd been asked to give a eulogy,

I wondered if it was in poor taste to tell that story at a memorial service. But I knew David would love it—after all, it had been *his* joke!—so I did, and the whole temple had cracked up.

Jennifer swung by once more, and I told her how G.G. and David had come through again in the same session. She said she was picking up on G.G. now too. "She's showing me a magazine spread with an article about you. Your face is smiling out of the pages. You're going to get press for your book, she's saying. And that if she were here, she'd *kick your butt* about finishing it. 'Tell her to stop questioning herself. She's got it,' she says."

I laughed at the sudden profusion of butt-related info coming in from the Other Side. "That's very G.G.!" I affirmed. "Thanks, G.G. I needed that!"

Soon Jennifer announced that we were bringing the session to a close. I headed into the night chatting with Melissa, who was walking to the same train station as I. She told me, as we ambled along, that she was thinking about medical school. After we parted ways, I thought about that. I loved the idea that, through people like Melissa, Western medicine would likely be transformed, before long, to include more of an openness to intuition, to energy healing, to things presently experienced by many but not yet fully understood.

Riding downtown, my mind played over the events of the message circle. I was sure that some of my skeptical friends would explain away everything by saying that Jennifer and Melissa had used cold reading, or that the information they'd come up with could've fit most anyone. But in my view, neither of these things was remotely true. Neither woman had asked leading questions. Jennifer had come up with the names *Sal* and *Charlie* fully hatched. Everything they'd gotten about my grandfather had been accurate: his strong hands, his betting on horses, the cherries, and the connection with fish.

They'd likely say I was influenced by wanting to hear from my loved ones, that my emotions had colored my perception of what had been said. But that just didn't seem so. And as I walked under the unusually clear, star-studded Manhattan night sky, I felt in my gut, Reader, that I'd heard from Grandpa Sal, Uncle Charles, David, and G.G., too. And I couldn't help but feel touched, and elated.

My friend Rick had once told me that he didn't fear getting old—that in fact, he looked forward to it—and that he didn't fear dying; he couldn't wait to get to the Other Side! And I used to marvel at that, with more than a touch of envy. Open as I was to the "spiritual," it didn't mean that the idea of death wasn't still a little scary. OK, at times, more than a little. I'd had my share of moments, in the wee hours of certain dark nights, of existential crisis, of fear of self-annihilation, or worse, as I'd pondered facing the Great Unknown. But now, after all the experiences I'd been having, I was starting to understand how Rick felt. Because if the Other Side *was* real . . . if death was not an end to life, or consciousness, as we knew it . . . then what was there, really, to be afraid of? And if the loved ones I'd lost were all there . . . somewhere, in some form . . . how marvelous would it be to connect with them again? And how many more adventures beyond this one did each of us have in store?

I would have to call Rick and tell him about my latest adventures, I thought, coming up out of the subway station.

And when I got home, the check was in the mail.

8

ADVENTURES WITH
A SPIRIT
✳ OR ✳

"Heeeeere's Bobby!"

WHEN I WAS YOUNGER, DECADES BEFORE MY EXPLORATIONS officially began, and well before I'd ever met with a medium to contact those who had died, I had a habit I've never before confessed to anyone: When someone in my life had passed away, I would think about other friends or loved ones who were also deceased whom I felt might like to meet that recently deceased person—assuming they'd never met, in life—and mentally introduce them to one another on the Other Side. "Ed," I might say, speaking to my beloved friend who had died very young of AIDS, "meet Herman. Herman was a fantastic photographer. As an artist, Ed, you would appreciate his eye. Herman, meet Ed. You both *truly* loved beauty. And loved life. And I think you would have a lot to talk about!" Why and how I thought this process would work, Reader, I don't know, but I did it, and not infrequently. I performed this sort of connecting all the time *here*, I reasoned . . . so why not try sort of *projecting* it . . . *over there*? Wherever, or whatever, *"over there"* was.

And so, in my first reading with Christina Wright (who channels the spirit of Carl Jung), when she'd told me that I was a *connector*—someone, she said, who could put people together and orchestrate things—I had to acknowledge with a laugh that it was on many levels true. And then she'd also called me a *runner*. This, she explained, was someone who connected people with whatever it was they *needed*. I wasn't sure about being a runner, as I'd never heard the term before, but I *did* notice that often, when people in my life were in need, a means for me to help them would synchronistically appear. Such was the case with my friend Ben.

I met Ben around the time I attended that first message circle. I had just started my house-sitting stints at my brother's place at the Shore. They'd proven a great way to escape the frenetic vibe of city life and to get some writing done. Plus, after the wrenching year in which I'd had my breakup with West Coast Mike and lost my friend David, I felt drawn to the healing effects of sand, surf, seagulls—not to mention sandpipers, my favorites of the bird kingdom!—and an endless horizon.

The house was a once-stately Victorian with a double-decker front porch now in serious disrepair. My brother and sister-in-law had contracted a company to rebuild the porches, replace the rotting wood on the clapboards, and install a new roof and door. So all that winter and spring, coming and going from the city for one- or two-week stretches, I watched the work progress. As I did, I got to know the carpenters who tramped in and out to plug in power cords and occasionally use the loo.

Ben was a big, muscle-bound guy with a long, curly mop of blond hair and a handlebar mustache. His brother, Bruce, was smaller and wirier, with darker hair and a face that was usually clean-shaven. They were both sweet fellows, polite and friendly, and pretty chatty once I made it clear I was interested in getting to know them.

One Monday morning, after I'd spent a particularly lovely weekend at the house, I greeted them as they worked on the half-built porch.

"How 'bout that gorgeous weather Saturday?" I asked.

"Well," Ben said, with a somber expression, "Saturday was actually a pretty big day for us."

He held out his large forearm. It was emblazoned with an equally large tattoo of a pair of sunglasses, the kind Tom Cruise wore in *Risky Business*, and the words *RIP Bobby*. Below that was a picture of a dog . . . well, puking. And below that, in quotes, the words *Sick Puppy*.

I started to laugh. Then, "I'm sorry," I said, realizing that the *RIP* suggested that this was no laughing matter.

"It's OK," Ben said, with a faint smile.

"Who was he?" I asked.

"My best friend," he said.

"Ben—I'm so sorry. What happened?"

"Well, do you know about that thing on the pier . . . ?"

I had no idea what he meant.

"It was pretty big news around here. In all the papers. My friend Bobby . . . he was Bruce's friend too . . . he hung himself. Out on the pier. Saturday was the service."

"*That* pier?" There was only one pier in town, a few blocks from where we stood. I cast my eyes in its direction.

"Yup," he said, lifting a blue bandanna aside to wipe some sweat from his forehead.

Having no TV in the house, and not being a regular reader of news, I'd missed it.

"Oh, Ben," I said. "I lost one of my best friends, two summers ago. It's horrible. And *hanging* himself . . ."

"It gets worse," he said. "Apparently, he used the wrong kind of rope, or didn't really work it out right, and . . . he decapitated himself."

OMG!

"Some lifeguards saw it. They dove in and got the body, but . . ."

"Not the head?" I finished the sentence and I let out an awkward laugh. "I'm so sorry!" I said, embarrassed.

"It's OK," he said. "Truth is, Bobby would have found it funny. How do you think he got the nickname *Sick Puppy?*" He lifted his forearm to display the words.

The head, he told me, hadn't turned up. A forensics team had said that chances were good it *would* wash up, but no telling where or when.

Ben went on to say that there wouldn't be a day in his life now when he didn't think about Bobby, before turning back to his work. It broke my heart.

I set out for my beach walk that day with some trepidation. Visions of the head washing up at my feet as I strolled along the sand at the water's edge kept intruding into my thoughts. First, though, I went to the pier. There was a little memorial there with flowers and some handwritten notes. I stood there, thinking about this young man who'd taken his life on that spot, one of my favorite spots, as it happened, and felt overcome with sadness.

No head turned up. Not in the days ahead on that visit, nor in the trips I made in the weeks that followed.

About a month later, when Ben was working on the house again, I confided in him about my project. I'd mulled it over, and it felt like the right thing to do. Sipping a cappuccino I'd picked up from the Loving Cup, I told him I felt it was possible I'd contacted, via a medium, my own close friend who had died.

"Yeah, my brother buys into all that stuff," he said, shaking his head with a mixture of disapproval and indulgence as he finished hammering in a nail.

Then I told him about the experience I'd had at the message circle run by Jennifer Hicks. He listened, curious, but didn't offer much response beyond the occasional "*Huh.*"

A few days later, though, as I was heading out of the house for a swim, he surprised me by telling me he was thinking of consulting a medium himself. I told him I knew a few good ones in the city, and that most of them worked by phone. "You might want to do it in person, though," I said.

He affirmed that he'd prefer it, so I let it go at that.

But then something funny happened. At another message circle, about a month after my conversation with Ben, I mentioned to Jennifer that I'd been spending time on the Jersey Shore.

"Where?" she asked, saying she was a Jersey girl herself.

As I named the town, she smiled. "I go there a lot, antiquing."

I asked if she'd heard about a suicide off the pier. She hadn't, and was as shocked by it as I'd been. But that had been the extent of our discussion.

Not long after, though, as beach weather rolled around, whom should I spy on the coastal train, to my utter surprise, getting off at my very stop? Suited up in a sundress and wide-brimmed hat, Jennifer greeted me, and invited me to join her on the sand. Unfortunately, I said, I had plans that day; perhaps another time. But as I made my way to my brother's house, duffel bag in hand, my mental gears started turning. Jennifer was a medium. Ben was *looking* for one. And she'd said she came here often. How synchronistic was it that I'd run into her here?

I wanted to help Ben ameliorate some of his pain. I wanted to share the sort of experience I'd had several times myself now with someone who was grieving, someone who might not believe in mediumship but was curious enough to try it. But of course, Reader, I had a personal agenda too. I wanted to do a session that wasn't about someone *I* had lost, to look at it as analytically and unemotionally as possible. As convincing as the message circle had been, as time passed, my Jiminy Cricket skeptic was rearing his head again, tiny top hat and all, wanting, if not "proof," then at least some other *convincing* experiences. Experiences replicating my convincing results. And I honestly couldn't blame him.

The next time I saw Ben, I told him how I'd run into Jennifer. "I could ask her if she'd do a reading for you, here," I said. "I'd split the cost with you, if you'd let me sit in and record it . . . and possibly write about it."

He didn't need much persuading. "Let's do it," he said.

*

WEEKS LATER, I was seated at the large, old-fashioned dining room table in my brother's house, with Jennifer, simply dressed in denim shorts and a white T-shirt, to my left and Ben across from me, waiting for her to "bring Bobby in." It was a gray day, and rain pelted against the windowpane. Jennifer asked Ben if there was someone in particular he wanted to contact. Ben told her only Bobby's first name; that he'd been a friend; and that he'd taken his life. While he was speaking, he was interrupted by a strange sound: a beeper or buzzer. We all heard it, but no one could figure out what it was. I checked my phone, but I'd turned it off. Jennifer's was off too, as was Ben's.

"That's weird," I said. I went to check the coffeemaker in the kitchen, but it was off also. And I hadn't set any kind of timer. "I've never heard that before," I said. Then, *"He's heee-eerrrre!"* I couldn't help chanting—half kidding, but only half.

We all laughed. And then we began.

"OK, I'm gonna close my eyes and focus on Bobby," Jennifer said. "I'm not going into a trance, I'm just trying to pull him through." She paused. "I use a form of mental telepathy. I'm sending out questions, or requests. I'm saying, 'Bobby'—who I'm sure knows you're here— 'Earth to Bobby, come in Bobby.'" She smiled at Ben as she opened her eyes. "You're in construction, right? Working on this house?"

"Yeah," Ben answered.

"Anne told me that, that's not a psychic statement," she said. I appreciated her candor. "Was he also in construction?"

Ben confirmed that he was.

She closed her eyes again. "I'm seeing a man with blue eyes, but I don't know if this is Bobby."

"He had blue eyes," Ben said.

"I'm seeing a man with sandy-colored hair, light brown. But I don't think this is Bobby. I feel like I'm seeing another guy, also deceased. He may be pulling Bobby through. They do that, you know," she explained to Ben. "Different spirits have different communication abilities, and some spirits just seem to be better at making contact. I like to call them *escorts*. They often bring others, the ones being asked for, in. Did Bobby have sandy hair?"

"Uh, yeah. When he had hair." Ben chuckled, inadvertently, it seemed, running his hand through his own mop of curls. Jennifer reiterated that she could see this man, but she still didn't think it was Bobby.

That, to me, was impressive. Ben had confirmed that what she was getting fit Bobby's description. And yet, Jennifer was insisting it wasn't Bobby. If she had been faking it, doing cold reading, wouldn't she have taken the information Ben was giving her—that Bobby *had* had blue eyes and sandy hair—and run with it? Ben was telling her that the description fit Bobby, yet she was saying it wasn't him!

Ben tugged at his mustache. "Might be his stepfather, who he was very close to."

"Don't tell me too much," Jennifer said. "Did the stepfather have *large* blue eyes, like, round?"

"Yeah," Ben said. "Bobby did too."

"Because I'm not seeing squinty blue eyes, like, Paul Newman eyes. I'm seeing big, round baby blues, coming through from the Other Side. I think this is the stepfather, trying to pull Bobby through. But I'm not feeling Bobby quite yet. This man is talking about when Bobby passed . . . Was there a ceremony at the water's edge, or did somebody go to the water's edge and throw in something? A flower, maybe? I'm seeing a person or people standing at the water's edge."

"I mean . . . we did something, afterwards, at the pier . . ."

"Because they're taking me to the beach, and this man, the step-father, is acknowledging the thing that happened at the water's edge. In memory of Bobby."

I was attempting to play devil's advocate more than usual in this reading, trying to figure out what Jennifer could have gotten by any means *other* than mediumship. I had told her about Bobby's death at the message circle—which I'd disclosed to Ben. Bobby's story had also been written up in the local papers. I'd researched it myself to see what they'd said. I knew a lot of what Jennifer might come up with would be information she could have found online—what Bobby had done for a living, hobbies and interests, surviving family members. As for a ceremony at the water's edge . . . I hadn't found anything online about that, but it was a logical guess. Big round blue eyes, though? I hadn't found any photos of him on the Internet—and I'd tried.

Still, Jennifer *had* asked about Bobby's eyes in a way that might lead one to believe she was using cold reading. In other words, if Ben had said, "No, his eyes weren't blue," or "They weren't round," Jennifer, were she a skillful cold reader, could have backpedaled and found some clever way to elicit from Ben the kind of eyes Bobby actually had. As it happened, though, she'd been right.

"I see somebody drawing something in the sand, with a stick," she continued.

Ben shook his head, as if in disbelief. "I . . . I did that *last night!*"

"The stepfather is saying, 'I saw a person'—it must have been *you*, then —'drawing this thing . . . It could have been a heart. *I love you.*' It was like a message to Bobby you were drawing in the sand."

"That's exactly right." Ben shook his head again. He was, as I've said, a big, burly guy, a real "guy's guy," tats and all. That he of all people would write "I love you" to a guy friend, inside of a heart . . . well, it was disarmingly sweet, but more to the point, it wasn't something I felt Jennifer could ever logically have guessed Ben would do.

"I feel like the stepfather crossed him over," Jennifer said. "Also, is there a man Bobby was related to or friendly with, with the initial *P*? Like, *Pat*?"

"Not that I know of," Ben said, tugging his mustache again.

"OK. I could be wrong, or sometimes people think of it later." She paused. "OK, here we go. Here he is. He's calling your name. *'BEN! BEN!'* Here we go: *'How are ya, buddy?'*" She said it loudly and deeply. "Did he talk like that?"

Ben laughed and nodded. "He did call me *buddy*," he said.

"Thank you. For a guy who committed suicide, he's very upbeat." Jennifer tilted her head and adjusted her glasses on her nose, perplexed. "I feel this was a person who . . . I don't know about right before he went, but he was a fairly happy person for quite some time. I'm not feeling this was a person who, from childhood, was morose, sad, gloomy. I'm getting this happy, bubbly feeling in life, before things started to build up to the point where he took his life."

Ben said that this was true. *Score another for Jennifer!* I thought.

"He's talking about the gang of guys . . . hanging with the guys. Did he like to fish? Who's got the fishing boat?"

"My brother-in-law."

"Did you go out on the boat, did you used to drink beer?"

"We *would* drink beer, but . . . Bobby liked to fish, but never *caught* fish. And he would make a joke of that."

"He just said, 'Well, they're jumping over here!'" She grinned.

Hmmmm, I thought. Again, it wasn't a big leap to guess some of this stuff. Guys at the Shore would likely fish, drink beer, own boats. And admittedly, Jennifer was asking questions again. It always made me squirm when psychics or mediums did this, simply because it left them wide open to that accusation of cold reading. And yet, having talked to a number of them now, I could see that it was the best way for them to work. As Jennifer had told me, she got things mostly in images: symbols. It was like playing charades to decipher them. Getting the best possible reading, then, would take a joint, back-and-forth effort between the reader and the person the messages were for.

So yes, Jennifer *was* asking questions. Still, she'd hardly gotten anything wrong. The only thing Ben had *not* verified so far was the friend with the name like *Pat*.

She paused. "I know you're in construction. Accidents happen. But who got their hand smashed or mangled? Or broke their thumb or finger?"

"I do have a friend who Bobby met . . . It was at this 'guys' weekend.' A friend who got his hand caught in a chipper."

"*Ooooooooh! Noooooo!* Don't tell me," Jennifer squealed, holding up a hand. "I'm squeamish! *Squeamish!*"

Ben and I laughed. Dead people didn't bother her, but mangled limbs . . . that was another story.

"He's talking about the guy who hurt the hand. So he may just be acknowledging this trip. Did he go to shake his hand, and something happened?"

"Well, yeah, the guy, he didn't like to use that hand, but Bobby insisted on shaking it, to show him that he didn't care."

"OK, so I think what Bobby is doing," she said, "and dead people *love* doing this, is acknowledging the good times you had together."

She went on picking up images that Ben affirmed: first, a connection to Atlantic City—Bobby had actually won a lot of money in Atlantic City about ten years before, which I'd learned from the Web, so of course Jennifer could have too; then, a female close to him with the initial *T*, which Ben immediately confirmed. Then Jennifer got one that Ben *couldn't* confirm: Bobby standing on the pier, pointing to a full moon. Ben wasn't sure if there had been a full moon the night Bobby died, so Jennifer suggested he check. Curious, I later checked myself: The moon had been "waxing gibbous" that night, and looked almost full; the full moon had been the very next night.

Again, Jennifer could have researched this, but it seemed unlikely; she had a full-time, non-medium job—interestingly, in the field of science. Jennifer was a self-described "biology nerd," with a BS in biology and a master's in education. I loved that! I loved practitioners who straddled both the worlds of spirituality and science. To me, the two were, in essence, one.

Eventually, she cut to the chase. "OK, Bobby, *why* did you do this?" There was a long pause. "He said, 'I was miserable.' And I'm saying 'About what?' Did he have money trouble?" she asked.

Ooooooh . . . I was assuming she'd just gotten a huge miss. I knew about the money Bobby had won in Atlantic City—close to a million dollars. According to the papers, he was still due to collect a fifty-thousand-dollar annual payout for a number of years. But I was pleased she'd asked this question. I'd wondered earlier whether Jennifer might have Googled Bobby, or the guy who'd hung himself on the town's pier, and found out about his casino winnings . . . and everything else. But the fact that she was now asking this question made me doubt that she had. Because if she *had*, I reasoned, she would have known that he'd won all that money, and likely would have concluded—as *I* had—that whatever Bobby's troubles were, money *wasn't* one of them. All of which led me to feel that the other facts she'd picked up weren't things she'd Googled, but true psychic hits.

To my tremendous surprise, Ben immediately *affirmed* what Jennifer had said. Bobby *did* have money troubles!

Cripes! She was good.

Jennifer just nodded.

"When I asked what he was miserable about, Bobby said, 'Money. I couldn't see the way out.'" She said it again. "'I couldn't see the way out.'"

Ben got very still. "You just gave me chills on that. It's what he said *exactly*. He left some of us a DVD, saying good-bye, and he said *those exact words*."

"I don't know if he had debts that were crushing him. He's going like this." She gestured as if shielding herself. "Like he was under attack. Like predators were after him . . . He's saying, 'My heart was pounding in fear.' Some people have money problems and they're upset, but they're like, '*Nyeah!*' But he was just *so afraid*."

"Yeah," Ben said, sadness in his voice.

Jennifer said Bobby was now showing her a little red wagon, which did not resonate with Ben.

OK, I thought. *At last, another miss.* Or at least something Ben couldn't confirm. There'd been very few even of these so far.

"The money situation, did it also have to do with his parents or his family?" Jennifer asked.

Ben told her that Bobby had bought his mother a house with part of his winnings, but that he'd been a Union carpenter, with no work for *two years*, and that it was because of that. "He was trying to give his pension to his mom," he said.

"By killing himself? Oh my gosh," Jennifer said, sadly. She sighed a deep sigh and shook her head.

It was hard not to be moved by Bobby's story. I'd had my own share of money woes, and family woes . . . of heartbreak, and depression. There had been moments when I'd felt so desperately low that the idea of suicide had passed through my mind. But I would never actually have done it. For all my gut feelings about life after death— and quite probably an easier sort of existence than this one—I'd never wanted to leave this life behind, even at those times, because of the people I loved in the here and now. I wouldn't ever want to hurt them. I wondered if Bobby could have known how loved he was, and how much his actions would hurt the people who loved him. He was surely learning it now.

Ben seemed to be struggling with his words as he told Jennifer about "something of [Bobby's] that was missing" that he was hoping would show up. At first it didn't dawn on me what it was.

"He doesn't want to talk about that right now," Jennifer said, shaking her head. She said she was now seeing a very old-fashioned house, one with blue shingles.

Ben affirmed that Bobby *did* have a blue-shingled house.

Wow, I thought. But again, if Jennifer had Googled Bobby, she could have found out his address and house color. There was so much information so readily available these days, I thought, it was more and more difficult to determine, to many people's satisfaction, whether a psychic or medium was "for real." Did spirits realize, nowadays, that they had to outwit the Internet? Did they think, *Gee, I have to come up with some really arcane or personal details now, that no one could ever look up online, to prove I'm really here?*

And moreover . . . *did spirits really care?* Did they care to make themselves known to us, like those minuscule beings who lived on the dust speck in the book *Horton Hears a Who*, that Dr. Seuss favorite of my youth, shouting, "We are here! We are here! We are here!" in the hopes that Horton, or someone, would discover their unseen existence?

Jennifer was modest when I commented on how accurate she'd been. "Bobby's a good communicator," she said. "A lot of psychics will say, 'Oh, people can't communicate right after they die.' No way; they *can*. OK, he's taking me inside the house. The missing object, is it from the house?"

"No. I kinda feel like he didn't wanna talk about it," Ben said.

"Well, that's OK, I don't like to give up that easily." She laughed, and shifted in her seat. "Is there any kind of legal situation—Is somebody taking somebody to court over money owed?"

"Not that we know of. His will, actually . . . it wasn't filled out right."

"Also, the blue house, does it need work? Because that's part of the issue. Does it need to be painted?" she asked.

"Yeah," Ben said.

"Not only couldn't he pay the mortgage, he couldn't pay—even though he was a carpenter—to fix up his own house. And I think that added to his pain . . ."

Ben affirmed that too.

Jennifer said that Bobby was mentioning a nearby town, naming it. Ben said Bobby's union office was there. She told him that she felt the legal action involved the union, then.

"Also, is there a little girl he was fond of? A niece? Or is there a dead little girl? About four years old."

"We had conversations . . . He had a little friend, in kindergarten, that died. A girl."

"OK, 'cause he's pointing to a very pretty little girl. So he may be with her."

She asked Bobby again to show her the missing item, but apparently he was moving on.

"What's with the 'Irish wake' that took place afterwards? Because he's laughing now, showing me there was quite a bit of drinking after the funeral."

Ben said that this was true.

"Is there a Vince, or a Vincent?" she asked.

Ben let out a small guffaw. "Yeah . . . This guy Vince, he showed up, and we didn't think he was going to."

"Is the missing item associated with the Irish wake?" Jennifer asked.

"No . . . It's very personal. It might be truly gone," Ben said.

"I don't know why he would bring up Vince's name. They talk about what they want, *when* they want. I try to guide things, but . . . they're in charge. OK, this item, had it been hidden for a while, or tucked away in a safe place?"

"It probably . . . I mean, it's something he had *on* him," Ben said.

"I feel like it's tucked away or hidden. Did he wear a medal around his neck?"

"No, but that's funny. Just this week, his mom gave me some-thing . . ."

"He's going like that." Jennifer made a circling gesture around her neck. "I thought it was around *him*. His neck." She motioned again.

Just then, I understood what the "missing item" was. How had I not realized it? *Duh!* It was Bobby's *head*! It made sense now, what Jennifer was saying about it being hidden, or tucked away. We'd all decided it must be caught in a crevice, maybe in the underwater framework of the pier, or one of the nearby rock jetties.

To my surprise, Ben didn't pick up on the gesture. Here was Bobby, practically drawing a picture . . . but neither Ben nor Jennifer was get-ting it.

Not wanting to sway the reading, though, I kept my mouth shut.

Jennifer continued. "Was his wallet taken?"

Ben said no, Bobby's wallet had been on him.

"He's doing something with his wallet. Was he ever the victim of identity theft?"

Or was Bobby trying to say, I silently wondered, *that it was* him, *his* identity . . . *that the* missing item *was a part of his body? If so, very clever*, I thought.

Again, though, Ben wasn't picking up on any of this. I had to prac-tically gag myself with a table napkin to keep mum.

Ben answered Jennifer's query about the identity theft, saying there *had* been a time when someone had been trying to use Bobby's credit card, but it'd been caught right away.

"OK, he may be going to this to show that the person who took the missing item gets caught. You see? I think he's drawing a parallel between the two situations."

I didn't think that was what Bobby was up to. There was no *person* to get caught. But it was a good deduction on Jennifer's part. Though she'd heard me, months earlier, mention the hanging and even the decapitation, she either didn't remember, or hadn't connected it with

Bobby at all, or at least not with Ben's current question. Not surprising, if the latter; it'd taken me a while to make the connection myself!

"I kinda *don't* want the thing to be found," Ben said.

Poor Ben, I thought.

Jennifer didn't blink an eye. "Let's find out," she said. "By the way, was he taking painkillers? Oxycontin? I'm seeing a pill jar."

"No, he didn't like painkillers . . ."

Another miss. Unless Jennifer was misinterpreting this symbol, of course. But perhaps Bobby had uncharacteristically used something to take the edge off or to numb himself out a bit before committing the desperate act?

She paused. "OK, can you show me more on the missing item?" she asked Bobby. "He's doing it again, going like this . . ." She indicated someone slipping something into a crevice. "He may be saying it remains hidden. Is it possible that, after he was dead, someone took the item and went like that?"

"No. I think it's in the ocean," Ben said, confirming my suspicions that the item was indeed Bobby's head. "I think it's in the jetty."

"Also, did he have a weapon? He's talking about the thing that was a weapon."

"He had a big piece of rebar in his truck. When he was working for the union, he made forms for bridges, to pour the concrete into. Rebar is the metal that goes in and holds the concrete together. He'd go, 'If you hit someone with this, it'd really hurt.'"

"With the missing object, he keeps saying it's *hidden*. He keeps sliding it somewhere," she said.

Bobby's bringing up the rebar, the thing that helps support construction, made me think, again, that the *missing item* was tucked away in some underwater structure. There was a drawbridge a few miles south; it could easily have gotten caught in its underwater support structure. Poor Bobby—he seemed to be doing his damnedest to answer the question. And really, his clues were all rather ingenious.

But it took two to tango, and neither Jennifer nor Ben seemed to be catching on.

"I know it was in the ocean," Ben said. "I wanna know if it's gonna show up."

"Oh, like if it's gonna wash up," Jennifer said.

"Yeah, something extremely personal," Ben stressed.

I'll say, I thought.

Jennifer paused. "I'm getting a *yes.* But I'm not saying it's gonna wash up where it went in. Also, I don't know if it's gonna be one hundred percent identifiable, is the vibe I'm getting. Like, it's going to wash up, or part of it, but you can't identify it . . ."

Ben made a face like he was about to explode. "I really wanna tell ya now!" he said. I knew what he meant.

"Would you like to ask more questions?" Jennifer asked Ben.

Ben seemed to be struggling with some emotion. "It's more like . . . to *tell* him. That he's a jerk. You know, for *doing* it," he said.

"It's like he's here, so he can hear you. He just said, 'Yeah, I know.' He's hanging his head." She paused again. "Does he have a friend who worked at a gas station or is a mechanic?"

"Yeah. A friend Pazz."

I wondered if this might be the *P* name that Jennifer had been getting earlier.

"Was I picking up the *P,* a last name?" she asked, beating me to the punch. "I think that may be who I was hearing, when I said *Pat,* earlier."

Score, again! I thought. She'd gotten the friend with the *P* name correct after all, *and* his place of occupation!

"I think he's calling out to Pazz. I think Pazz tried to talk to him, said, listen, chin up, try to hang in there. What he's saying to me is that people were pushing him to do something else for a living . . ."

"Yeah," Ben affirmed.

"But I feel like he was being very rigid . . . Like, 'This is all I do, this is what I know how to do . . .'"

"Yeah, a very good friend was trying to get him some work, but it would be at, like, a non-union wage . . ."

"And he didn't wanna do it," Jennifer said.

"Yeah."

"Now he's acknowledging that this was wrong. He's sorry that he didn't accept help. He's saying, 'I could have pulled myself out of that situation.'" She placed her palms on the table in front of her and shook her head.

"Now I hear your brother saying, I psychically hear him saying, 'What a waste.' I don't know if your brother actually *said* that. 'What a waste that he took his life.'"

"Yeah, he did," Ben said, slowly nodding his head.

We all fell silent for a moment. It was too sad for words. I didn't really know Ben that well, nor Bruce—and I'd never even met Bobby. But this tragic story now felt like something I was a part of. I found myself feeling surprisingly connected to them all.

Jennifer broke the silence, saying that Bobby was now moving back to the Irish wake. "Were there people who stayed up drinking all night long and saw the sunrise? I thought at first he was talking about a *tequila sunrise*, but he said, 'No, the *real* sunrise.' The hardcore ones that stayed up . . . he saw they were drinking shots! And it doesn't look like vodka to me, it looks like it's a darker liquid."

"Whiskey shots. We were," Ben affirmed.

"And then, did you all break into song? Was somebody singing?"

"There were a couple of people who walked off, and they are very much 'singing' type people. But I didn't see them doing that."

"You may wanna ask. He says they were singing about him." She paused. "He wants his mom to know he's sorry. He says, 'I was protective of her when I was young.'"

"Yeah. And he was protective of anyone he felt was a friend."

"That is just so sad, that he took his life. He's definitely sorry he did this."

Jennifer asked a few more questions about Bobby's personal habits that Ben wasn't sure about. Then, "He's saying that before he started thinking about suicide, he was planning on moving south. Maybe Carolina, Florida. Like, when he retired."

"Yeah . . . Mexico. That was his whole plan, to retire down there. Oceanfront property. It's getting sold right now. He would've had money, but . . ." He sighed.

"Couldn't he have sold that to solve his problems?" I had to ask.

"It *was* in the process of getting sold, by him and his partners in it. The problem was, the Mexican government, getting things done . . ."

"I'm seeing two-hundred-fifty thousand dollars," Jennifer said.

"That was the total, that's *exactly right*! He was getting half of that, with the partners getting the other half." Ben put his hand to his head. He looked stunned.

"He probably could have talked to his mortgage company and said, 'Look, there's this property I'm trying to sell.' They might have worked with him . . ." Jennifer said.

"I feel like he just decided to give up. He had it planned, the suicide . . ."

"Don't tell me any more," Jennifer said, putting her hand up again. "He's saying that Pazz may have been suspicious or felt something was brewing. I think he may have tried to talk to him."

"Well, he was with him twenty-five minutes before it happened. And I believe he is still truly upset, that he didn't realize it just then."

"Yeah, that's one of the most upsetting things about suicides, people afterwards saying, 'What could I have done?' . . . OK, Bobby's back," she said. She paused. "He's saying that you'll know he's around because you'll start noticing something unusual about a bird, or birds. Has this already happened?"

"*Yeaaahhhh . . .*" Ben said slowly.

"He says, '*That's me.* That's me communicating with you.'"

Ben was practically jumping out of his chair now. "Wow! I was sitting right here, when I first arrived, and I looked out the window. And across the street, in the pouring rain, there's a crow, just sitting on top of the telephone pole, looking this way, and . . . I'm very much into nature, and . . . birds get out of the rain. They go under branches, under leaves. They don't stand out in it and . . . *Wow.*"

"He's going to continue to use birds to communicate with you," Jennifer said.

"*Wow,*" he said again. "I thought directly of him when I saw that bird, because . . . I was camping a month ago, where he and I used to camp. There are always hawks flying around. And I did a little toast to him, and a hawk came right through my clearing, screeching. They never do that. And I directly thought of him. So when you said that, I felt something go through my whole body."

"*Wow.*" It was *me* this time.

"Dead people love using birds as communicators, 'cause they're mobile, and they can do things like that," Jennifer said. "Birds are gonna be his way of communicating with you, as compared to lights going on and off, and things like that."

"On that same camping trip, I was by myself again—I called my brother and told him about it—a butterfly comes into the clearing. And it flew around me seven times. And then it just stayed in the little clearing of our campsite for a full fifteen minutes."

Jennifer asked if this had been right after Bobby had died, which Ben affirmed. "I feel that you're gonna have more experiences like that one. Butterflies, to me, fall under the same category; it's almost like dead people can manipulate them."

Huh! I'd heard it said that birds and butterflies were often signs from the dead, and I'd always assumed that it meant dead people somehow *appeared as* these creatures. I'd never really been able to swallow that.

But the idea that they could, perhaps energetically, *manipulate* them—now, that made more sense.

As I ruminated on these odd notions, the reading drew to a close. Quiet fell over us, as if we were all exhaling. I hoped Ben had been as impressed as I'd been by Jennifer's reading. And as exhilarated. And as touched. I'd gone into it wondering if it could more definitively convince me that mediumship was real . . . and indeed it had.

Ben sat there at the table for a while; he seemed to be soaking it all in. When he finally stood to go, I asked him if we could meet for a follow-up chat at some point, and he agreed. Then I ushered him and Jennifer out. The rain continued to drum softly against the house, misting the air and rustling the boughs of the nearby tree, where the wet, deep-green leaves had taken on a slightly silver sheen. I looked up at the phone wires to see if any birds were hanging out in the downpour. There were none to be found. Since that day, I always look for birds sitting out in the rain, and I've yet to see a one.

MONTHS LATER, Ben was back rebuilding the wooden risers and steps of my brother's porch—I was doing a self-imposed writing retreat at the house while I supervised—when he called to me at the front door.

"Did you do this?" he asked, pointing to a small screw on the doorknob of a screen door he'd recently put on the porch's side entrance. It had come almost totally unscrewed.

"I haven't touched it," I said. "Could it have come loose by itself?"

"Naw. That's really odd. I screwed that in, tight, just the other day."

That *was* odd. There'd been no one else in the house. I wondered if it was Bobby, playing tricks. According to Bruce, he'd been quite a prankster. But could spirits actually move a physical object? Well . . . if they could energetically *manipulate a bird*, as Jennifer seemed to think, I didn't see why not.

I checked the screw for a few weeks after that, but it didn't come loose again, and eventually I forgot about it.

It took me about six months to get around to transcribing the tape of that remarkable session with Jennifer. On the day I did, I was house-sitting again at the Shore. It was a day filled with the voices of Jennifer and Ben, and the presence of Bobby. In the midst of it, I took a break and went out on the porch. As I tried to go back inside, the door-knob wouldn't turn. A bit panicked that I'd locked myself out—no one nearby had a spare key—I tried the knob again. No luck. More panic. I took a deep breath, twisted the knob again, *hard*, and finally got the door open, only to see that the very same screw had come loose; that was what had kept me trapped.

"Bobby!" I said. "Are you screwing around with me?" I found a screwdriver and tightened the screw, wondering if he was pissed at me for writing about him without his permission. But if he hadn't wanted that to happen, would he have showed up for Jennifer? As I finished my bit of handiwork, I became aware of what I was doing: standing in a foyer, trying to psychoanalyze a spirit who might or might not have been responsible for the little bit of home repair I'd just had to perform. What would my friend Frankie say if he could see me now? *A loose screw, huh? Are we talking about you or the doorknob?*

Well, so be it. To me, it was another opportunity for a test. "Bobby, if you're around, loosen the screw again. But don't let me get locked out," I said.

Well, that never happened. Had it simply been a weird case of syn-chronicity that it had occurred on a day I was so steeped in memories of, and voices from, that reading? Or had Bobby really done it—and then, having satisfied his need for hijinks, taken off for poker games and slot machines in loftier realms?

✳

LIFE BEING WHAT IT WAS, it took me more than a year to ask Ben to sit down with me for that follow-up chat. I invited Bruce, too. Ben seemed noticeably happier, lighter. Time seemed to have had its healing effects. I wondered if the reading had helped.

Over beers, they answered my questions. Yes, there'd been a lawsuit, as Jennifer had predicted, to do with Bobby's estate. As she'd also predicted, there'd been legal action to do with Bobby's union, too! Ben said the union was having a lot of suicides; nearly every two months, some guy, due to lack of work, was taking his own life.

Ben had forgotten about Jennifer's mention of the red wagon, and said he hadn't noticed one around, nor had he learned anything more about painkillers Bobby might have taken, or the little girl who'd died. As for the head, it had never washed up. Ben told me that a forensic specialist they'd recently consulted had said that, at this point, it probably never would—at least not recognizably. The salt and the motion of the water would by now have eroded it. That fit what Jennifer had said about it possibly washing up but no longer being identifiable.

Ben told me that he was still experiencing "weird bird things," and he wasn't the only one who was. "Bobby's cousin, who's my brother-in-law, he's had them now too," he said. He told me how this cousin and some friends had been out on a fishing boat forty-five feet off the Jersey coast, and found themselves accompanied by a flock of little birds whose behavior was exceedingly odd.

"First off, you never see little birds like that," said Ben. "That far out, the only birds you see are seabirds. These were not that type of bird. And they said the birds were coming right up, sitting on their shoes . . . One fell asleep on top of the microwave!"

"Yeah!" Bruce jumped in. "One of the friends said he was standing on deck, smoking, and the bird did a sort of backflip on his chest!"

"And they had a really good catch that day, like the birds had brought them luck."

I smiled. My inner Jiminy Cricket had been silenced by Jennifer's reading—at least for now. And the thought that Bobby was finding ways to be in touch with his friends, and that perhaps they were now more open to the idea that in some sense he was still around, gladdened my heart. Ben had wanted to reconnect with his BFF, and the Universe had turned to make it happen—to deliver Jennifer to Ben, and to Bobby, via me. I felt privileged to have been a part of it.

More and more I was feeling it, and seeing it—how we were all connected. Like actors on a stage, the Universe had placed us in one another's paths, to create something I was pretty certain none of us would easily forget.

"So Ben," I said, "you were pretty much a big skeptic when we met. Would you say that this experience, the reading with Jennifer, and what's happened since, has opened you up at all to the possibility of Bobby still being around?" I didn't mean to "lead the witness" with my question, though I knew some would see it that way. I truly wanted to know. In any case, Ben was not the kind of guy who could be easily led.

He paused, nodded, and in his usual understated way, declared, "I'd definitely say that."

✳

I WAS TYPING the last part of Bobby's story on the Southern Crescent train to Virginia, where I was heading to see my friend Griffin. As I'd been pursuing my metaphysical explorations, Griffin had proved invaluable—answering my questions, recommending books, and sharing information from his own years of in-depth reading and studies. I was looking forward to reconnecting in person and telling him about my latest experiences, including Jennifer's reading for Ben.

I nestled farther into my seat, gazing out the window at the passing scenery and thinking about how to end Bobby's story. His head had never turned up, the memorial on the pier had been taken down, and in that sense, his tragic tale seemed to have been put to rest. As I picked up my reading glasses, which I'd temporarily placed over my thigh, I found them broken; the screw holding one of the earpieces in place was gone. *Odd*, I thought. I'd been wearing them for hours and hadn't even noticed it was loose.

"Crap!" I said. (I'm known among my friends as a feeble curser.) I really was helpless without my reading glasses, and I pictured Griffin, throughout my entire trip, having to read menus, price tags, and text messages aloud to me, like some latter-day Annie Sullivan in drag. Before I could fret further, though, a glint of silver winked at me from a crack in the seat cushion: *My screw!* Relieved, I plucked it up. And then it registered: *Another loose screw!* More synchronicity? Or Bobby screwing around again? After all, I'd *asked* him to do it again . . . and I'd never specified *when*.

Three-quarters of me believed it was Bobby. And if so, whether he'd meant to or not, he'd given me the perfect ending to his chapter. Maybe he wasn't pissed off at me after all. I'd come to feel a surprising sweetness toward, and attachment to, Bobby. I'd never known him in this life. I'd never even seen his photo. But now, across the dimensions, or whatever separated us, I felt we, too, had connected . . . had become friends. I wondered, with a chuckle, to whom I might introduce him—perhaps my friend David, who might appreciate his prankster ways—over there on the Other Side. And I wished him well in his own continuing adventures.

"Very funny, Bobby," I said, smiling out the window as the blindingly bright sun filtered through the many-hued leaves of tree after passing tree. "And thanks."

9

ADVENTURES WITH
A GHOST-WHISPERER

✳ OR ✳

She Sees Dead People

DO YOU BELIEVE IN GHOSTS? WHAT *ARE* THEY, ANYWAY? AND what's the difference between a ghost and a spirit? Is a ghost a spirit that's trapped in this level of consciousness, and can't move on? And if so, why?

These are questions I've pondered after hearing the ghost stories of my friends. I mean *personal* experiences. And believe me, *many* of them claim to have had them.

These friends who say they've seen ghosts, they've seen them in all kinds of places—in a graveyard, in one case, but also in their own bathrooms and backyards. In most cases, they've been people I've known for a decade or more, people who've proven themselves sane, reliable, and truthful. They've never been arrested, institutionalized, or appeared on a reality show. In one case, two married friends of mine, Elspeth and Will, a professor and a computer programmer respectively, saw the same ghost at the same time—a figure dressed in old-fashioned businessman's attire, topped by a tall hat, striding self-importantly beside them as they strolled along Charlotte Square in Edinburgh, Scotland—till he vanished before their eyes. They were able to verify the details of this mind-boggling experience with each other, and later learned that the square was famous for such "spirited" sightings.

In the case of Elspeth and Will, the occurrence was fascinating, and provocative—especially to Elspeth, who didn't believe in ghosts, yet couldn't write off what she'd seen as a case of indigestion—but not particularly frightening. But of course that's not always the case.

I used to watch a TV show on A&E called *Psychic Kids: Children of the Paranormal*, about children and adolescents who were tormented by ghosts and apparently dark spirits. These . . . let's call them *entities* . . . apparently scared the bejesus out of these kids, approaching their beds at night, sometimes as headless bodies or shadowy, ghoulish forms that accosted them on predawn bathroom runs. On the show, they'd bring in a child psychologist from an Ivy League university, as well as a psychic. The psychologist would listen, counsel, and provide emotional support to the kids, while the psychic would suss out the invaders, usually managing to drive them away by having the kids confront them—who knew the dark forces were so obedient?—all to the blessed relief of the parents, who were understandably disturbed as their children experienced what looked to be very real distress. I saw some of the kids and their parents on *Larry King Live* once, and my two cents: Reader, I believed them.

I also read a terrific book called *Holy Ghosts: Or How a (Not So) Good Catholic Boy Became a Believer in Things That Go Bump in the Night*, which my mother had heard about on her favorite late-night radio show, out of California, about all things metaphysical, *Coast to Coast AM*. The author, Gary Jansen, a writer and editor on religious and spiritual topics, had no particular belief in ghosts until he moved back to his childhood home—a Long Island house his mother had insisted was haunted—with his own wife and child, and experienced them for himself. While Jansen has an obvious sense of humor—he uses a quote from the show *Scooby-Doo* as one of the book's opening epigraphs—his intelligent and thoughtful book, which describes the year in which he and his family were, he makes the case, visited by ghosts, is at times thoroughly creepy. Picture toy cars and talking stuffed animals turning on and off; "electric surges" that felt like arms running up and down his body; dark shadows floating about; and doorbells that rang by themselves. If I ever thought it might be "fun" or "interesting" to live in a haunted house, this fascinating book changed my mind, and I highly recommend it.

The closest I've come to meeting a ghost myself—and admittedly, it's not very close—was, two times, hearing voices. And I don't mean that little inner voice that whispers things like, "Do you really *need* a third brownie?" or "Two frozen margaritas on a work night is really quite enough." I mean true, disembodied voices. *Otherworldly* voices . . . though I'd rather call them simply *unexplained*.

The first of these experiences took place in my Greenwich Village apartment. I'd lived there for at least fifteen years at the time, and nothing like this had ever happened before. I was in a semi-awake state—definitely not dreaming—late at night, tucked up in my futon bed. I heard a woman's voice, as loud and clear as if she were in the room with me—but at the same time, it seemed to be coming from inside my head. I didn't know the language she spoke; maybe Portuguese, I later thought. She sounded young, and she was sobbing as she spoke. I jumped out of bed and walked up and down the old, wooden plank floors the length of the apartment, to see if someone was there—the voice was so immediate. But I was alone. It wasn't coming from a nearby apartment. I'd often heard my neighbors laugh, argue, and watch TV through the walls. This was completely different—clearer, and far more distinct.

The whole thing lasted maybe twenty seconds, but it shook me up so much that I couldn't sleep for hours. I wondered if it was a vestige of someone who'd inhabited my apartment, and I toyed with trying to investigate whether someone had died there who'd spoken Portuguese. But I had no idea how to do so. And the voice never came back.

Almost ten years later, I heard my second voice. I was at my brother's house on the Jersey Shore, in bed again but not asleep, when I heard:

"You have cancer." Again, it was a woman's voice, this time speaking English, but with an accent. It sounded like the voice of my great aunt's home-healthcare aide, who was from Nigeria, and I wondered if it was some kind of psychic flash. Aunt Sarah didn't have cancer, but it ran in the family. Was I hearing some future news about her? Or was the news meant for *me*? But neither of these felt right. As it turned out, I didn't have cancer, nor did Aunt Sarah. And I never did find out exactly what those voices were . . . But no question in my mind, they were *real*.

The one additional *otherworldly* thing I experienced a few times in my apartment, not disturbing but puzzling, was a very intense smell of fresh-cut oranges, or maybe freshly squeezed orange juice. Go on, laugh—but I've read about people experiencing spirits through smells: a pervasive scent of roses after a loved one has passed, or the stink of a dead uncle's cigar, years after the dearly departed has departed. So why not *juice*?

"Are you sure it didn't come from a restaurant near you?" asked my mother. Of course, that would be the logical explanation. There were restaurants aplenty near my building. But I'd never smelled that smell before, and those establishments had been there for years. Plus, the smell was not "normal." It was heady and intense, and so delicious I wanted to drink the air: Orange juice to the *n*th power. Orange juice from heaven.

"They make orange-scented stuff to mop floors with nowadays," she added. Despite my mother's curiosity about things metaphysical, there were places where she drew the line. It seemed that ghostly smells was one of them.

Well, that *would* be a good explanation, I told her, except that I'd never smelled it before, and had only smelled it one time hence, maybe a year later. If my super was using orange-scented cleanser to mop the halls, I'd have hoped he did it more than once a year. And cleanser, even orange-scented, doesn't smell so divine you want to lick the floors.

Not long after that, I'd read about the phenomenon known as *clair-gustance*: the ability to smell scents and taste flavors that Spirit sends to you. Which made me feel a bit better . . . till I told my friend Frankie about it.

"Maybe it's the ghost of O. J. Simpson," he offered. "You know, *The Juice?*"

"Wait, is he *dead*?" I asked.

"No," he admitted, "but he *should* be."

Anyway, there you have it. Those small, strange incidents comprise the extent of my own otherworldly encounters, at least those unaided by psychics or mediums.

And while I really don't wish for a ghostly encounter, part of me envies those who have had them—the less terrifying sort, anyway. Because they've really borne witness to something. They have *seen, felt, heard from* the Other Side, and know it to be real.

I often wished that I could talk to some of those "haunted kids" on that now defunct TV show. I was fascinated by their experiences. Perhaps I could look up the show's therapist or psychic, I thought, once I'd started my explorations. But I never got that far. Because, as with so many things I wished for involving my exploratory project, a former "haunted kid" was delivered up posthaste—in the form of a young woman I'll call Rebecca.

I REMEMBER THE DAY I met Rebecca. I was still house-sitting at the Shore, and had headed into the Loving Cup café with my laptop to write. It was early summer, and local businesses were staffing up in preparation for the coming surge. As I ordered my latte, Young Ethan introduced me to an even younger woman beside him behind the counter. She was tall—a good five ten or eleven—and a bit stooped in her posture, as if self-conscious of her height, with curly reddish hair pulled back in a pony tail, topped by a forest-green bandanna, a smattering of freckles, and an intelligent look in her hazel eyes.

"Anne, this is Rebecca," Ethan told me. "She'll be helping us out this summer before she heads off for a semester in Italy in the fall."

"Hi, Rebecca," I said, and shook her hand. I'd chosen a small table, covered with a blue-checked cloth, that was close to the counter, so between the sparse customers, Rebecca and I conversed about her present art studies and her upcoming trip. Eventually, our talk turned to what I was writing. I told her it was a book about the world of spirits and energy . . . psychics, mediums, past lives, et cetera, et cetera, et cetera. I always braced myself for people's reactions when I told them this. Rebecca's expression wasn't easy to read. She seemed startled, more than anything, and a bit flustered.

"Today I'm working on the chapter about ghosts and apparitions," I continued. "I have a lot of friends who've had experiences with them. Though not me, personally."

"Wow," she finally said. Her face had gone pink, and her voice had a slightly different tone: hesitant, but excited. "I might like to talk to you about that."

Antenna up!

"Really? Did you live someplace that was haunted?"

"Well," she said, "every place that I've lived in was haunted. Or I guess you could say, I'm a haunted person." She pushed back her bandanna, and I could see a fine sheen of sweat on her smooth, unlined forehead.

"So, when you say, 'haunted person,' you mean you didn't just see things in the house where you lived? You saw them everywhere?"

"Yeah," she said. She proceeded to tell me about seeing a boy—a ghost, spirit, or what-you-will—in the home of one of her friends. "Ironically, it was at a Halloween party, but it wasn't on Halloween. I happened to go and fix my makeup in her bathroom. And there was a little boy standing there. He was probably between eight and twelve years old, and he had a mushroom cut . . . with brownish-red hair."

"*Mushroom cut*, meaning, like a bowl?"

"Yeah. So I told my friend, because she believes in that stuff. That was when I was around fourteen, when I was picking up that stuff a lot. I asked her if her house was ever haunted, and she said they'd felt a bit of something like that, because her mom's sort of sensitive. And, like, two years later, she said, 'You know how you said you saw something in my house a few years ago?' And I was, like, 'Yeah, the little boy.' And she was, like, 'I found a newspaper in my attic, and it turns out a kid about eight years old died in my back woods.' Like, way back, probably the early nineteen hundreds."

"Wow. Was there a picture of the kid?" I asked. "There probably wasn't a *photograph* of him, back then."

"I'm not sure, but she said it matched what I said I saw, so there must have been at least a description," she said.

"Did he say or do anything?" I asked.

"Just stood there. He seemed kind of scared."

"Probably of you." I laughed, and so did she. But I didn't feel she was making it up. She seemed smart and stable, and didn't appear to be after attention—not needy, nor a drama queen. She was, for her age, rather adult and serious.

Rebecca glanced up at a customer coming in—an elderly woman in a "Life's a Beach" T-shirt, who stood a bit shakily with a cane as she searched for a table—and I remembered that she was working. "So," I asked, "could I interview you sometime?"

"Yes," she quickly said.

※

REBECCA AND I MET at a bench on the boardwalk soon after, on a gloriously sunny day. I arrived first, taking in the heather-like vegetation on the dunes, and beyond that, the sand, reflecting almost silver in the light, and the deep cobalt blue of the sea. She startled me as she pad-ded up on her sneakers so quietly I didn't hear her at first, and then I greeted her with a smile. I invited her to sit as I set up my tape recorder and took out a pad and pen. I'd once been told by a tarot reader that because I was quite psychic, electronic devices around me would have a tendency to malfunction. Whether that was the cause or not, com-puters, CD-players, and cable boxes did seem to weird out on me with maddening regularity.

Finally, against the gentle roll of the surf, we talked.

"How did it start?" I asked her. "Do you have a first memory of it?"

"Yes," she said, "but it's kind of graphic. Basically, when I was about three or four, I remember waking up . . . I always had this sense of dread in my room. And you'd think, normally, as a kid, it's maybe like the boogeyman or whatever. Just a child's imagination. But I saw two little girls on my floor. Almost like twins, next to each other. But one was just ripped to pieces, like a rag doll. It's still almost burned in my memory."

Eek!

"You were so young," I said. "You must have freaked out."

"Yeah, and, to me, a little kid can't come up with something like that. Can they? I always try to play the role of the skeptic. I mean, if it's something that *could* be my imagination, then it probably *was* my imagination."

"Did you tell your parents when that happened?" I asked.

"I told them a few times, but they just thought I was a little kid being a kid. Also, I commonly saw a man that just stood in the corner of my room and stared at me."

Lordy! "So . . . what did you do, if you were already in the room with him, or *it?*"

"I never hid under the covers, because I liked knowing what my surroundings were. I'd rather see and be able to defend myself if I had to, than, like, hide."

"That was very . . . *aware* for a little kid," I said. "Because usually the first instinct for a little kid is to hide."

"I still never hide from anything. It doesn't make things go away," she said. She turned a ring on her finger. "So, those are probably the first memories. When you're a kid, you're always told that things like this aren't real. So I wasn't aware of what was happening, I didn't understand it. And I would usually stay really quiet about it."

Rebecca said she'd shared her bedroom with her sister, who slept above her in the top bunk. But her sister never saw the ghostly visitors, she said when I asked. Nor did anyone else in her family. "Although . . . my sister stayed in my room a few months ago, and she's like, 'I will never stay in that room again. I kept seeing shadows and I heard footsteps.'"

"And was it just like seeing a person, in terms of their physicality? Could you *see through* them? Or . . . was there less solidity to them than a normal person?"

"With the man, yes, it was kind of transparent, translucent. The little girls that I first saw were just like people. Flesh and all. To this day, it completely varies. I've seen completely solid people, but I've also seen shadows, and transparent things. I think people who see things, we're like a magnet to these spirits. I have never recognized anyone I've seen, *ever*. So maybe they know that I can see them, and they want to say something or get someone's attention."

I nodded.

"The problem I have is communication," she said.

I told her I'd been wondering about that: whether any of them ever talked to her.

"Rarely. I've been touched a few times and had screaming in my ear. I can't remember a time that I've actually heard someone say something distinct."

"You hear about kids who see spirits when they're little, who actually play with them; I mean, the spirits are friendly," I said. "You never had that kind of thing?"

"No." She paused, seeming to recollect. "It used to be like, I didn't know what it was, I just knew it was bad. And then when I was thirteen or so, there was this period where it became so prevalent, every single night I'd be kept up. I finally had to tell my parents, 'Listen, this is real, this is happening. And I don't know what to do.'"

I looked at Rebecca, sitting there in her cutoff shorts, "Jersey Shore" T-shirt, and worn, maroon Converse sneakers. Though technically, legally, an "adult," and tall and mature as she was in her bearing, she still seemed vulnerable to me. *What would I do*, I wondered, *if I had a child who seemed to have abilities of this kind?*

"So your parents," I asked, "at what point did they acknowledge, if they did, that this was real? And did they try to get you some help? Are they open-minded about this kind of stuff?"

"They're pretty open-minded, but . . . Part of it is, I've always loved horror movies, so they thought it was just in my mind. But I can totally tell when it's my mind playing with me because I've just watched *The Ring* by myself at night. If it's something that actually touches my soul and tells me, "Be afraid". . . I just *know*. You *know*. My parents, though, when I straight-out told them, they didn't say they didn't believe me. It was obviously something that was really, *really* troubling me. So my dad, through his company, had a number that I could call, for someone who dealt with that kind of thing. He worked for a big pharmaceutical company."

"A *number*? What kind of number?"

"They have emergency numbers . . . for, like, therapists and things like that."

"Oh! Duh. I thought you meant for, like, an *exorcist* . . . like, the GlaxoSmithKline spiritual hotline . . ." I laughed. I was glad to see that she did too.

"Basically, my parents started researching it and trying to come to an understanding of what I might be dealing with."

"Did you call the hotline therapist?"

"I did. She gave me the stereotypical answer, 'Tell them to go into the light,' and whatever, as if it was totally in my mind. I tried that once, and it kind of blew up in my face. Which is why I'll never do it again."

I asked her what she meant.

"I ran into something that was not so good, actually here in town. There's, like, a children's park that's by the lake down there." She pointed farther south, and I knew where she meant. "It sounds like a movie. I saw a little girl in a Victorian outfit, but something was, like, *way* off. I had never seen something like that in my life. I was just hanging out with friends and, all of a sudden, I'm kind of drawn to this corner. And then I see this thing . . ." She paused. "And it starts coming in my direction, and something inside me was just like, '*Run, run now . . . Get out, get out, get out, GET OUT!*' And you know, at that point, I had seen so many things, so many times . . . Sometimes you get alarmed, and sometimes, if they're not threatening, you let it pass by. But that day, I literally ran out of the park, screaming bloody murder and crying. And my friends probably thought I was nuts. I was like, 'There's something there, there's something *very, very, very bad.*' That therapist woman had told me, 'Confront it and tell it to go to the light.' And I remember, like, mentally, when it was coming toward me, I was like, 'It's OK, just go to the light,' and that *totally* did not work. To me, that probably irritated it."

"Wow. So . . . it looked like a child?"

"Yeah, but it was just *real bad news.* And then some of my friends who are very Christian decided it was some kind of demon, and forced me back into the park, like, 'The power of Christ compels you' . . . whatever. And I lied to them and said it was gone because I just didn't want to be there. That kind of thing really aggravates me. Not that I don't consider myself Christian, but I knew it wasn't gonna work."

I told Rebecca that I'd heard that this town, which was founded in Victorian times, had a lot of ghosts. A friend had sent me a clipping about a number of workmen who had seen the same ghost—

a soldier in a old-fashioned uniform—while doing reconstruction work on an auditorium that was one of the town's largest original structures. Interestingly, instead of jumping on that potential bandwagon—as I'd have expected if she were making it all up—Rebecca told me that for her, the incidence of these experiences there in town, where she'd spent many summers, was actually very low. "I'm wondering about the suicide-on-the-pier thing, though," she said, referring, I knew, to Ben's friend Bobby. "I'm thinking about going to the pier one night . . . but I don't know if I have the guts to go alone."

"I'll go with you!" I sang out, jumping on the opportunity. "I know the guy who was his best friend, so if you got any kind of information . . . Do you ever pick up psychic information?"

"I've never tried to, like, call upon it. I have no control over it, so I really don't want to stir anything up that I don't know how to control. You could be calling someone specifically and get someone totally different. I'm not trained by any means to handle that. I'd totally be willing to go to the pier and see if I felt anything; if someone wants to make themselves present, they will. But I'm not gonna go asking for it."

I asked Rebecca if her ability was something that she wanted to learn to utilize.

"Absolutely. As I said, I've never gone to an actual psychic. I've always been afraid of that whole crazy factor, like it could really just be all in my head. But I've gone over certain situations, like the little boy in my friend's house, and how she found that paper in her attic. There's no way I could have known someone died in her back woods."

"Did you ever watch that TV show *Medium?*" I asked. On the show, a drama based on the life of medium Allison DuBois, memorably played by Patricia Arquette, Allison was continually having dead people pop in uninvited, much like what Rebecca had described.

"Yeah. I used to be obsessed with things like *Ghost Hunters* and *Paranormal State*, because I was searching for a sense of comfort, that this kind of stuff does happen. And searching for someone to relate to, I guess. I'd be curious to see what a psychic had to say about me and . . . how much of an ability I have."

I told Rebecca I'd be happy to introduce her to some of what was now becoming a veritable posse of "psychic friends." She said that she would love that.

"Having verification that it's not just all up here"—she pointed to her head—"would be so relieving. Even though I really can't see it *not* being real. I can't see it being, like, 'Oh, I watched a scary movie and I saw a girl in a Victorian dress' . . . That would *not* cause me to run out of a park screaming, in front of all my friends!

"You know, especially at home, I still do not feel comfortable with the lights off in my room. And I still have to have some kind of background noise. I literally sleep with the light on; every time I turn it off, I feel really uncomfortable and really vulnerable.

"I've been to a few friends' houses where I can't sleep," she went on. "One of my friends from down here, Mia, I went to her old house. Oh, man, I had such a bad experience there. There was this really tall man that was just like . . . it was so eerie, because she had the TV on, and I could see—you know how you can see the reflection of light out of people's eyes? I could see it bouncing off . . . like he was a flesh-and-blood person, and it scared me *soooo* bad. I literally was grabbing my friend's leg. That was the *one* time I've actually hidden myself, I just could not bear to look at it, because I hadn't seen something so solid and so . . . real. It's one thing to think your eyes are playing tricks on you when you see something transparent. And that's what, honestly, I do a lot, I just trick myself into debunking it. Like, I'll see someone walk by, and I'll just be like, 'Oh, I was staring at the TV for too long!' Just so I can get to sleep. Because if I think, 'Uch, there's another ghost in my room,' I'm not gonna be able to sleep."

We chatted a bit more, and then I snapped off my recorder. As we stood, Rebecca reminded me about going to the pier to see if she could pick anything up.

"What would make you even want to do that?" I asked.

"I think I've become a little bit more brave . . . I've had a big change of heart recently, just because I think I'm kind of growing up in every aspect of my life . . ."

"How old are you, again?" I asked.

"Twenty-one. And, a lot of the artwork I did this year had to do with fear. And I genuinely believe the only way you'll get over your fears is if you face them."

I looked down toward the shore and watched as a man and a little girl ran across the sand, laughing as they struggled to launch a bright pink kite. One try. Two. Then, finally, it set sail.

"Yep," I agreed. "I'm a big believer in that."

WE MADE PLANS TO MEET a few nights later at the pier. The sun had just set, and the sky had an almost violet hue just above the water, with thin streaky clouds here and there, giving way to a clear expanse above. Rebecca was sitting on a bench with another young woman, whom she introduced as Mia, the friend who'd been with her when she'd seen the man with the TV reflected in his eyes. I noticed that Rebecca had changed into red-white-and-blue flip-flops for our beach expedition.

"So, are you feeling anything?" I asked her.

"I feel like he's not around here anymore. Like he's moved on. But we haven't walked down to the spot where he actually did it."

Rats. I'd secretly hoped she might pick up something spectacular that I could write about. But this added to my feeling that she wasn't a liar or trying to get attention.

I took off my sneakers—I loved to feel the evening sand, soft and cool, on the soles of my feet—and we made our way to the spot on the pier where Bobby had jumped. Then we climbed down to the water's edge, as close as we could come to where he must have gone in.

"Nothing in either spot," Rebecca said, after a few minutes of silence. "But I *am* getting a really bad feeling about *that* guy." She screwed up her forehead and pointed to a man up on the pier.

"Like he's thinking about what Bobby did. And maybe about doing the same thing."

I gazed up at the guy she was pointing at. He'd been idling around the pier for a while now, near Bobby's makeshift memorial, which was still up at the time.

"I'm really worried about him," she said. But what could she do? Walk up to a stranger and say, "Excuse me, but I sense you're going to kill yourself. Please don't." Allison DuBois, at least as portrayed on the show *Medium*, did stuff like that all the time. But Rebecca . . . she'd have to just sit with her feelings, I supposed. And try not to feel guilty if she read about this guy's suicide in the paper the next day.

✳

A FEW NIGHTS LATER, I emailed my psychic friend Frank Andrews, asking if he might be willing to talk with Rebecca. He'd once told me that, being Sicilian—like me—he felt compelled to "take care of the world." For him, this had included raising several Vietnamese orphans, for which I truly admired him . . . and which made me think he might be willing to help Rebecca, somewhat of an orphan, in the invisible world, herself.

While waiting to hear back from him, I phoned intuitive counselor Maggie Moise. She'd been very generous with her time and talents, and I needed a little help myself. One friend that I'd told about Rebecca said he believed she was a compulsive liar, and making it all up. Though that just wasn't my take on her, it was possible, of course. It was also possible that she could have some sort of mental imbalance that caused her to "see" the things she saw as hallucinations, or to somehow just *think* that she'd seen them. I knew very little about schizophrenia or other such psychoses. My gut feeling was that Rebecca didn't fall into this category either. Still, she herself had said that she feared she might be crazy, so I thought I'd run it by Maggie, one of the most accurate intuitives I'd met, to get her impression.

Maggie was quiet a few moments. Then she told me that, yes, Rebecca was the real deal. "She's a *postcognate*," she said, in her clear, melodic voice.

"A *what*?"

"A postcognate. She can see things that have happened in the past."

Oh. Postcognate, *as in* postcognition. *As in* precognition, *but the other way around.* It made sense, given the old-fashioned boy in the bathroom and the girl in the Victorian dress. Note: I hadn't shared any of those details about Rebecca's experiences with Maggie.

"Would you be willing to talk to her?" I asked. "She's never talked to a psychic or medium. And I think it'd help."

"I actually am interested in what she can do," Maggie said, sounding excited. "It's not something I'm good at, and there are some things I'd like to know about, in the past, some things I'd like to ask her. If she was interested, we could do a barter."

A barter! Rebecca would flip. I knew that she didn't trust her own abilities yet, and figured she'd find the idea of doing a reading for someone else—a professional psychic, no less—completely daunting, as my friend Katarina had. I told Maggie this, but she assured me she'd help her through any fears.

"You're going to work well together," she said then. "You have a good rapport."

"We do. I'm looking forward to hanging out with her. There's a Ghost Tour they give in the next town. I'd love to see what she could pick up at those supposedly haunted spots. Plus, she wants me to come when she talks with you. I might like to write about that."

"Sure," Maggie said. She paused, obviously back in receiving mode. "There's going to be a point, though, when she's going to just disappear.

She'll do it very suddenly and without explanation. And you'll be left wondering what happened."

"Really?" I asked, a bit dismayed. It seemed so unlikely. Rebecca appeared so eager to talk, as if she'd been waiting for someone like me to cross her path her whole young life.

"Don't take it personally," Maggie said. "She's just not ready to deal with it. She's going to, one day. But not until later . . . Like, maybe when she's forty or so."

Oy! This was beginning to sound like Katarina all over again. I could totally understand it, and yet, how maddening and disappointing if it proved true!

Maggie then told me that Rebecca had had a very hard time with her gift in childhood, and reiterated some of the things that Rebecca herself had told me about that.

Pleased with my talk with Maggie, I beelined it to my laptop to email Rebecca and let her know. When I got there, I found a reply from Frank Andrews; he'd be delighted to talk with Rebecca, he said. *Yes!*

I dashed off an email to Rebecca, asking her to call me, and sharing this cornucopia of good news.

I was sure she would get back to me quickly; after all, it was so exciting! But when I checked my inbox, and my phone, over the next two days . . . as a friend of mine likes to say, "Crickets."

I waited a few more days and wrote to Rebecca again. Again . . . crickets.

Could Maggie's prediction already *be coming to pass?* My gut was telling me that yes, indeed it could.

I informed Maggie, who suggested I give it some time, so Rebecca wouldn't feel pressured. But she, too, seemed to think my new friend was already pulling back, and that what Rebecca and I had shared thus far would be the sum of our work together.

I tried to contain my frustration, but I was seriously tweaked. Was this to be my fate: to meet a passel of Reluctant Psychics? Was it that merry prankster, Synchronicity, playing with me again for sport . . . or maybe to teach me a lesson? Like, *Quit sponging off other people's intuition, Anne, and get to work on developing your own?*

I let time pass and avoided the Loving Cup when I was visiting the Shore. I didn't want Rebecca to feel weirded out or pressured. I finally wandered in, about a month later, to find her behind the counter, now very much the pro. When an opportunity arose, I approached her and told her that I'd been surprised not to hear back from her.

"Oh, sorry! I've just been totally swamped," was her somewhat sheepish response.

I wanted to take her at her word. But I didn't believe it. I hoped she'd get past whatever her reservations were. As a few more weeks went by, though, with little time left before she'd be off for her semester abroad, I sent her one more email.

"It's totally OK if you don't want to do this . . . Just please let me know."

"That's not it at all," she wrote. She still wanted to do it but was just "so swamped."

But she never did get back in touch. Maggie had been right.

At summer's end, I wrote to Rebecca and thanked her for sharing her story. I told her I'd be there if she ever changed her mind, and wished her a bon voyage. I also asked if I still had permission to use the material from our interview.

She wrote me back, sweetly thanking me. Yes, of course, I still had her permission, she said. And that was the last I heard from Rebecca.

All of which brought me to the question: Was this type of ability a blessing or a curse? Certainly, in Rebecca's case, it had seemed to be the latter. But aside from all the scary stuff, was being open to other levels of consciousness or beings in other realms something I would really want? Most people, I'd found—at least those who were open to the existence of intuition—thought that being psychic would undoubtedly give you an edge in life. And certainly that *could* be true. It had helped Katarina pick lucrative stocks—and that had likely been the tip of the iceberg in terms of how her gifts might have beneficially been used. But then, Katarina had ended up choosing to disavow them. And now, here was Rebecca, apparently doing the same. It seemed that having an open receptor to other realms wasn't always all it was cracked up to be.

As for me . . . well, I'd never really doubted that being "sensitive" to the invisible realms could have its downsides. I'd been warned by some, throughout my explorations, that there were "dark energies" out there, and I'd never questioned that. After all, our human world was full of some pretty dark energies too. I was sure the invisible realms were every bit as complex as this human one . . . and then some. And while I never felt fearful during my explorations, it was important, I believed, to keep one's wits about one, and to tread carefully, no matter where one was treading—and that included other realms and levels of consciousness—and to work with trusted, experienced practitioners.

I tried contacting Rebecca one more time, about six months later, just to say hello, but got no response. So, as with Katarina, I had to let it go. I thought she was a brave young woman, given all that she'd told me. And I hoped that, one day, she'd feel ready to explore her abilities and learn to control them better, so they didn't wreak havoc with her life. I'd heard the old saying a lot recently, "When the student is ready, the teacher appears." I'd certainly experienced that myself since starting my exploratory project—and how, and more than one!

I trusted that, when Rebecca was ready, she'd meet hers.

10

ADVENTURES WITH
A SOUL MATE
✳ OR ✳

Accidentally In Love

"HEY, BABY . . . HAVEN'T WE MET SOMEWHERE BEFORE?"

It's the oldest pickup line in the book.

But is it possible that what causes that intense, often instantaneous attraction to someone we sometimes experience is the fact that we *have* met before . . . as *soul mates*?

Anyone who's ever used Match.com, OKCupid, eHarmony, or any other dating app or site, has witnessed the hordes of singletons out there desperately seeking theirs. But do soul mates really exist? If so, what are they, and what does it mean when we find one? Is it a promise of happily ever after, or its own special circle of dating hell?

When I started my exploratory project, I didn't know much about the idea of soul mates. From what I gathered, one of the tenets of reincarnation was that souls reincarnated together in groups, or "clusters." Thus, soul mates were those souls with whom one connected, again and again, across many lifetimes—and not just as lovers, but as parents, children, siblings, friends, and yes, even enemies.

The basic idea was this: that souls, with the aid of spirit guides, signed up for human incarnations in order to expand—to have new experiences in which they would learn and grow. In order to do so, they recruited other kindred souls to play the necessary parts. Thus, a soul mate might be "cast" as your mother in one lifetime, your daughter in another, and your husband in a third. You, in turn, would sign on to play similar roles in *their* various lifetimes. Think: Earth as a massive stage, the Universe as central casting, and our souls as a sort of endlessly revolving repertory company.

After my past-life explorations with Marianna Lead and Rev. Kev O'Kane, I put aside my wonder-lust about reincarnation for a while. Eager for a definitive experience as I still was, I had many other topics to explore. But then I met Sam. And if there truly were such things as past lives, I was sure he and I had tripped the light fantastic in more than a few of them. And so I found myself thrust back into my wonderings.

I couldn't say I hadn't been warned about Sam. Back when Maggie Moise had told me that I was going to experience a man-storm, she'd seen me meeting "a young *boy*, maybe thirty-two or so," who was "not emotionally *ripe* yet," but who would make me feel really *good* about myself. She'd pulled two cards: the Knight of Swords, indicating periods where he'd be charging forward, full of enthusiasm, and the Hanged Man, indicating alternating periods of great stagnancy.

To my shock, Maggie had been right about the storm. Not long after, with no action on my part, there'd been a sudden profusion in my life of interesting men. I'd enjoyed all of their company, and had kissed and even canoodled with a few, though I never fell in love. And then, one by one, as Maggie had predicted, their red flags began to flap too blatantly to ignore, and I bid them each good-bye.

It was amazing: I was actually learning.

And then I met Sam.

I'd decided to try a new restaurant that had just opened not far from my brother's summerhouse at the Shore. When I walked in, no one was there to greet me, so I seated myself at a small, bare table. Several young waitresses behind the counter ignored me for a good fifteen minutes. As I was about to leave, thinking the place was just "not ready for prime time," Sam appeared with a place setting, a menu, and a disarming smile. He apologized for the fact that I'd been waiting, swiftly and efficiently set up the table, and fetched me coffee, chatting affably all the while. *Well, at least* someone *here knows what he's doing!* I thought.

Over the next six months, and as many breakfasts, we started to get to know each other. Sam was friendly and outgoing, kissing me on both cheeks when I came in and asking about my writing as he end-lessly refilled my cup. He told me he was an artist and a glassblower, which intrigued me. I remembered how Patricia Masters had gone on about glassblowers; I'd hadn't ever actually met one. We discussed showing each other our work—*his* idea, let me note—and exchanged phone numbers, though neither of us ever used them.

For my part, I was simply busy, happy, enjoying my explorations and the storm, such as it was. I never thought of Sam as part of it. Hav-ing lived in Greenwich Village and worked in theater and publishing for so long, I assumed that any guy as sweet and charming as Sam was likely gay.

Besides, he was younger. A lot younger. Not that I wasn't attracted to younger men; I *was*—probably because I felt so young myself. I had that headline from a newspaper article I'd cut out, "50 Is the New 25," tacked up on my fridge. Still, I never thought of Sam as someone who'd be interested in anything with me beyond friendship.

But then one bright, Indian summer afternoon, I was walking on the boardwalk—in my camouflage skirt and a *scarlet* T-shirt, as it happened—when I heard someone shout my name. There was Sam, shirtless, atop his slightly battered-looking bike. He didn't look like a waiter anymore; he looked like a *guy*. And a pretty cute guy, at that. I headed over to him, smiling.

"I was checking out the women," he said, "and I was checking *you* out, and I thought, *Hey, I know her!*" He laughed. I was flattered. Maybe it was all my years of feeling inhibited about my body and unattractive to men, but I never thought any shirtless young dude would be check-ing *me* out. As we chatted, he mentioned his *ex-girlfriend—twice.* The second time, it hit me: Not only was he *not gay,* he was trying to *flirt* with me—he'd been trying since we'd met! Before I could process that surprising thought further, he looked at me. The sun was hitting his eyes, turning them an electric turquoise blue, and the world seemed to freeze for a moment. "Anne . . . you're *so beautiful,"* he said. And then, forward as you please, he kissed me. And not on the cheek this time.

Ay, caramba! In all my years, no man had ever done that. I'd always had to assure a guy, the first time, that it was OK to kiss me, or kiss him first myself. And no man had ever called me *beautiful* like that. Sam's forwardness made me relax, because it made me feel so clearly wanted. But there was something else. As soon as he kissed me, I felt a particu-lar energy flash between us, something I'd never felt before, yet some-thing *so familiar.* Before I could think about it, I'd kissed him back. As he leaned in for another, though, I backed away. "That's enough of *that*!" I said and walked off, feeling his eyes on me.

It was lunatic. It was insane. I couldn't stop smiling.

To my surprise, I didn't hear from Sam after that. I finally texted him, too curious to stop myself. "How old are you, anyway?"

"Thirty-five," he shot back. "You?"

"Fifty-one."

"You don't look it," he wrote, with a smiley face.

A few texts later, he still hadn't suggested we get together, so I asked if he'd like to meet some afternoon. He said *evening* was nice, upping the ante, and I agreed. I didn't know what to expect, but after that kiss, Reader, it was something I had to explore.

A few evenings later, I sat on the boardwalk watching a small figure in the distance grow larger. Sam was wearing a backpack containing, I soon found, a blanket, a bottle of wine, and two lovely, unusual gob-lets he'd made himself. We took off our shoes and walked down to the cool sand in the moonlight. Within minutes, surf lapping at our feet,

we were hugging. We kissed again, and this time I had the most powerful sense of coming home, to someone I'd known, and *loved*, before.
Oh! It's YOU! I thought, shocked at the strength of the feeling. I didn't
want to let go.

Though Sam, I'd later learn, had once been very interested in
religion—he'd read the Bible and explored the Rastafari way of life—
he had no interest, and no apparent belief, in things like psychics,
mediums, or past lives; he thought it was "cute" that I did. But later,
when I confessed to him what I'd felt that night on the beach, he told
me that he'd felt the very same thing himself.

TWO DAYS AFTER that first evening with Sam, I attended one of Roger
Ansanelli's sound-healing and meditation classes at his Hoboken studio. I arrived early, and as I waited in a nearby park with a stunning
view of the Manhattan skyline, across the river, my cell phone rang.

"How are you, Annie?" asked one of my cousins in her singsong
voice.

I told her I was great, and that, to my shock, I'd met someone.

She said she was happy for me, that I deserved some good love, and
we chatted a bit more about Sam until it was time for my class.

"Please don't repeat any of this to my family," I said. "They'll think
I'm insane. He's so young. It probably won't last. And I don't want to
hear their *I told you so*'s."

She assured me that she'd keep my secret.

In class that day, Roger set us on a guided meditation in which we
entered a clearing where a circle of our "elders" sat. We were to go into
the center of the circle and "peel away the layers" of ourselves, like the
layers of an onion, to see what would emerge. As we silently meditated,
Roger walked around the room, playing his crystal bowl and crooning
his unearthly melodies. As was his habit, he'd pause to deliver messages from the angelic realm when they came in.

Perhaps it was my happy, excited mood causing me to "vibrate" higher than was my norm, but I found the mental images coming in more vividly than usual. I could see, *feel*, gauzelike layers peeling off me, then a stiff, hard substance, like dried wax. When I got to my core, I found it was simply *light*. It felt freeing, astonishing. As this light, I began to dance, in the most joyful, celebratory way. And then, like something from that old Disney film *Fantasia*, the light that I was began morphing: I became a fountain of sparkling water; a white bird, soaring; a white horse, galloping and rearing up on its hind legs; brilliantly colored fireworks; and then a woman of translucent white, dancing.

My eyes still closed, I felt Roger stop in front of me. There was amusement in his voice. "They're saying, 'How can you sit there so still, when all you want to do is dance and run around? Your *secret* is out! And *fuh*—excuse me—*frig* 'em if they don't like it!' Meaning *your family*," he said.

Oh. My. God. Not only had "they" picked up on the dancing images in my head, they'd picked up on the "secret" I'd shared with my cousin, and my fears about my family's reaction to Sam!

After class, I approached Roger. I told him about Sam and about the conversation with my cousin. He grinned as he listened, then grabbed me up in one of his viselike hugs. As he let go, he paused. "They're telling me to tell you: *'Anne . . . let it rip!'*"

✳

MY YOUNG MAN and I became involved in an on-and-off, roller-coaster way. We were giddy whenever we were together. We laughed constantly, when we weren't kissing and hugging. My history of being rejected by men, and my recent relationship with West Coast Mike, who said he loved me but wasn't sure he was attracted to me, had left me feeling as if something was wrong with me. Sam instantly changed all that. When I hugged him, my body fitting perfectly into his so that my head rested on his shoulder, he emitted happy little squeaks, little groans of delight. He told me I was "perfect," which touched me; no man had ever said that to me, not even my father. He said there was *nothing* about me he didn't like—save for the calluses on my feet, which he discovered once while rubbing them—but that he loved my *brain* most of all. How could I resist?

Sam was a goofball, a nutcase. He had a penchant for juvenile humor and a very "youthful" lifestyle, which might have put many women my age off. To me, though, probably because I'd dated so little when I was younger, it was appealing, fun. His mind worked differently from other people's—"I'm *so* ADD," he'd explained when we met—but I found his offbeat way of thinking stimulating, unique. He showed me his sketchbooks, played me his music. I showed him the children's book I'd written and illustrated in college. He tried, unsuccessfully, to teach me to dance. Normally, I was so self-conscious I wouldn't dance with a man, but with Sam, I felt safe; he pronounced my lack of coordination "adorable." He would follow me into the bathroom if I let him, because he didn't want us to be apart.

Sam was shocked that I didn't have men chasing me. "When you used to come into the restaurant, I'd get so excited. But I was sure you had some Harley dude at home."

"*You're* the only dude I've ever been with, Dude," I said, laughing.

He couldn't believe I'd never been married, had never even lived with a guy; though so much younger, he was by far the more experienced one in terms of romance. I told him once, not very long after that day we kissed on the boardwalk, that I'd been "very old" before becoming seriously involved with a man.

"*How* old?" he asked.

"*Very!*" I said. "Let's leave it at that." I'd always feared telling men this deep, dark secret of how late a bloomer I actually was, sure that they would think I was a freak. But now that I'd opened my Pandora's Box an inch, Sam's curiosity was piqued. He started to guess numbers. I knew he was being playful, but I could barely look him in the eye.

Still, I knew that he loved me—I could *feel* it—and it made me feel safe; it allowed me to trust him. So when he reached the actual number, I admitted my embarrassing truth.

When I'd confessed, I could tell that he was shocked.

"But *why?*" he asked. I still couldn't meet his gaze.

I told him I didn't really know. I told him about my parents' unhappy relationship; about my struggles with my weight, and with anxiety and depression; about the many men I'd chosen who'd just not chosen me back. I told him how many years I'd been in therapy trying to figure it out. By that time, some old feelings of pain and shame had surfaced, and I was crying.

He squeezed my hand so tightly that I almost jumped, and I looked him in the eyes.

"Anne," he said, with the most earnest and open of expressions. "*I love you.*"

Now *I* was the one who was shocked. Not that I hadn't felt it. But I was startled that he would actually *say* it.

"You're so awesome," he said, stroking my hair. "Don't ever let anyone make you feel you're anything else." He kissed my hand, and all my hurt and shame melted away.

"Where did you *come* from?" I asked, wiping my eyes.

"No, where did *you* come from?" he asked.

I felt like he'd been dropped by an angel, exclusively to heal me. And maybe he had. Sam made me feel seen, really *seen*, for the first time in my life. And as Maggie Moise had so presciently predicted, he made me feel really *good* about myself.

But Maggie had been right on another front too: This peach of mine, for all his sweetness, was decidedly *unripe*. In the same breath that he told me he loved me, he told me he was terrified I'd break his heart. He kept me "in a box," never mixing me with his friends or his family; his parents, he said, "wouldn't approve," because of my age, and that seemed to carry an enormous amount of weight. He'd disappear for long periods of time. When he popped up again, often many weeks later, he'd apologize, but seemed powerless to stop it. One of my girlfriends took to referring to him as "the Phantom." I dubbed him "Houdini," for the speed with which he escaped. It was extreme, immature behavior —definitely that of a "boy." Was I maddened, frustrated, hurt, and distraught when he ran? You betcha. There was a red flag flapping as big as a bedsheet. But I'd never felt such joy in the presence of someone. Not even close. How could I help but want more?

Alas, Sam's fears went on and on. "Relationships—once they get serious, they always turn bad," he said. I knew that he'd had a long relationship that had recently ended. Though he was far from blameless, I was sure, it was clear he'd been deeply hurt by some things that had occurred, and it seemed to have left some scars. Also, he said, he had nothing to offer me, couldn't *provide* for me the way I deserved.

I told him I wasn't looking for any of that. "You make me *happy*," I said. But I couldn't seem to make him understand.

Of course I had fears of my own. That I'd grow too wrinkled, too saggy, too gray. That he might want to have a family, something *I* could no longer provide. I'd had a short, sweet dalliance with a younger man whom I'd met through work some years before. He was extremely open and sensitive—there was something different about men of his generation, I found, men who'd been raised by parents who'd come of age after the feminist revolution—and it had been a lovely connection. I'd felt surprisingly crushed when he ended it abruptly to date someone his own age. I wasn't eager to go through that again.

"He's a *lot* younger," I told Edward Ragosta about Sam, in a reading I had at the time.

"Is he legal?" he shot back.

"*Yes!*" I said. "He's thirty-six."

"Stop thinking like a human!" he said. "We are *spiritual beings*. When it comes to love, age really doesn't matter."

Well, I did believe that. Still, in the life we two were experiencing *now*, whatever others we might have experienced, children *were* an issue; Sam quickly admitted it when I asked. "I'm supposed to marry the perfect woman—*my parents'* idea of the perfect woman—and give them grandkids."

"But what do *you* want?" I asked.

His face wore that look of happy delirium he had whenever we were together. "I'll get married, have kids. And after I'm divorced . . . I'll come find *you!*" He laughed his goofy laugh, but I knew he was half serious. He was also, I thought, half cracked.

Fall soon came, and with it Hurricane Sandy. At my mother's house, where I chose to weather the storm to make sure she was OK, I saw the devastation of the Jersey Shore on the evening news. I tried to contact Sam, but no luck; many towns, I knew, had lost power. When at last I heard back from him, he told me his house had been flooded. The seawater had destroyed many of his possessions, including much of his art, which broke my heart.

When I finally made it back to the Shore—a ravaged place I barely recognized, though my brother's town had fared far better than most—I dropped by the restaurant where Sam worked. It was far enough from the shoreline that it had survived Sandy intact. There he was, pulling his pen and pad from his pocket, as I headed for my usual table. He stopped in his tracks when he saw me—"Baby girl!" he cried, which was funny and endearing, since technically I could have been his mother—and swept me up in a massive hug.

We met the next evening. He brought me a glass candleholder he'd made, in the form of a breaking wave, pulled from his home's wreckage. I scavenged for a candle, lit it, and we fell into each other's arms. Later, he told me his hurricane tale. True to form, he'd tried to wait out the storm at home, despite the rising waters. He'd had to evacuate in the end, carrying his cat out, to safety, on his head.

That night, Sam pulled back the covers of my double bed and went about tucking himself in, patting the mattress beside him, as if we'd been doing it our whole lives. And maybe we had. By this point, Reader, not only did I feel that I'd known him—known his *soul*—before, I felt sure I'd been *married* to him. It was as if I'd lost my husband, and now here he was, back from the dead, a beer-drinking, duded-up Lazarus. I couldn't bear losing him again.

Sam and I talked a few times after that. "Anne, it's snowing!" he texted me at midnight like a happy kid as the first flakes of the season fell. But soon, the old pattern resumed. I knew he was busy finding a new home and putting his life back together, but his periods of radio silence went way beyond that. Perhaps some women could handle such uncommitted love affairs, but I was beginning to get depressed. I started to behave in ways I wasn't proud of, alternately needy and angry, texting him too often and demanding to know why he was acting as he was. Several of my friends suggested that perhaps we had reached our expiration date, and it was getting harder to ignore them.

Still, I couldn't walk away. *If Sam and I* had *been together in a past life, or lives*, I wondered, *why had we met up again now?* Was this story of doomed, star-crossed lovers our fate? Was it some sort of cosmic test? If so . . . it really sucked.

By mid-December, I knew I had to end it. I'd worked too hard to overcome depression in the past to let it get me in its grip again. Sam and I made a plan to meet. As I waited for him, listening to blues on the stereo and drinking a bottle of a local beer, I grew sadder by the minute. By the time he arrived, a bit late as usual—when Sam worked, he focused so hard, he never wanted to stop—I was positively morose.

"I'm feeling kind of down," I told him, as he shrugged off his army-style jacket.

He said that I was a writer, I was supposed to get the blues. As we stood hugging, my head on his shoulder, I blurted out that maybe we needed to end things.

Sam looked at me, distress in his eyes. He led me to the couch and stroked my hair. "You've got to know that, what I do . . . it's not because I don't love what we have. It's everything I've wanted."

"But you can have it!" I said, incredulous. *"Here it is! Here I am!"*

He shook his head sadly and said that ours had to be "a different kind of relationship," one of two kindred spirits sharing a moment. He said that I was so perfect that if he let himself really be with me, he'd get lost in it, and never be able to move on.

A stronger woman, I knew, would have run, screaming. But I wasn't that woman. I was the woman who thought she could grab her few moments of joy, a joy she'd been waiting for her whole life, and let the chips fall where they might.

Sam got up, swapped out my blues CD for some bouncy reggae, and reached down to pull me from the couch. I still couldn't really dance, but I took his hand.

*

SAM AND I MADE another plan to meet up before Christmas. I was happy, excited; I'd rarely had a man in my life at the holidays. I bought him a gift and wrote out a potty-humor card I knew would make him laugh. On the designated day, though, he sent me a short, disjointed text, saying he had to leave town, that something had come up.

I stared at it, my stomach bottoming out. He'd said very little, but I could feel the fear and panic behind the words. Still, that didn't stop the pain and anger *I* felt—at Sam, at his parents, at the *Universe*, at whoever or whatever was in charge. Embarrassed even as I did it, I blasted him with furious calls and texts, which—no surprise!—he didn't answer.

I wanted to pour out my heart to a friend, but most of them were tired of hearing about Sam. "You deserve so much better," they'd say. Or, "Even if he's a not a bad guy, he's certainly not careful with your feelings." And I totally understood. I knew he wasn't treating me well, and I knew I deserved better. But because I could see that his actions were coming from his *fears*—because I could actually *feel* those fears— I held out hope that he could overcome them. Was it because we were souls who'd been together, many times, before? Or was it because I was still dysfunctional and codependent when it came to men? Or was it, perhaps, both?

I called a neighbor, asking her to join me for some holiday cheer, and I tried to be merry and bright. As we walked home from a local music venue along hushed streets, I thought I saw a shooting star. It was a beautiful, crisp, unusually clear night, and I mentally patted myself on the back for not letting it go to waste because of a man.

"Did you see that?" I asked, craning my neck. "A shooting star! Look, there's another!" I thought I must be imagining it till I saw a third, and she saw it too.

"It's a meteor shower," she said, in a hushed tone.

I stood, lost in space, watching the brilliant bodies appear out of nowhere, whiz across the sky, and disappear. In all my years, I'd never seen the like of it. A Carl Sagan quote, "We are made of star stuff," flashed through my mind. It wasn't a metaphor, I knew, but a statement of fact: The chemical elements in the atoms of our bodies had been forged, billions of years ago, in the hearts of stars.

As I came back down to Earth, my thoughts gravitated to Sam. Was he looking up at the same wondrous event that I was? Was he thinking of me, as he had when the first snowflakes fell?

Back in the city again, the holidays past, the gift I'd bought him shoved to the back of my closet, my chest literally ached. January came and went, and no word. I wondered if the fallout from Sandy had pushed him over the edge, left him post-traumatic-stressed out, the way 9/11 had left me.

I was still making frequent visits to the Shore. I tried to take my daily walks whenever I was there, but it was a different landscape now. The boardwalk where Sam and I had first kissed had been torn apart by Sandy's monstrous surges. Metal rails were bent, boards strewn, large areas roped off. The pavilion where I'd once stood waiting for him to pedal up and meet me no longer existed. As I picked my way along the bleak streets of a neighboring town, littered with debris, I knew I should be grateful: that I had a home, that my loved ones were unharmed. There were so many people who had lost so much. Yet I couldn't help thinking what a fitting visual metaphor it all was for my emotions, or for whatever relationship Sam and I had once had.

✳

ALL THIS TIME, my informal experiment was underway. Sam started popping up in my readings without my even asking about him. I supposed it was because I was thinking so much about him. Or maybe because our energies were still so intertwined.

"There's a *young man* here," Frank Andrews said, turning over the very first card of my reading about a month later. "Wow. Good for you! Now, this is a good guy. But when they're young, they're young. See, you've got a problem. You're locked in at around *thirty-two* in your *mind!*" He flipped another card. "Aquarius," he said. *Sam's sign!* "So this could be on again, off again, on again, off again. The next card says, 'Reunion.' So it's not over."

My heart leaped a bit. I hadn't told him we'd broken apart.

"Now, can I be very blunt?" he asked. "Sleep with him if you want, but don't fall in love. I *like* the guy. But I don't want to have to pick you up off the floor. Because you're talking about *youth*, here. Maybe not so much in *age*, as *in the mind*. And you seem to have had a strong influence over him. See? But I don't want you being his mommy. Or his therapist."

"I haven't!" I protested.

"Yeah, I don't know if I believe you." He grinned. "This is the card for tears . . . that's you, crying. Next to it is the Hanged Man." It was the same card that had come up with Maggie Moise when she'd first seen Sam as part of the man-storm. "Meaning that the relationship is in a state of suspension. In order to make this work, you need a lot of will power. You can't be weak. I know you *think* you're *Wonder Woman* . . ."

He flipped more cards. "Now, if you said to me, 'Frank, do you think he really has feelings for me?' I'd say, '*You bet!*' This guy's not using you. This is *all about love.*"

Now, one might suspect psychics of saying this sort of thing because it's what clients want to hear. But I'd asked plenty of psychics about plenty of men over the years, and I'd *never* been told that. Much as I'd felt it, with Sam, and trusted those feelings, it was still good to hear.

"But he has his own demons," Frank went on. "The baggage he carries is very heavy. See, this boy—and he *is* a boy—was *conditioned*: He's supposed to find that perfect woman and have children. That's in the back of his head. Also, money: Men feel kept, they feel anger, if they don't have finances. For men, that hurts."

Holy sum-him-up-in-a-nutshell, Batman! It was exactly what Sam had said.

"I'm not gonna say forget about him. But try to focus on making money and finishing your project. Because, my feeling is, even if he comes back, he's gonna leave again." He paused. "Let me put it this way: When the phone rings, I want to hear you say, 'Oh, who is this? Gee, I didn't recognize your voice!' Then you know you're free from it, and then maybe you can deal with it," he said.

✳

DURING A PHONE SESSION with Christina Wright, I hadn't mentioned Sam—that day or ever before—when she said, pulling cards, "You have the Lovers in front of you. And here's an air-sign man, or a young man."

I told her I *had* met a younger man—an air-sign man, at that.

"An Aquarius?" she asked.

"Yes!" I said.

"OK, Let's look at *the dude* . . ."

I laughed, and told her I'd called him that myself.

"I find him a gentle soul. How old is he?" she asked.

"Thirty-six, now," I told her.

"Oh, he's more like *twenty-something*, emotionally! But you know, part of him is delightful. I find him stimulating . . . his energy."

I beamed. I'd been so angry at Sam, yet here I was, feeling *proud* of him—like a doting wife or, God help me, a mother. Had I *been* his mother in some life too? It wouldn't have surprised me a bit. Or perhaps this was Hypatia, the sacred prostitute, in me, still trying to bring out the light in men through loving them.

"What I hear is, 'Good for the moment!' And he did give you a gift; he soothed your soul. Somebody's standing next to you, stroking your hair . . ."

I told her that he'd often done that, and how lovely it had been. And then he'd disappeared.

"Well, his *behavior* isn't really lovely. I kind of like him, though."

Ha, I thought. Sam could charm women without even being there.

She said that Sam had low self-esteem and felt he wasn't good enough; that he wanted to make more money, to be able to give more. As an artist, he hadn't gotten much support. "Also, he made a decision—he wasn't gonna take any woman seriously, no one was gonna hurt him again, he was gonna be *tough, strong*—and then he ran into *you!*"

I laughed. "How do you do that, Christina? When you get into the mind of someone that way, I mean, basically you're just—"

"*Spying* on them!" she said, gleefully. "The women love it!"

I *did*. But was it ethical?

"You can only get what the person asking needs to know, what the person they're asking about maybe should have told them. I get what I'm allowed to, for everyone's highest good."

She returned to Sam. "He's marriage material, but doesn't know it—a bit of a 'walking wounded.' His ex, she changed him . . . disappointed him. But he *likes* your relationship, he likes your time together. You know . . . it's *magic*."

Ah, that was it exactly. After all my friends' disapproval and dismissiveness, it was gratifying that someone understood.

"And you've had some past lives together."

Ahhhhh! I was thrilled to hear her say what I'd felt so strongly myself.

Like Rev. Kev, Christina could apparently access past lives directly from the Akashic Records. "He was a soldier and you were gonna get married, but he had to go to war. He could have a little *soul memory* about that. Like, 'Oh, it's not gonna work, I have to flee.' But that's not true."

I told her Sam was afraid he was going to get hurt.

"Or *die*, even, because he died young in his last incarnation with you. He suffered. Oh God. He lost limbs before he died . . ." Also, she said, there'd been another life where we'd been a couple, and *I'd* been the one who'd tragically passed away.

Had we truly been through all that? If so, it would certainly explain Sam's intense fears about relationships—and my own.

"Goodness, now we're getting another lifetime. He was there when you and I were sisters together," she said, referring to *our* past life together, which she'd told me about previously, as nuns in the South of France. "He was a monk!"

Ha! Sam was certainly no monk now! But I thought of his interest in religions. Had it been a carryover from that lifetime?

"You know, you have other men around you, in your future," she said. "But you have time ahead of you, you and the Aquarius. And if it doesn't work out, there *is* life after Sam." She paused. "But this one . . . this one is strong!"

Well, I knew she was saying that, about the other men, to make me feel better. But I didn't want to think about other men. I didn't want to think about "life after Sam."

✳

PSYCHIC READINGS, I discovered while working with my Team, could be very addicting. If one said something promising, or disappointing, I always wanted to run it by the others, to see what *their* take was; it was simply part of conducting my experiment. But I had to admit that, when it came to Sam, the urge to "cross-check" had become far more personal than that.

"He's dazed and confused, and unsure of his future," Edward Ragosta said. "He's wearing a suit of armor at a nudist camp. Meaning, he thinks he has to protect himself, but there's really no need . . . and he's only screwing himself. In love *and* in his career. He's trying to find himself, but he has to take his head out of his ass to do it."

I laughed. Edward always had a way with words.

"He has a lot of unresolved anger from childhood. He may *look* happy, but he's *not*," he said. "Believe it or not, he *does* love you—but he doesn't allow that. He's blocking it with his mind. He *waaaaaay* overthinks things and blocks his own happiness.

"There's the Hanged Man," he said, flipping a card. It was the third time this card had come up regarding Sam now, with three different readers! In my experience, thus far, this was rare.

"More *is* possible for the two of you, but not till he goes through a process he needs to go through."

Yes! My heart soared.

"How do you do that, Ed? Is it mind reading?" I asked.

"I wouldn't call it '*mind* reading.' If anything, I'd call it '*energy* reading.' But, to me, it's just what I do.

"I'm looking to see if you've had past lives with him," he said, without my bringing it up. "When there's someone in your life you know you should walk away from, but you can't, it's usually a past-life thing." He paused, flipping cards. "OK. Put it this way. As many positions as there are that you can have sex in, that's how many lives together you two have had."

LOL! But there it was again, my own feelings confirmed!

Edward said we'd had a life during the Renaissance that was directly affecting this one. Sam had been an entrepreneur, traveling and selling his wares. He'd visit me whenever he was in port. "He loved you, he loved his time with you. But it was an occasional thing, separate from the rest of his life. He's doing that same thing now."

My heart sank a bit. "Was I unhappy about it back then, too?" I asked, feeling a surge of solidarity for my past-life self.

"Of course," Edward said.

WHEN I GAVE Dana Marie Sam's first name, she was perplexed. I'd told her only that he was someone I was in a relationship with. I neglected to add, "of sorts."

"I'm trying to pick up his energy but, for whatever reason, I'm not getting a strong energy from him," she said. "Usually when I look at relationships, I get the energy of both people. I don't know if he's been resistant to certain things you're doing, or questioning things, but spiritually, and in terms of emotional intimacy, I'm getting him being *absent*, like he's just *checked out*."

I told her that was it precisely—that he'd recently disappeared.

She paused, homing in. "OK, it's like, he overthinks and overanalyzes the situation so much, his mental hard drive crashes." *Huh! Just what Edward Ragosta had said.*

"You—you're an emotional person. He *can* be emotional, but he's more a mental-type person, who wants to find a rational, practical answer first. Like, 'I don't want to hear about the emotions, I don't want people getting upset, I just want the facts on whether or not this is gonna work.' The question is, where does this go? I don't feel it's necessary for you to break things off, but you may have to try to relate on his level, just like *he* has to try to relate on *yours*. If he can understand that you're not having crying fits on a whim, that there's a good reason why you get emotional, he'll be like, '*Ohhhh*, now I understand.' And if *you* can step into *his* shoes and think, *as Sam*, knowing he has that logical mindset: *Would I want to continue this relationship if I were him?* You know, would *you* want to date you?"

She had a point. Getting angry and upset with him, pushing and pressuring as I sometimes did from sheer frustration and *wanting* to be with him, wasn't helping. I appreciated how Dana Marie supplemented her intuitive take with practical advice.

"It looks like there are some abandonment or rejection feelings, from his childhood," she said. "Like nothing he did was ever good enough."

Just as Frank Andrews had said.

"He's afraid you're ultimately going to reject him, when you two get really close, on that deep, deep spiritual level," Dana Marie said.

She said Sam wasn't an angry person, but because of his childhood baggage there was a lot of anger there. "I don't see this as a completion with him. If you let him be for a while, one day he's going to show up with his head hanging; he's gonna be like, 'Oh, I did it again, I'm such a goofball, I get cold feet, I'm always chickening out, I know you probably hate me, can you forgive me?' And you're gonna be like, '*Dude*'"— she, too, had picked up on Sam's dude-ness!—"'if there's a problem, before you disappear, you've got to talk to me about it.' And I think he needs to hear that."

✳

REV. KEV STARTLED ME by giving me a very accurate and specific *physical* description of Sam, from his being "not much taller" than me, to his "not very broad but extremely *strong* shoulders and chest"—the result of all that glassblowing. "The feeling I get is, he's *forward, outgoing*." That was certainly true! "You can relax around him because he makes everything feel safe. Also, he's been through some difficulties. Nice guys can get rolled over, and it hurts. As far as his feelings for *you*, he's seen the wonderfulness here, but it's scaring him. Because with women in the past, wonderfulness turned to nastiness." He paused. "He's a very hard worker, very conscientious. He's also caring and loving. If you two got together, after a while he'd work more than he'd be at home. He's not a workaholic, but he really, REALLY concentrates on what he's doing. So when he's at work, he doesn't want to stop."

I couldn't have described him better myself.

"So with the things I'm feeling about him, I kinda would say, *Go for it!*" Kev concluded.

Well, I was trying to. But Sam had been underground for more than a month.

"It's definitely not the end for you two," he said, when I told him that. He did a few more exhales as he tried to tune in to Sam. "OK, he's all about the fear right now. Like, 'I'm gonna get hurt again, but this time more than any other because of the way I feel.' The vision I'm getting is of him leaning against a bar, drinking a beer, thinking about you, and then finally getting to the point where the pain of not being with you is more than the imagined pain of possibly being hurt."

Sam did go to bars and drink beer on a regular basis. Of all the men I'd dated, he was actually the only one who did. *Bravo, Kev!* I thought.

I asked Kev, too, whether what he did was a form of mind reading.

"Energy can be felt specifically so that it *seems* like mind reading. The more a client has focused on a subject, the easier it is for me to discern what's being thought by that person. If you have no connection to the person asked about, I can't read his energy, because it's not any of my business." *It was almost exactly what Christina Wright had said.*

"From the beginning, he said he was afraid of getting his heart broken. And I was like, 'No, *I'm* the one who's gonna get *my* heart broken.'"

"I want to give you a suggestion: Stop thinking that way. Because both you and he are *manifesting*. Even with what I'm saying, anything can change. You can manifest a broken heart for both of you. You *can*," he said.

I did think it was possible to manifest—that is, *create*—things with one's thoughts and feelings, though I wasn't sure it was as simple to do as the massively successful film and book *The Secret*, by Rhonda Byrne, made it sound. Still, I firmly believed that one's thoughts affected, or even created, one's reality. There was the placebo effect, just for starters. A wonderful book by science-journalist-turned-bestselling-author Lynne McTaggart I'd recently been reading, *The Intention Experiment*, was all about very legitimate scientific studies done at highly respected institutions on the power of thoughts to influence all kinds of things—from plants, to animals, to machines like random-number generators, to other people—and it was thoroughly intriguing stuff.

"I don't want a broken heart," I told Kev now.

"So don't manifest it. When we focus on what we don't want, we get what we don't want. Manifest love, happiness, the two of you being together."

My hopes were buoyed. I would certainly try.

But would Sam?

MY TEAM WAS in agreement about Sam—that he felt he wasn't good enough, wanted to make more money, was overthinking things, and had childhood baggage and parental pressure. They nearly all described him as "emotionally younger," and said I'd had a strong influence on him; that on some level, he saw me as a teacher or mentor.

Unanimously, they also said he truly loved me, and that things weren't over between us.

As to whether things would ever *change*, though, their opinions varied.

"I don't believe it could ever be what you want it to be," Frank Andrews said. "I wish it could. 'Cause, see, this would've been the great love story we could write about. But unfortunately, his childhood baggage . . . his whole being is preventing it."

"I don't even think he's aware of it," Dana Marie said. "And he's not going to be aware of it, unless he gets to a turning point where he realizes he needs to heal, and unless someone tells him . . . like a psychologist!"

Rev. Kev O'Kane was far more positive. "Talk to him, reassure him. He'll come around to seeing there's no scary downside on this." To my shock, Rev. Kev told me he saw a *possible marriage* between us. It was hard to believe, given the present state of things. And yet, Kev had described Sam so accurately . . .

"I don't want to give you false hope," Maggie Moise said. "But he *could* make a decision to change his behavior. When he calls, after he disappears, you need to not be so nice to him. Be cooler. One-word answers. 'Yes.' 'No.' 'Fine.' You've been cutting him too much slack; a lot of people, especially women, have done that. You can't let him think what he's done is OK."

Well, that was good advice, but I couldn't seem to heed it. I was, once more, letting down the drawbridge for a man who couldn't cross over. Then again, at his age, I'd had an impenetrable suit of armor myself. Would he ever grow out of it—the suit *and* the behavior? And if so, would it happen before *I* was wearing Depends?

✳

I WAS AT MY BROTHER'S summerhouse that spring when I found a bag of homemade cookies at the door. After asking everyone around there I knew, I concluded that it had to have been Sam. It had been six weeks since I'd attempted contact. If he *was* making a gesture, and I didn't acknowledge it, would he think I never wanted to see him again? I emailed him, and he texted me right back. My heart gave a little *ping* as it popped in.

"No, it wasn't me," he wrote, with a weepy face. "Can we talk?"

The next day, we met at a nearby bagel place. As I pulled open the door, I could hear my pulse thumping in my ears. He stood up as I came in, and we hugged. Cool as I tried to play it, there it was: that deliriously happy feeling I couldn't deny.

"I'm sorry. What I did was asinine and immature. You didn't deserve it," he said, without prompting.

He lowered his eyes and thanked me for "being the mature one."

I took Dana Marie's advice. "Homie," I said—I'd taken to calling him that, too, because he felt so much like home—"when that happens, please *talk to me* about it."

He promised he would. "I got overwhelmed. I know I need to work on it. I just screw myself. Afterwards, I spiraled into a little depression."

He told me how much he cared about me, as a friend, in addition to all else. "Will you give me a chance to try? To work on myself?" His eyes lifted to mine.

Call me a hopeless romantic, Reader, or call me worse—I said that I would.

✳

AS I WATCHED the debris being cleared from the boardwalk on my Shore visits, it seemed a time of new beginnings. I was trying to see things from Sam's point of view, and communicate my needs and feelings, as my Team had suggested. Sam still had silent periods, and we had long stretches between visits, but I gave him his space, and focused on my work and my writing. I'd always been told I was very independent—*too* independent, my female friends said, citing this as one reason for my continual trouble with men. If he was reliving that Renaissance life as a traveler, visiting me when he was "in port," well, I could do the same.

Sam found a new house, moving in with some younger coworkers. His room was papered with geographical maps; he seemed to be slightly obsessed with them. As I sat on his bed one day gazing at the multihued land masses and stretches of blue ocean, I thought of what Edward Ragosta had told me about Sam's life as a Renaissance traveler, selling his wares and visiting me when he was in port. Could it be true? For all I'd now read about patients who healed from past-life regressions, and children with verifiable past-life memories, and for all my own gut feelings, I *still* couldn't help, at times, questioning it.

I'd recently read another of Brian Weiss's books called *Only Love Is Real: A Story of Soulmates Reunited*. It was a remarkable tale of two patients Weiss was treating for grief and relationship issues with past-life-regression therapy, present-day strangers born in different countries who, under hypnosis, described, in great detail, what appeared to be *the very same past lifetime*. When Weiss became aware of this astonishing fact, and after struggling with the ethics and implications of doing so, he introduced them. And the two fell in love and married . . . resuming what eventually appeared to be their shared history together across many centuries and lifetimes.

"You may be awakened to the presence of your soul companion by a look, a dream, a memory, a feeling," Weiss wrote. "You may be awakened by the touch of his hands or the kiss of her lips, and your soul is jolted back to life." It was such a precise description of what I'd felt on the boardwalk, and the moonlit beach, with Sam.

Intrigued by the story, I resolved to delve more deeply into my own possible past lives with Sam. I turned again to Rev. Kev O'Kane.

"Do you know what just came to mind?" he began in our phone session. "A scene from an Emily Brontë book. The two of you standing on a cliff. Him standing there, stalwart, holding you; your hair blowing in the wind; both staring out to sea."

"Oh my God." I laughed. "*Wuthering Heights* was my favorite book when I was younger," I said, referring to Brontë's tale of tortured, otherworldly love. "Only it was the moors, not the sea, in that book," I said. Heathcliff, a homeless beggar boy who'd been taken in by the young Cathy's father, had never thought himself worthy of his intense love for her . . . until he'd gone away and made his fortune, coming back a changed man.

"His name was probably Heathcliff then," Kev said. "Yes, of course you've been together." He told me about two lives: In the first, Sam was a successful fisherman who went out on ships. We were married with three children, a happy, drama-free life. "The name coming in is *Bournemouth*, England; somewhere on the coast. Time-wise, I would say between 1870 and 1880."

The next life Kev saw was in ancient Greece. Again, Sam was a man, I was a woman. He was upper-class, I was lower. And we met in secret. That was funny, I thought, considering how Sam had kept me "in a box" in our present-day life.

"*Again*, he was a seaman. But this time he went on longer voyages." I flashed on the maps in Sam's bedroom. I thought, too, of Roger Ansanelli's words, in that session before I'd met Sam, about a new guy coming in who loved boats and sailing. Had he been picking up on Sam—picking up on his past lives?

"You two ran away and got married. You ran to Africa, because your father would never find you there; he never did. Neither of you ever saw your family again. You lived a relatively happy life. One time, though, he was hunting and got mauled by a lion. But he lived. I'm seeing him as an old man—back then, that was anything from thirty on up—farming. He has a combination heat stroke and heart attack, and that takes him. But you're stoic, and you accept it. Also, you believe in reincarnation, so you know it's not the end.

"You've had other lives together too. So yes, it's a strong connection. One reason you have the age difference now is that, so many times, there's been the age difference in the other direction. You two wanted to see what it was like the other way around."

Later, when I Googled *Bournemouth*, I found it'd been a Victorian seaside resort—much of the architecture still remained. The resemblance to the Victorian seaside resort town where Sam and I had met was uncanny. I'd never told Kev where on the Jersey Shore we'd met.

WHILE SAM HAD been missing in action, I was still visiting the Shore whenever I could. I'd made a few other friends there now, including a man named Jonah. Jonah and I had an easy rapport from the start. A bespectacled man with a deep, raspy voice and long, dark hair, often pulled back in a ponytail, threaded with gray, he did technology work for a nearby hospital by day, writing screenplays, which was his passion, by night. He loved talking about indie movies, which we did whenever I ran into him at the Cup.

Jonah and I definitely clicked, and the possibility of dating hung in the air. But much as I liked him, it felt more like friendship to me than potential romantic partners. As he never made any moves, I assumed he felt the same way.

About a month after we'd met, I confided to Jonah about Sam, and all our ups and downs. To my surprise, he got a bit growly about it. "I understand sharing a moment. But he's not treating you well. Why would you ever want to see him again?"

"It's not that simple," I said, explaining all the good things I'd gotten from knowing Sam, and also all of his childhood "issues." Jonah didn't want to hear it.

A few weeks later, I ran into Jonah again. He told me he'd learned that a young woman he knew worked at the same restaurant as Sam. While eating there one day, he'd questioned her about Sam, mentioning my name.

"You did *what*?!" I couldn't believe he'd done such a thing without my consent. What if it got back to Sam? I felt Jonah had stuck his nose way too far into my business, and had way overstepped his bounds.

"I was looking out for you!" he said, miffed. Then he told me—not suggested, but *told* me—I needed to forget about Sam.

Well! I told him not to tell me what to do; he told me not to tell him what to say. We parted ways, steam coming out of our collective ears. And then a stalemate ensued.

I felt terrible. Back in the city, I emailed him, trying to smooth things over. But he was distant, prickly. He made it clear he was cooling things off between us for good.

At the time, I had another reading with Kev O'Kane. Puzzled and sad about Jonah's behavior, I wondered what Kev could pick up about his role in my life. Telling him nothing about the situation, I gave him only Jonah's first name.

"OK," Kev said, "he has been a brother of yours in a very recent life, probably late 1800s, early 1900s. You were his sister. He's still a bit strict, in that he wants the best for you. If you want a friendship, you can have it, but it's never going to be a friendship like you'd have with anyone else because of this brother thing; it'll always be, 'I'm the older, more mature one, I'm watching out for you.' He's going to want to *protect you* because he still thinks he knows much better than you do."

My jaw literally fell open as he said it. Kev had aced it, big time.

"Older brothers can get their feelings hurt. They try to do the right thing, and the person they're trying to protect gets mad at them."

Hearing it all, I softened. If Jonah *had* been my big brother, his behavior made perfect sense. I actually felt touched. Though I had four brothers, one of them older, none of them had ever been protective of me in the least. Nor had my father.

Kev said that if I wanted to continue the friendship with Jonah, I'd have to be the one to reach out—make a gesture, invite him for coffee, something like that.

I did, and—*huzzah!*—soon all was well between the two of us once more.

Kev's reading, though, had been profound in another way. If I had told Kev what had happened between Jonah and me, and *then* he'd said what he said, that would have been one thing; but given that I hadn't told him anything at all, well, it was one of the most convincing things I'd experienced thus far in terms of the validity of past lives.

Of course, Kev *could* have been picking up what had passed between Jonah and me from my energy field, if such things could be done—and it seemed more and more clear that they could; it didn't necessarily follow that Jonah and I had *shared another life*. Yet coming on top of all the persuasive material I'd read in Brian Weiss's and Jim Tucker's books, and alongside all the undeniable feelings I'd had of having lived in nun's and monk's cells, and of knowing—and loving— Sam, or his soul's incarnations, before, Kev's reading felt like the cherry on the sundae of the personal experience I'd been seeking, bridging the gap between what I'd felt in my gut and what I could rationally accept in my mind. As I heard Kev nail the situation with Jonah and me so precisely, I could sense something in me shifting. I could feel my own "belief system," wherever in my brain it lay, stretching to incorporate the experience, like an amoeba I'd once viewed under a microscope in a high school biology class engulfing its prey.

PONDERING IT ALL LATER in my threadbare armchair, I asked myself: If Rev. Kev had been so on target about Jonah, could I accept that I'd lived all those other lives he'd seen with *Sam*? I thought again about the similarities between Bournemouth and the Jersey Shore town where Sam and I had met. He wasn't from the area, nor was I. Had we two been drawn there because it felt like home, a home in England we'd once happily shared? And if so, what then? What was one supposed to *do* about these past-life husbands who popped up again in the present?

If soul mates were in our lives to help us to learn lessons, to have experiences for our soul's expansion and growth, then what was Sam here to teach or show me? He'd helped me to heal and to learn what it was like to feel truly loved. But was he also here to teach me what I needed to learn about heeding red flags, as Maggie Moise had said? Despite my many protests and talks, and despite my understanding of his childhood pain, in forgiving Sam's behavior and especially in continuing to want to see him, wasn't I condoning that behavior? If so, then I was ignoring the lesson he'd come to teach me—the lesson that I, ostensibly, had *asked* him, in spirit, to teach me when we met up again in this present life.

Moreover, if Sam *was* part of my soul group, with whom I incarnated again and again, chances were good that *Jonah* was too. Was *he* back in my life to help me accomplish what was obviously so hard for me to do *myself*: to walk away, once and for all, from men like Sam?

In a way, it seemed clear that that was what I needed to do. But as Roger Ansanelli had once said, "Pisces know what they have to do, and then they do something else." I couldn't help thinking back to Patricia Masters, when she'd talked so specifically about glass and glassblowing, and told me I'd one day have quite a collection of glass myself. Had she been seeing my future with Sam? Of course, I wanted to believe that. But hadn't she also said that I needed a man who knew how to take care of me, the way someone would take good care of glass?

Reader, it jangled the mind!

My Team members had all said that Sam and I had time ahead of us. I knew that time, like the tide, could rip us asunder, or gently lap at our ankles as we embraced in the surf. No matter how many psychic readings I might have, there was no way of being certain which it would be, because there was no predestined future; in fact, I'd come to believe, there was no one, single "future" at all.

The idea was maddening! Yet it was also totally liberating. It meant endless possibility, endless hope. And after all, if we really could know our future, if we had no power to affect it, by our choices and actions, by what we learned—or *hadn't* learned, *yet*—what would be the point in living? Never mind living again, and again?

I'd had a few psychics tell me that their guides didn't want to reveal a particular answer just yet; that, for whatever reason, they felt it should not be shared with me at the present time. Maggie Moise had explained that some things needed to unfold as they would—to be left, for the moment, as a mystery. "Sometimes you're not supposed to control absolutely everything," she'd said.

There was no getting around it: Life *was* a mystery, a glorious mystery. My experience with Sam had brought that home, big time. I felt so certain we'd been together before, many times. But even if so, that was no guarantee we'd be together now. And even in those lives when we *had* been together, there'd apparently been difficulties, even tragedies, more often than not.

Yet here we were—or so I truly believed—playing it out one more time! And whichever way things went down, I had a feeling it wouldn't be our last. The Dude, I had a feeling, would abide.

Perhaps that was part of what Sam was here to teach me. And Jonah, too. If reincarnation was real, then there was always another go-round. No tragedy was really quite so tragic. No ending really an ending.

So perhaps my future, or lack of future, with Sam was one of those things that had to unfold as it would, without my foreknowledge and without my probably wrongheaded attempts to affect or control it. Sam had said, that night when I'd feebly attempted to break things off, that we were two kindred spirits, sharing a moment—and, hard as that concept could be for us humans, there was definitely something to be said for that. Each life was, after all, only a chain of present moments; each one, as it beautifully, miraculously unfolded, was what we were here for, and really, all that we had.

11

ADVENTURES WITH
CHRISTOPHER
✳ OR ✳

The Spirit Is Willing

I WAS IN MY LATE THIRTIES THE FIRST TIME I SAW THE
Thornton Wilder play *Our Town*. I knew that it dealt with small town
life, and had a reputation as a corny, even saccharine affair. So I wasn't
prepared for the impact it had on me when I finally saw a production.

In one of the final scenes, Emily, the female lead, who has just died
in childbirth, attends her own funeral. As she goes to join the dead,
she's told that she must now forget the life she's just lived. Instead, she
chooses to go back to Earth to relive just one day, her twelfth birthday,
fourteen years before.

Emily arrives, on the dawn of that day, outside her childhood home.
As she watches her mother cook breakfast and chat with her father
about the usual mundane things, it's more than she can endure, and she
breaks down sobbing: "I can't go on. It goes so fast. We don't have time
to look at one another . . . Take me back—up the hill—to my grave.
But first: Wait! One more look. Good-bye, Good-bye, world. Good-
bye, Grover's Corners . . . Mama and Papa . . . Do any human beings
ever realize life while they live it—every, every minute?"

That scene has never left me. And lately, it's made me wonder: Do
spirits of the departed ever miss this life, and us, as much as some of
us here miss them? Is that why those spirits who come through with

mediums, or express themselves in other ways, do what they do? Or is it, rather, that they know how much we're missing them?

I'd witnessed my carpenter friend Ben's reunion with the spirit of his best friend, Bobby, and heard from a number of my own departed loved ones through mediums myself. More and more, I was starting to feel that death was not an end but simply a transition—as psychic Christina Wright once described it, "Like getting out of one car and getting into another." Less and less, I feared it. And yet, for all my increasing lack of fear about what happened after death, my loss of the loved ones who had passed, in my day-to-day life, was still palpable. Was it the same for them?

I had numerous friends and acquaintances who'd claimed to have seen dead loved ones, without a medium involved. I'd wondered, when they told me their stories, whether these individuals somehow had a more open channel than those of us who lacked such experiences. Or if it meant, perhaps, that these spirits were more hell-bent (if you'll pardon the expression) on contacting, or making their presence known to, the loved ones they'd left behind.

Once, when I was sitting in my friend Bonnie's unusually large Manhattan kitchen, her brother Joe was visiting from Indiana. His big frame stretched out on one of her ladder-back, carved oak chairs, he asked me what kind of writing I did, and I told him about my explorations. I expected him to laugh, or tease me—Joe was another big, burly, bearded guy who, like Ben, worked in construction, and I figured he wouldn't believe in such things. Instead, he surprised me by telling me he'd once clearly seen the spirit of his late uncle.

"Yeah . . . Uncle Rudy. I saw him, on the farm, after he died. He was standing there in his straw hat, with his cane. Out in the yard. He kind of nodded to me."

"He was our dad's brother," Bonnie explained, with a slightly stunned look, processing this news she'd apparently not heard before.

"He never married, and lived on the farm all his life. Joe lives there now."

I asked Joe if his uncle seemed to know that he'd been seen, and if he had acknowledged the incident in any way.

"Oh, he knew I saw him," Jim said, stroking his beard. "Definitely so."

"Did he say anything?" I asked.

"No. Just gave a long look, right at me," he said.

We chatted a bit more, and Joe admitted that, though the incident had happened many years earlier, he'd never shared it with anyone else. Funny enough, a few weeks later, Bonnie called me to say that upon his return home to Indiana, Joe had shared the story with their brother Pete, only to learn that Uncle Rudy had made a similar appearance to him at about that same time, which Pete, too, had kept a secret all these years.

There were other friends with similar experiences as well. Some, like Joe and Pete, had briefly seen the departed loved one; others had felt the loved one sitting on their bed, and even tickling their feet. But for all the tales I'd heard, I'd never heard as many connected with a single individual as with the son of one of my mother's best friends.

Jeanne had been my mother's close chum since they'd been sorority sisters in college. I'd known her my whole life. She and her two children, Jamie and Christopher, were like extended family. I hadn't seen Chris often as an adult. Still, I always heard what he was up to, via his mother, via *my* mother. She and Jeanne talked constantly on the phone.

When we were both in our forties, Christopher, who'd become a professional chef, had passed away; shockingly, he'd choked on a mouthful of food while teaching a cooking class. When I heard what had happened, my heart went out to Jeanne. Chris had been her only son, and if ever a mother and son were close, it had been Jeanne and Chris.

"Christopher telephones Jeanne every single day," my mother used to tell me—a little enviously, I thought. And it wasn't just his mother Chris had been close to; he'd been very tight with his sister, Jamie, too, and had been adored by many, many friends.

Soon after Chris's death, Jeanne and Jamie, and other people who'd been close to him, began experiencing uncanny events. I'd heard about them through my mom. A few years after his passing, when I found myself in the midst of my explorations about the afterlife and other realms, I asked Jeanne if she'd talk to me about them herself, and she kindly agreed.

As I sat across from Jeanne in her cozy Upper East Side apartment, nestled into one of her comfy, highly tufted armchairs—threads all well intact—her standard poodle, Lucy, at my feet, I marveled at this woman's resiliency. When my mother had heard the news about Christopher, she'd said, "I really don't know how Jeanne is going to go on." And yet I could see that she was carrying out her very full life very well. I marveled both at her ability to talk so easily about Chris's death and to smile and even laugh as she did so. I wondered how much Chris's apparent after-death contact had helped with that.

"I wanted to have a closed coffin," she told me, after I'd switched on my recorder, recalling her son's jam-packed wake, which I'd attended. "But people kept bringing stuff to put in there. You know, Christopher loved rye bread, and the butcher brought a loaf of bread to put in the coffin. All these people were bringing things to put in—jewelry, pictures . . ." After he died, many of his friends got tattoos with his initials, she said, or with the word *Chef.*

"And he knew everyone, wherever we went!" she said. "It seemed like, if he met someone, he kept in contact with them, and they never forgot one another, which is very rare in life." She paused. "He was an adorable son."

"He *was*," I said. Chris had always been a cute and charismatic person. I'd had a crush on him for a while in childhood, though as always, I'd been too shy to let on. "So, as you know, I've heard, from my mom, about a lot of . . . *unusual* things that happened after Chris died. And I wondered if you could tell me those stories yourself."

Jeanne was quiet a minute, her big brown eyes shifting upward as she seemed to search back for where to begin. I cast my eyes about the room. Jeanne had, I recalled, owned a pottery studio for a time, where she'd hired me to work one summer. Her apartment's furnishings reflected her playful spirit and her love for color and art. "He had just died, and my friend Lara was on her way to the funeral parlor. I've told you about Lara before . . . she's the one who's a psychic."

"Yes," I said. I'd always been curious about Lara, though we'd never met.

"And Lara said she was on a subway train, and Christopher came in and sat down next to her. And he said, 'I want you to tell my mother I'm all right, and not to worry.' And she said, 'Yes, I will do that.' And then he walked away."

I asked Jeanne if she had believed her friend.

"Yes, I did," she said, thoughtfully. "She does have that ability, I think. So that was the first thing that happened . . . Then, about a month after that, I was in the Metropolitan Museum with my friend Vera. I was, naturally, feeling upset and depressed. And so we went to the museum, because they were having a show with a lot of Renaissance paintings." She thought the beauty of the art might lift her spirits, she said.

"So they had this picture of the Blessed Virgin, in a little room. Vera and I walked in, and there was the most gorgeous young man. He had blond, flowing hair and blue eyes, a beautiful white shirt—the shirt was *fabulous!*—and a beautiful crucifix around his neck. And he was looking at the Blessed Virgin so adoringly it took my breath away.

"Well, I'm looking at him, and he turns around, and we started to talk. He was a Catholic priest," she said.

Jeanne, I knew, was Catholic herself.

"And I asked, what was his name? And he said 'Jamie.' And I said, *'Jamie'*?"

Jamie, of course, was Jeanne's daughter's name.

And he said, 'Yes, I'm Father *Jamie Christopher.*'"

"I said, '*What?*' And Vera said, 'Would you say that again?' We were stunned.

"I said to Vera, 'With that shirt and that hair, he looks like Jesus Christ!' So I told him about Jamie, and about Christopher, and he said, 'Don't worry. I can tell you, Christopher's fine.'

"So now, he walks out of this room. But then Vera said, 'Oh, let's find out where he's from.' And there was a stretch ahead of us, and then there was nowhere he could have gone, right or left, because there *was* no right or left. So I said to Vera, '*You* saw him, didn't you?' She said, 'Yes, I did. I mean, we're not nuts.' But really, I mean, how many people are named *Jamie Christopher?*"

The story reminded me of my synchronistic encounter with Drew at the museum in Amsterdam. I wondered if it was possible we'd manifested these things, to help us with our own healing. That is, if Father Jamie Christopher *was* a flesh-and-blood human, and not some type of angelic being or spirit. As Jeanne described it, one had to wonder.

Jeanne paused and sipped her coffee as Lucy padded around the room and then came back to sit at her side. "And then . . . a friend of Christopher's was riding his motorcycle," she said. Chris, I knew, had been an avid biker. "And he skidded, it was wintertime, and he thought he was going to be dead. And he told me later, 'The strangest thing happened. The motorcycle just went out from under me, and Christopher came along and picked me right up and put me down.' He was saved."

"Wait—did he feel like he actually *saw* Chris?" I asked.

"Oh, yes, he said it was unbelievable. He said, 'Christopher came from behind, picked me up, put me down, and then he disappeared.'"

She told me about a few other incidents in which friends of Chris's felt they had been "visited" by him. One woman had been rocking her baby, feeling sad that she couldn't make it to Christopher's funeral, when the lights in her breakfront, which had never worked, had gone on. They had continued to work from that point forward.

"Oh, and then I dialed a phone number, a number that I always dial . . . And it turned out that the number I *reached* was something totally different! Like, none of the digits were even the same! Not even close! And this girl says, 'Hello,' and it's *a friend of Christopher's*! And she said she'd just been thinking of him, and wondering how we all were."

"And the person you were actually dialing wasn't connected to her, or to Chris?" I asked.

Jeanne said no, the person she'd been calling had no connection at all to either one.

"Would you have known this girl's number, the one who answered the phone and turned out to be Chris's friend? And dialed it accidentally? You know, sometimes you think you're dialing your mother, and you dial your sister by accident?"

"No! I didn't know her number at all! I didn't have it! I'd never dialed this girl's number in my entire life! I'd *met* her, once, briefly, but just that."

"And it wasn't Chris's cell phone, or something like that, with the number already programmed into it?"

"No, it was my own phone, this phone right here!" She pointed to a portable phone on a table across from us.

"Wow." I pondered that. "You hear that a lot, the idea that the energies of spirits can play around with lights and other electrical or electronic things," I said. "After one of my mother's cousins died, his wife told us the lights in the house went completely wild. Things going on and off, and blinking, for days. And you know, my mother is obsessed with looking for signs from my father. She's always asking him to flicker the lights. It did happen once or twice, though not that dramatically. But then, my mom's good friend from childhood—Rita, *you've met her!*—died. And the day we were going to her memorial lunch, the lights in Mom's dining room chandelier went absolutely bananas! They blinked on and off like fireworks for about twenty seconds! My sister saw it too, which was lucky because I'm not sure anyone would have believed me if it had been just me."

"Yes." She nodded. Then she asked me if my sister was as interested in the spiritual stuff as I was.

"I think she believes, to some extent, or is at least open to it. She's had some strange experiences herself. Though she can be pretty skeptical, too."

"And your mother does," Jeanne said.

"Well, she does and she doesn't. She wants to believe in an afterlife, of course. But then, she's scared about some things. She's really afraid I'm going over the top with all my explorations. She's worried some kind of evil spirits will get hold of me. Probably she's more afraid of them getting into her house and getting hold of *her*! And she *hates* the idea of reincarnation! She doesn't want to come back as somebody else, and when she gets to heaven—I think she's hopeful she'll get to heaven, though she's got fears about that, too—she wants my father to be ready and waiting. Not back here as somebody's teenage boy . . . or for that matter, teenage girl!"

Jeanne laughed.

"I recently tried to get her to agree on a sign that she could send me after she dies," I went on. "But she said that she's been so forgetful lately that, even on the Other Side, she probably wouldn't remember it!"

Jeanne laughed again. She'd always had a fantastic, big, and very unique laugh. Despite everything she'd been through, that hadn't changed.

"But speaking of electronics," I said, "there was one story Mom told me that really intrigued me, about you and Jamie on a bridge, and something with the car radio?"

"Yes, yes, *yes!*" she said. "I don't remember it exactly, maybe because it was just so *bizarre*. Like, it had nothing to do with reality. You know, sometimes when things are *so* strange, you block them out." She paused, stroking Lucy's velvety head. "We were driving over a bridge, and we had the car radio on, music was playing. And we were having a conversation about Christopher. We were talking about some topic, and asking each other, 'What would Christopher say?' We still play that game, like, 'What would Christopher think about this restaurant?' So the music was playing, and then this voice interrupted, and *said something* . . . I mean, it was completely pertaining to what we were asking! It was as if Christopher had *answered* us! And we were both like, '*What?!*'"

"And did it go right back to the music after that?" I asked.

"Yes! And we got frightened. It was just so weird. We weren't really afraid, but it was very shocking. I think we both blocked it out, because it was just so . . . *different.*"

That story, I thought, was like something out of a sci-fi novel. Jamie affirmed it later, though she, too, couldn't recall the words that had been said or the topic they'd been talking about. She seemed creeped out just remembering it.

I asked Jeanne then to tell me about the time she'd seen Christopher herself.

She paused, gathering her thoughts.

She was at her kitchen sink, she said, when she felt a strong sense of a presence behind her. "I live alone. So that was a little strange, right? So I turned around . . . and *there was my son.* Just walking, straight ahead. So I saw his side view pass by. He was wearing jeans, a shirt, and the sneakers he always wore . . . his normal attire.

"It took me a minute to come out of the kitchen. When I did, he was no longer there. Well, I was shocked. Because he was really there. Solid. It wasn't an apparition, this was a solid *being* walking by. And you know, I couldn't comprehend right away."

I asked if it had scared her.

"Oh no! I thought maybe he came for dinner, because he really liked my cooking, and we always talked about food!" She laughed.

Christopher hadn't acknowledged her at all, Jeanne said, just walked straight ahead. "That's the only time I ever saw him. I've dreamt of him. I remember that day, I was feeling so bad, and that made me feel better, even though he didn't stop to say hello."

That, to me, was so odd. Why *hadn't* Christopher said hello? And how had Jeanne been able to see him? Had Christopher been able to somehow intentionally project himself into Jeanne's level of consciousness, from wherever he now was, and had Jean been open enough, somehow, to receive it? But if so, why hadn't he acknowledged her? I'd read about the idea of different levels of consciousness or different dimensions at times intersecting, and talked to Griffin about the notion of things from other dimensions "bleeding through" into this human level of ours. Perhaps this had been such a case.

I knew from my mother that a friend of Jamie's had gone to see TV medium John Edward in a large-group setting, and apparently heard from Christopher. I inquired next about that.

"Yes, this good friend of Jamie's had tickets and asked her to go, but I think my daughter was a little afraid. So, at the show, John Edward points to the area in the audience where this friend was sitting—and he came up with the name *Lucien*. So, Christopher had his restaurant, as you know, Dirty Pierre's," Jeanne said. "And Jamie's friend knew that restaurant. But she didn't realize that he'd had a restaurant *before* Dirty Pierre's, called Lucien's. She didn't know—a *lot* of people didn't—that Christopher's father's name was Lucien, and that it was actually *Christopher's* real name too. *Christopher* is his middle name."

I did know this. I nodded.

Jeanne continued. "So, John Edward starts talking about a restaurant. And so Jamie's friend is thinking, *Huh!* And then John Edward said the restaurant was named for this person who died, and that the name was also the name of this person's *father.* 'But he goes by another name,' he said. And that's when her friend realized that maybe he was talking about Christopher. And once she told that to John Edward, he started talking about how the restaurant is famous for their mussels . . . which is absolutely true!

"And then John Edward said that this person coming through was talking about the person with the turtle pond in the backyard. And that was Jamie! I mean, nobody would have known Jamie had a turtle pond. She wasn't even there!"

The turtle pond! I flashed back to my first reading with medium Jennifer Hicks, who'd gotten so many details right about my departed family members. She'd gotten the name *Christopher* and said she was seeing frogs or turtles. It seemed that this was one of Chris's identifiers of choice. I reminded Jeanne about that, pointing out that, once again, he'd come through that day—and I hadn't even asked! She nodded, obviously pleased to remember it.

"He also said that Christopher was all right. And not to worry. And to continue with the restaurant. And Jamie *has* continued with it," she said.

"That story really impresses me," I said, "because Jamie's friend wasn't directly connected to Christopher, and *she* bought the tickets. There was no way the people at the show could have found out about Christopher by researching obituaries with *her friend's* name in them on the Internet, or anything like that. And the friend didn't even *know* the name *Lucien,* or the fact that the restaurant used to be called that—yet *that's* what John Edward picked up. I know some wonderful magicians, they're called Matt and Prakash, who do mentalism as part of their act. And they swear that these TV mediums are charlatans. They say that they're eliciting information in various ways: by researching the names on the credit cards when people buy tickets, and also something called *cold reading*." I explained to Jeanne what that was.

"But I've watched John Edward's show so many times, and I know about cold reading, and while I see why these friends think that, and I'm sure in some cases things like that are true . . . well, if you watch the show a *lot*, which I have, there are many, many times where I don't see how either of those methods could be going on. The personal details he comes up with sometimes are *so* specific, and he hasn't gotten them from anything the family members have said. Once, he told this woman that her dead husband was showing him an image of her putting his shoes out on the fire escape, because they were so smelly. And the woman said, 'Oh my God, I had to do that every night!' Another time, he talked about a dead person showing him a figurine, Mickey Mouse, I think, on a shelf in someone's closet, and it was true. How are you going to get that online? He knew exactly which room in the house, and in which direction you had to turn to get to the closet.

"You know, my sister got us tickets to see John Edward," I continued, "when he was in Staten Island once. And it wasn't as if he got a lot of stuff wrong, live, and they just edited it out of the show, which these friends have also suggested. He was very accurate. There was a lot of flap at one time in the media—rumors, I mean—about his audience members being interviewed before his show, being asked to fill out cards about themselves, and so on, but there was nothing at all like that going on as far as I could see," I said.

Apparently, no one had asked Jamie's friend to fill out any forms when she'd attended the show either. I'd checked with her later, highly curious.

"Speaking of mediums," Jeanne said, "there was that other man that *you* put me in touch with, in Long Island . . ."

I'd given her Jeffrey Wands's info a while back, and she'd booked a session with him. I'd heard that she'd been floored by it. I asked her to tell me about it now.

"Well, I went in," she began, "and Jeffrey said hello. And I said, 'I've got to use the ladies' room first.' So when I came out of the bathroom, I opened the door to his office, and he's standing behind the desk, turned so he's in profile. And, as if he's tipping a cowboy hat, he says— and this is just what Christopher would always do, and say, kidding around, about himself versus his sister—'And I'm *still* the favorite!'" She drew in a breath. "It was amazing—he captured it *exactly*!

"You know, Christopher loved hats, he had a whole collection of them . . . And I said, 'Oh my God! How could this man have *said* that?' *It was Christopher.* I almost couldn't concentrate on anything else after that. Even though there was a lot more . . ."

"Christopher really used every means possible, didn't he, to come through?" I said, petting Lucy, who was putting her paws up on my lap. "And wait, there's one we forgot! The Central Park story. About the *little boy* . . ."

"Oh, *the little boy*!" Jeanne said, her face lighting up. "It was Christopher's fiftieth birthday, and Jamie and I were going to celebrate. So before we did, we sat on Christopher's bench in Central Park." Jeanne and Jamie had made a donation to have a plaque put on a bench there, in his memory.

"We didn't have anything indicating a birthday. And this adorable little boy, on a scooter, came right up to us, and said, 'Happy birthday, my lad,' or 'Happy birthday, my boy.' Then his father came, and we were going to ask him about it, but they went the other way. You know, this little boy, he came out of this underpass about fifty feet from the bench, and rode *directly toward us*. He could've gone *this* way, he could've gone *that* way; people were sitting here, people were sitting there, but he came *right* to Jamie and me."

"And neither of you was a boy, or a lad!" I said. I was loving this. "Chris has sent you a lot of messengers. You know, I read that the word *angel* means *messenger.*"

"Yes," Jeanne said, smiling.

I switched my recorder off after that final story, pleased with how much Jeanne had remembered, and she fed me a delicious pasta and salad lunch before I departed, good cook that she was. As I left her apartment and rode the elevator down to the lobby, I thought again about how Christopher would call Jeanne every day. He was someone who made sure, day in and day out, to connect with his mom. It was remarkable that now, in spirit, he appeared to be the very same way.

I'd heard it said that when our consciousness continues, after we pass from our human form, who we are, in our essence, remains intact. Our soul, I supposed. And Reader, isn't that something we all want to believe? Jeanne's experiences with Christopher seemed to me, quite strongly, to affirm that. Now that I'd heard all of her wonderful stories for myself, it seemed clear to me that a large part of Jeanne's ability to "go on" in the face of her devastating loss was due to Christopher's unparalleled attempts to "reach out" to her—and to all his loved ones—after death, just as much as he had in life.

✳

SOME TIME HAD PASSED since I'd sat with Jeanne and Lucy. It was Easter, and the bright golden daffodils and violet crocuses were abloom in my mother's front yard, where we sat in the sun before Mass. I hadn't slept well, and despite the beauty of the day, I was feeling cranky.

"Are you sure you unplugged the iron after you finished ironing?" my mother asked.

"Yes," I said. "And I turned off the water on the washing machine, and I didn't leave anything burning on the stove."

She flashed me a look, and, guilty, I averted my eyes. After all, it was Easter Sunday. But I'd been staying with her for nearly a week, and her fearfulness and anxiety, and habit of talking to me as if I were six, were getting to me.

"Did I tell you about the Easter card Jeanne got from Christopher?" she asked. "I'm not going to get it straight. You should call and let her tell you. It's a good story!"

Well, that made me curious, so I pulled out my cell, and ran and got my trusty little recorder, which I'd lately gotten in the habit of taking along pretty much everywhere I went.

"Put her on speaker," my mother said when I returned. She was constantly warning me about the dangers of brain tumors from cell phones. Irritated, I waved her away.

"Happy Easter, Jeanne!" I said, as she picked up.

"Put her on *speaker*," my mother said again, and this time I flashed *her* a look. But I did it, so she could hear too.

We all exchanged Easter wishes, and then Jeanne told us the tale. "Well, a while back, I had a dream of talking to Christopher about three people," she said. "One was his friend Danny—he's so sweet. The second was *my* friend Barbara . . . a darling. She's always broke. And the third was an old family friend . . . he's poor too. So Chris is talking about how these three people need surprises. You know, I used to surprise my kids with little things, food, clothing—it was a thing I did. So he says, 'You should get them surprises.' And then I woke up.

"So then Jamie calls me, and I tell her, and she says, 'You should get the surprises.' So I got a gift certificate for Danny for a clothing store. And Barbara needed her hair done, so I got her a certificate for that. The third person, I couldn't find, so I couldn't do it for him. But I told the other two, 'This is a surprise from Christopher. He told me to do this, and I hope you like it.' And they did.

"So about a week before that, I had gone through some trunks and I found a lot of Jamie and Christopher's old children's books, and I took them out and looked through them. I had given my friend Anita a bunch of them; she has a cute little boy.

"I'd been feeling bad again, about Christopher . . . sad. And I called Anita when I had the dream, and told her about it. We made a plan to have lunch. So I went to meet her for lunch, and she gives me an Easter card. And inside *her* card is another little card . . . *from Christopher.* She had found it in one of the children's books! And it says, 'Dear Mom, Happy Easter! I didn't forget! Love, Chris.'"

I could hear the joy in her voice.

"It was so odd," she said. "I'd looked through those books, all of them, but I'd never seen it. Anita told me that when she found it, she showed it to her husband, and he said, 'That's *Jeanne's* surprise.'"

"Wow," I said. "*That* is a wonderful story!"

I looked over at my mother, who gave me an *I told you so* smile.

After we hung up, I sat there in the sun with my mother, thinking about that story. I began to feel bad about my earlier crankiness and impatience with her. And not just because it was Easter. I realized how lucky I was to be there with my mother now, how very much I loved her, and how lucky we were to have this time—this beautiful day, this beautiful life—*together.*

And I thanked Christopher for reminding me of that.

It was, I thought, *my* surprise.

12

ADVENTURES IN
CHANNELING
✳ OR ✳
Divine Secrets of the Woo-Woo Sisterhood

I'VE OFTEN FELT THAT, AS THE BEATLES PUT IT, I GET BY WITH a little help from my friends. It's kind of been my personal theme song.

Though I'd never faced hardships like hunger, homelessness, or a debilitating disease, by my late forties I'd struggled with family problems, financial problems, weight problems, anxiety, depression, and many broken hearts. My hair had fallen out in patches from stress, two separate times, in my teenage years, and later in life I'd suffered with severe insomnia and panic attacks. There were many times when I couldn't have made it through without my friends.

But there had been times, too, when I seemed to get help of a different sort—when there was danger at hand, and it felt as if some *unseen* friend had my back. Once, while doing a work-study stint as a stagehand for my university's theater department, I'd tried to move a "sky horse"—a heavy, crane-like piece of equipment—on the stage of the school's brand-new theater, without asking for help. Totally idiotic—which I realized, heart hammering, body gone clammy and cold, as I watched it teeter toward the first rows of brand-new, built-in seats. My fate—in this case, doom, expulsion, and lifelong notoriety as the student who single-handedly broke the spanking new theater—seemed sealed. Somehow, though, against all odds, two tool-belt-wearing stagehand-dudes had scrambled over, grabbed the thing—to my utter relief—and managed to right it. It must have weighed a ton, and had been on its way down. What kind of strength would it take to right something that massive, against the pull of gravity? It had seemed impossible—or as if something or someone unearthly had saved me, big time.

Many years later, I was crossing Sixth Avenue, a broad main artery in Greenwich Village, where I lived, one rainy night, an umbrella pulled down low over my head. I was highly distraught about something— probably a guy—and quite literally lost in my thoughts. Suddenly, I became aware that I was crossing against the light, as I heard the thundering roar of a Mack truck—it was so close that I could see the small name delineated on its front grille. I remember thinking, *This is it. I'm gonna die, right here, right now!* No way it was not going to happen.

Yet, it *didn't*. Somehow, the next moment, I was standing, physically shaking, on the other side of the street, clueless as to how I'd gotten there. I'm sure I stood like that for a good five minutes. I couldn't immediately process what had just occurred, or even walk the remaining fifty or so yards to my door.

There had been other incidents too: a near-mugging one night in Times Square; three separate times when my hair had caught on fire but I'd emerged unscathed; a gas leak I'd found in my kitchen after being out of town, which, according to the Con Ed man who came to my rescue, could easily have launched me into firsthand explorations of things Beyond the Beyond. (He seemed amazed that it had not.)

I'd heard of guides—spirits who were assigned to us, or perhaps volunteered, to protect us and help us on our way. Since I'd started my explorations, psychics had told me a number of times that I had many dead relatives and friends acting as my guides. It made me highly curious about what guides, if they existed, *did*; how they operated; and whether I had other guides whom I hadn't known in life—

as Rev. Kev O'Kane had suggested—who were helping me specifically with my writing and my investigations.

As with the angels, it seemed all I had to do was put the wish to meet them out there, and my guides quickly found *me*.

SINCE EARLY ON in my process of writing about my explorations, I'd been using the working title *Adventures in Weird Stuff* for my manuscript. I wasn't sure it was the right title, and was curious how it would hit people. Some friends I'd shared it with loved it . . . others not so much. I was toying with using the term *woo-woo* in the title. A friend of mine was fond of using it when talking about things like energy healing, the spiritual world, and other New Age stuff. But did most people even *know* the term *woo-woo*? If I used it in my book title—say, *Adventures in Woo-Woo*—would anyone know what the heck I was talking about?

I searched on Amazon to see if the term had ever been used in a title. Up popped a book called *Woo-Woo: Becoming a Psychic at Fifty*, by Janet E. Alm. *Coolio!* I was fifty myself, edging toward fifty-one. *What would it be like*, I wondered, *to have a psychic gift emerge at this point in life?* It reminded me of Katarina, who'd been in her forties when she'd been told by Patricia Masters that she was a medium. I knew how her story had ended. I was curious to read about Janet's, which was obviously very different, so I sent for a copy of her book.

I found it to be a page-turner. An academic, I was later to discover, with a B.S. in elementary education; two masters degrees, in library science/folklore and intercultural studies; and a Ph.D. in recreation resource management, who'd had no interest or belief in things woo-woo at all, Janet began picking up telepathic images and messages a few years after her mother died. While initially she didn't always understand them, she believed that they were coming from her mother, and worked to develop a means to decipher them. One of the

first things her mother was directing her to do was to heal the lingering pain from her father's old war wounds by laying her hands on him.
Janet was dubious, but did as her mother instructed. To her shock, it
worked. This led to her beginning a healing practice, and then, with
time and work, to offering her services as a medium, and also channeling a spirit guide called Eia, who offered clients wisdom and counsel
from another dimension.

For the author of a book dealing with other realms, Janet's approach
was refreshingly down-to-earth. I appreciated her sense of humor, too.
But what I liked most about *Woo-Woo* were her detailed explanations
of the process by which all of this had occurred: how she'd picked up
information; what, specifically, she'd seen, felt, and heard; how she'd
sometimes misinterpreted data; how she'd improved, over time and
with practice; how bizarre it had felt to be doing this, especially for
someone who had a scientific background and worked in the academic
world—a world which she knew was likely to brand her a crackpot—
yet, at the same time, how gratifying.

I perused Janet's Web site, noting that she looked like a more cherubic version of the actress Kathy Bates. Then I emailed her, telling
her how much I'd enjoyed *Woo-Woo* and asking for a reading. I didn't
tell her that I was writing a book, or anything else. Jan, as she called
herself, wrote back, telling me that she worked as a university librarian
and did readings by phone only one night a week. But she had a slot
open in a few weeks so, elated, I grabbed it.

As the evening of my reading approached, my excitement grew.
While some of my Dream Team apparently channeled information
from beings in other realms, I'd never met a practitioner who actually channeled an entity with a specific identity, and, I assumed, a
specific personality. It put me in mind of Seth, the nonphysical collective entity famously channeled by Jane Roberts, in Upstate New
York. Roberts authored a series of books about the experience, in the
1960s and '70s (and, with her husband Robert Butts, published a book

or two dictated solely by Seth). I'd been given one of the Seth books by a friend in my twenties, and had found it beyond fascinating: Seth's explanation of the nature of personal reality, the subject of that particular book, had truly boggled my mind. Recently, as I'd begun my explorations, my friend Griffin, who was a huge fan of the books— and in my opinion, a real Seth scholar, having read even the massive body of unpublished channelings—had gotten me into the Seth books again. Out of the many, many books in the genre that I'd been reading, I'd found them among the most impressive.

As I punched Jan's number into my cell phone, I wondered what wisdom Eia might have to give me. Would she know, simply because she was in the spirit world, what was going on in my life? I'd read in some books by mediums that the spirits of our departed loved ones could indeed see us do everything we did, if they so chose. The title of one of them, *Do Dead People Watch You Shower?*, by medium Concetta Bertoldi, and her answer—basically, "They can if they want to"— pretty much said it all. But what about a spirit who had no connection to me? Had she checked Jan's appointment book and done some quick surveillance? Or could she access the Akashic Records—like stepping into a library, or hooking up to the Internet—and do a crash course before I called, on the topic of *moi*?

And what about my own spirit guides? If Jan could channel Eia, could she channel my own personal spirit guides too?

Jan, who was living at the time in Mattawan, Michigan, greeted me warmly when she picked up the phone. She sounded highly intelligent and thoroughly unpretentious, with no more of the "mystical" about her than a hand-knitted afghan or a bar of Ivory soap. She asked what sort of reading I wanted, and I said that I'd like to talk to Eia, and also to meet some of my own guides, if that was possible.

"Very possible!" Jan said. "If someone wishes to connect with their own guides, I usually start with Eia, who then typically introduces the person's primary guide, who I can then channel. That's always fun because the guides all have their own personalities and outlooks, and some of them are very humorous. But the common thread always is their love and support for their human partners. Guides often explain that their reason for being our lifelong companions is to support us and do all they can to make our human experience as positive, meaningful, and loving as possible."

In Jan's book, she'd talked about getting information from her mother in video-like form—in her head. So I was curious as to how she communicated with Eia. "When you do this," I asked, "are you *hearing* her speaking, or do you *see words*, or . . . how does it work?"

"Sometimes I hear words, and sometimes it comes as a *concept*. That seems weird when I try to explain it, but sometimes you're just handed this ball of . . . a concept. And you *get* it! But then you have to sort out the *words* for it."

Huh! That reminded me very much of what Roger Ansanelli had described to me as *conclusive thought*.

"And sometimes Eia will make a reference to something that *I* understand, and say, 'Explain that to *them*.'" She laughed.

"It's like with a computer . . . she *downloads* it into you," I said, and she agreed.

"OK, before readings, I take twenty minutes or so to clear my mind and get a connection going," Jan said. "It's not uncommon that I get some concepts beforehand, too. I jotted down a few before you called. They may or may not connect to you. One of them referred to . . . I assume it would be *you*, as *an author*."

"That would be true," I said. The skeptical part of me—and yes, there still *was* one, especially when it came to new, untested practices and practitioners—had mixed feelings about that. Jan had my name and could easily have Googled me and found that I'd written some books. She and her book seemed decidedly sincere, so I doubted she'd done this, but of course it *was* possible.

"Also," she said, "I heard the word *general*. And then the name *Lee*. Possibly in connection to it. General Lee would be a Confederate. You're not a Southerner, are you?"

I told her that I wasn't, but that I'd gone to school in the South. I also told her that I had a friend named Lee, and that I'd been speaking to him a few days before.

"OK, so we don't know about that one, then. I also got: *Some concern about the fact that you are aging.* Is that you?"

I laughed. "That's *everybody*, isn't it?" But, I told her, a few days before, I *had* been talking to a friend about aging, and about younger men and older women. "It could be connected to that."

"Or, it could not be connected to you at all!" Jan said, self-effacingly. "OK, another thing was, an image of and the word *dragonfly*."

"Ah, that does have some meaning. I have a very close friend . . . *Dragonfly* is part of the name of her business, a name I actually helped her pick." I'd recently been in touch with her, too. Also, I told Jan, a few weeks before at the Shore, while walking on the boardwalk, I had found myself surrounded by a cloud of at least a dozen dragonflies—a very unusual occurrence, which had been quite memorable and magical.

"Then the last thing was the name *Tim*, connected to the idea of a husband's name. What I specifically got was: *husband Tim*."

"Ha! That *is* my *sister's husband's* name," I said. "I'm with him a lot."

"OK, well there weren't any *total* clunkers in there, then."

"No!" Everything she'd said had borne some relation to me. *Why those particular items?* I wondered. They seemed fairly random, but in a way, they could be seen as a brief survey of my conversations, thoughts, and interactions over the past few weeks.

She took a few deep breaths. "OK, Eia's already talking," she said. "Typically she starts by talking about you, in the third person. And here she goes. She says, 'Anne is an angel. She brings light and love into so many relationships around her that people welcome her into their lives and are very open about sharing their intimate emotions and experiences with her. She is an extraordinary listener and supporter, and even those who cannot see her, um, or, *cannot see it for themselves*, can sense that she has an extraordinary aura of light and goodness that pervades the space, and can enlighten, or *lighten'*—Eia says, 'Doesn't matter, either one—whole rooms when she enters.'"

"Oh my gosh. That's very flattering!" I said. I was almost embarrassed by the description, as I surely had my downsides too. Compliments aside, though, I had to admit that she had hit on something true: Of all my personal qualities, the most marked *was* probably my ability to listen and be a supportive friend—hence my father's "professional friend" comment.

"Thank you, Eia, that was beautiful," I said.

Jan continued. "She says, 'Anne is on a journey, a very enlightening and joyful *experiment* in reaching out beyond herself into the spirit world . . . ' Now she's waiting for me to describe the image she sent with that. It's of you reaching a hand out toward the Universe, or toward stars, and your hand and your arm are sort of glowing themselves."

Jumping Jupiter! I hadn't uttered a word to Jan about my project, nor was it written about anywhere online. And she'd even used the word *experiment*, the word I often used for my exploratory project myself.

Jan paused. "My brain is butting in here and saying, 'Is this a *hard* journey?' And Eia is saying, 'On the contrary. It's a journey of meaning and experience. It involves music.' She says, to *you* now, Anne, 'You are hearing'—in quotes—'*the music of the spheres.*' And she's doing this sound of what I would call an *angelic* kind of music."

Well—that was exactly what I'd been experiencing in my sessions with Roger Ansanelli, melodies from the angelic realms.

"She says, 'Yes, you're learning a great deal. But the heart of your journey is the joy of reconnecting to your sense of self-awareness. And by this I refer to your *true* self, not your *human* self . . . but the *spirit* who you really are.'"

Once again, I thought of what Roger Ansanelli had said: that my book, and my journey of writing it, were really about my *own evolution* more than anything else.

Jan paused. "Eia, is there anything else? She says, 'No. It's Anne's turn now.'"

I chuckled, as did Jan.

I told Jan about my project and my book-in-progress. She was surprised, and pleased that Eia had been so on the mark. Jan had written in her book that Eia was more of a counselor than a prognosticator, so I thought I'd ask about a conundrum I had, to see if she could offer some higher-dimensional perspective and advice. I'd recently made a friend who told me he had some psychic abilities. While I did not distrust him on that—I'd done a few tests with him, and he'd done extremely well—I felt he was making up some things he'd told me during an interview with him I'd conducted, things he supposedly was channeling about my past lives. My sense was that he was doing it in order to impress me. I hadn't confronted him about it, as I didn't want to embarrass him, but I wasn't sure whether to include that information in my book. It was interesting information, *if it was true*, but my gut said that it wasn't.

I wanted to see what Eia would come up with on her own, so, "I'd like to ask if she has any advice for me on my book" was all I said.

"Eia, you heard it! Any input?" Jan asked. She paused. "She says, 'You need to trust yourself more. You have very good instincts about what rings true—and what is bogus.'"

Yowza! Eia seemed to be reading my mind, or more likely my energy field, as I'd now learned.

"She says, 'You are able to immediately distinguish individual practitioners who are insincere. That characteristic is very much on your radar. But you also find yourself questioning some of the practitioners whom you have interviewed, and have at times had a certain level of . . . ' Let's see, what's the word? *'In-cred-ulity.'* She says, 'It is inevitable as a spirit works with a human conduit that there are levels of unintended, and sometimes *intended*, inaccuracies. My point is, trust your instinct on that.'"

Amazing! Eia had hit on my precise concern without my voicing it. Also, she knew that I was interviewing practitioners. That wasn't a given; Jan's book, for example, on the same basic topic, didn't include interviews with other practitioners at all. And of course, my concern about my friend's truthfulness *was* specifically connected with my experience of interviewing him, just as she'd said.

Having received such on-point and helpful advice, I decided to press for more. "I also wondered, as to the book's structure, if she had any thoughts about that."

"OK," Jan said. "Go ahead, Eia." She seemed to have to say those words to switch herself back to channeling mode. "She says, 'In some ways, your book is reminiscent of Jan's. Your decision to set it within the framework of your own personal experience and exploration is *brilliant*.'"

"Thank you!" I said. Again, very flattering, but that aside, I was impressed once more with Eia's accuracy. My book *was* very much like Jan's, a very personal account from a first-person perspective. I hadn't told Jan any of that.

"'Your reader is essentially in your shoes as you describe with honesty and openness the mysterious and surprising events that you wonder about, and then begin to explore,'" she said.

Again, Eia had totally hit the mark. I told this to Jan, who seemed pleased.

"Can she introduce me to any of my guides now?" I asked.

"OK, Eia. Hear that? Anne would like to know who she's got on her team." She paused. "Ha! This is really cute. She says, 'Oh, there's a wonderful fellow!' I've never heard her talk like that about a guide. She says, 'This is Anne's primary guide. He's a consummate gentleman.' That's a funny way to describe a guide, Eia! A *gentleman*? Then she says, 'What's the matter with *that*?'"

As I listened to Jan debating this way with Eia, I knew that many people would find it ludicrous, and possibly even question Jan's sanity. I can only say that, during this session and in numerous talks we later had, Jan was always supremely rational and intelligent, with a healthy sense of humor about this unusual second career she'd taken on in midlife.

"She says, 'This guide's name is *Wallace*, and he is the most loving, gentle individual . . . you could possibly call into your life. He has of course been with you since you came to this Earth incarnation. He is utterly supportive. He has brought you through, uh . . . one main danger or difficulty after another.'" Jan drew in a breath in surprise.

I understood that. To Jan, I probably seemed like a happy-go-lucky sort who hadn't had too many "dangers" to escape from. But to me, Eia's words made sense. I told Jan, briefly, about the sky horse, the Mack truck, the near mugging, and the times I'd accidentally set my hair on fire. I told her how I'd felt, each time I'd somehow come through miraculously unscathed, that I was getting help from some unseen entity. Had it been Wallace?

"She says, 'You can talk to Wallace yourself!'" Jan exclaimed.

I told her I'd love that, drawing in a breath now myself.

"OK, the general shape that I'm getting here is that he's strong. Kind of reminds me of a football player, but not pudgy. But just . . . *strength*. Of course, the physical description is just a way for them to portray themselves to us.

"OK, Wallace says, 'I'm so proud and so happy to be part of your life, and that you invited me to be your guide before you . . . departed on this adventure.'"

I got chills. The word *adventure* was a crucial word for me in the writing of my book. I'd already decided to structure the book in terms of my various "adventures" exploring different topics and phenomena. Each chapter would be titled using the word. Jan had no idea of that.

Jan continued. "He says, 'I'm not the only guide who has been watching your project with interest. You have a writing guide—*Celeste*—whose goal is to aid you in the narrative of your story, and she is very excited about this project. I chose her and called her in to help you in this way.'

"OK," Jan asked then, a question in her voice. "Now, who says that? OK, *somebody* is suggesting, and I'm not sure if this is Wallace or Celeste or another guide, but somebody who's interested in your project is saying that you should interview . . . magicians."

"*Hahaha!* I actually *have*! I've interviewed two magician friends. They're brilliant magicians called Matt and Prakash."

Matt and Prakash performed feats of mentalism in their act, I explained, and I'd talked to them about that, and about the possible existence of psychic abilities. For the record, based on their own experiences, they said that they didn't believe in them.

"Why are they saying that?" I asked. "I had my own reasons for doing it, but . . ."

"OK, this is Celeste. She looks like a pretty little blond-haired angel figure," Jan told me. "She says, 'There are many reasons for including magicians in the telling of your explorations. The first is that many people have experience with them who do not have experience with spirit communication, so it provides a bridge for their understanding. Another rationale is that many people know of the . . . Great Randi . . .'"

"Oh, my gosh, he's a big figure on my radar, for sure—James Randi, the *Amazing* Randi. Do you know who that is?" I asked.

Jan said she didn't know his real name, but had heard of him. She continued.

"She says, 'For many people who are skeptics or on the edge of skepticism, they immediately think of magicians as debunkers . . . with the Great Randi in mind. And so that is linked in people's minds, and it would be appropriate to address that. And you know, magicians are not immune from belief in the spirit world,' she says."

I agreed. I knew Houdini had been interested in the spirit world, and attended many séances, hoping to contact spirits, although he'd famously been a debunker, too.

"You know, I'm hearing the name *Frank*, now. I think this is from Celeste."

"That's a good friend of mine, I call him Frankie! He's a writer too," I said. "A comedy writer. He's also in my book, as a sort of skeptical Greek Chorus. And actually . . . this is funny, now that I think of it . . . he's my connection to the magicians, Matt and Prakash!"

I asked if Celeste was saying anything about Frankie in particular, and Jan said no, that she seemed to just be calling my attention to a good friend.

"Well, he is that," I said. "I was just speaking to him. His birthday is next week, and I want to take him out."

Once again, nothing Celeste had picked up was off the mark. Time was running short, so I thanked Celeste and Wallace, and said I hoped to speak with them again.

Of course, I couldn't let a reading end without asking about my love life. Since Sam had gotten his new place, I'd seen him a few times. I was trying to enjoy the moment and manifest that positive future for us that Rev. Kev had seen. But at the same time, I had to brace myself. I knew that, having run so many times, Sam would likely run again.

"I'd like to ask Eia if she has any wisdom about my love life, or lack thereof," was all I said.

Jan giggled. "I can relate to that." She paused. "Eia says, 'Anne is a very lucky girl. She has a very fun love in her life right now. This is a fellow who, while he, at this point in their relationship, is not . . . uh . . . wholeheartedly committed for life to the connection, still he is open and . . .' I think the word is . . . '*reverent* and kind to you.' OK, this part's without words, so I'll describe it to you. She's showing him as being kind of a joker and somebody who's really a positive, upbeat person."

I was impressed at the accuracy of this, especially since basically I'd just said to Jan that I *had* no love life. As for Sam's being positive and upbeat, it was true, except when it came to his fears about us.

"OK, now Eia is saying, 'Anne, what's your question?'"

"My question is, right before Christmas, he—his name is Sam—completely disappeared. It hurt a lot, but I felt it was all about fear. Just recently, we got back in touch. I would love if we could really resume things but . . ."

Jan paused briefly. "OK," she said. "Is he *thirty-six*?"

"*Yes!!!*" I was floored. "He had a birthday *two days ago*, and turned thirty-six!" I hadn't seen Sam on his birthday, but we'd talked by phone. I'd had to roll my eyes a bit as he'd described a drinking game going on in his living room, among his twenty-something roommates.

"You know, Sam, you're a very *young* thirty-six," I'd said.

"Thank you!" he'd replied. And I'd laughed; I hadn't really meant it as a compliment. Still, that youthful spirit was a big part of what I enjoyed about Sam.

But I didn't tell Jan any of that. "His age—was that from Eia?" I asked.

Jan told me she'd just gotten the feeling of me being older, and then had seen two "big round, fat numbers" right in front of her. Interesting, again, that she picked up on me being older, especially as I hadn't told her my own age.

Jan went on. "She says, 'There's no doubt the relationship scared him. Sam has the self-concept of a younger person; he still sees himself as about *twenty-four*, and cherishes that youthful sense he has in his approach to life. So, yes, he is a little scared. When he's with you, because of your age difference, he perceives himself as self-censoring to be more serious, and that rattles him a bit. And he is so attached to his youthful . . . self-perception . . . that simply growing older is a bit of a shock to his system. He clearly likes you and adores the fun and crazy things you talk about and share; he enjoys the intellectual company. But you will find him attempting to bring more'—Eia's laughing now—'juvenile antics into your relationship.'"

True, I told her. But I wished he wouldn't feel the need to censor himself.

"'It's really a huge compliment, because it's an indication that he values your relationship for more than . . . a keg and a one night stand.' She's saying that 'you represent to him the maturity that he possesses, but is not quite ready to own yet.'"

I laughed. But I had to ask: "Does Eia think he can ever overcome his fears, so we can have a real relationship?"

"What about that, Eia?" Jan asked. "She says, 'Yeah, he's open to maintaining a relationship with you, and it will naturally evolve into a more mature one. Whether that ultimately leads to you two becoming long-term partners remains to be seen. He's sensing his own . . . *maturity* creeping up on him, and is beginning to see the value of embracing that, but at the moment, he's still holding it off with one hand.'"

"With one hand . . . and with a pint of beer or a joint in the other," I added.

"She didn't put that in the picture," Jan said, laughing.

"Oh, believe me, it's there!"

"Eia says, 'Sam is very sensitized to the fact that you are nearby and that you two are in contact again. She says, 'Don't push things, but he'll definitely be open to spending time with you, in friendship or in . . . hanky-panky.' That's funny, I've never heard her speak so colloquially before."

It was funny to *me* that Eia had used the term *hanky-panky*, an uncommon, old-fashioned term that I often used myself.

"She says, 'You know, dear . . . you are a person who truly thrives on having her own freedom, and relationships do bring trade-offs."

She's giving me one of those thoughts I'm supposed to explain. Do you know the 'Spenser' detective books by Robert Parker? Spenser's sort of an *intellectual* tough guy, with a heart of gold. His girlfriend is a therapist, and they each have their own house, but it's a totally committed relationship."

"Perfect!" I said. "Is she saying that she sees something like that for me?"

"She says, 'Anne got it. In many ways that would be ideal for Anne, who is, um, both an intellectual and a very independent soul. To share in a committed relationship without giving up her freedom would be a development . . . fervently . . . to be desired.' She's telling me that you have the power to bring in that kind of relationship again. But basically, she's not gonna give you any names or places."

Well, fair enough. Jan *had* said that Eia wasn't a prognosticator. But her words buoyed my spirits—so to speak.

Jan and I chatted a bit longer, and then I thanked her, and Eia, for a truly dazzling experience, and we said our good-byes. After I hung up, I sat a while, absorbing it all. Had I actually just met two of my spirit guides? Had Wallace truly had my back in all those close-call situations? Was he really a spirit BFF, whom I'd asked to be my guide, on a soul level, before I was born? And was Celeste really helping me with my writing, without my being aware of it?

If it was all to be believed, I was indeed acquiring—or at least becoming aware of—a new family, *a family in other realms*, just as Patricia Masters had once said. And, too, I was acquiring a new family in the gifted practitioners I was meeting—which was especially gratifying as, more and more, my own family was concluding that I was seriously off my trolley.

It was fascinating to meet Jan, who, like my friend Katarina, had awakened to her gifts in midlife—and unlike Katarina, had pursued them. I found it inspiring. I wondered if it was possible I might ever experience such a dramatic increase in my own intuitive abilities. Now *that* would be an adventure!

Jan's Midwestern life and mine couldn't have been more different in many ways, but I'd felt a surprising kinship with her, an ease, and a sense of great familiarity. I was thrilled when she invited me to call her anytime to chat about things metaphysical, and I planned to take her up on it. If Christina Wright and I had been nuns together in the South of France, I was pretty sure Jan had been there too, laughing and crunching away on those contraband apples with us.

Maybe I was imagining it, of course. But the next day, I was talking by phone again to Christina, and I mentioned my reading with Jan. She said, almost nonchalantly, without any prodding from me, that Jan had been "one of us" sisters too!

Huh! I thought, wondering if Jan would prove to have some sort of "apple connection"; Christina had told me, back when we'd first spoken about it, that the former sisters she'd met again in this lifetime always seemed to have one.

And so, Dear Reader, imagine my delight when I called to get Jan's address to send her a check—which I'd forgotten to do the day of the reading—and she said that she lived on Apple Lane.

13

ADVENTURES WITH
GUIDES
✳ OR ✳

Help, I Need Somebody . . .

FROM GUIDANCE COUNSELORS TO MENTORS TO BODYGUARDS, we often turn to those with more experience, more connections, or bigger pecs when the situation warrants it.

Having been introduced by Eia to my spirit guides Wallace and Celeste, I was curious to learn more about these higher-dimensional beings we apparently had working on our behalf. I did a little online research and then ordered *Ask Your Guides* by Sonia Choquette, as I'd read and greatly enjoyed a few of her other books.

Ask Your Guides, as it turned out, was actually to a large extent about angels, too. The book talked about guardian angels, saying we all had them, that they were with us as our "personal bodyguards" from birth—or perhaps even conception—onward, and escorted us to the Other Side when we died. She said that angels were the only types of spirits helping us humans who could actually materialize here on Earth, which they often did to help and protect us. *Ah,* I thought. So guides stayed put wherever it was that spirits hung out, whereas angels could walk among us . . . as they had in Lorna Byrne's book *Angels in My Hair.* "Although you only have one guardian angel," Choquette wrote, "it can reveal itself in any number of costumes, at any age, and in all shapes and skin colors. You see, contrary to popular belief, guardian angels don't necessarily appear with silver, flowing robes, or flaxen hair—sometimes they look like homeless people or rock stars."

Homeless people. I remembered the homeless man who'd handed me that newspaper I'd been seeking, telling me he was my guardian angel, outside a deli, many years before.

I delved further into the book, learning about archangels, the head honchos of the angelic realm, who apparently packed the biggest punch, and the "ministry of angels," who could aid us with all our needs—from finding a parking space to fixing a computer to finding the perfect pair of party shoes—if we simply called on them for help. In fact, Choquette wrote, angels *wanted* us to call on them; they were sensitive, and got frustrated when we ignored them. Well, funny as this sounded, I'd heard it said before: Lorna Byrne had written that there were a great many "unemployed" angels these days, because no one was utilizing them, and how frustrating that was for them. Similarly, Roger Ansanelli had declared in our class one night, referring to the angels who often popped in on him for a chat, "They're saying you all don't ask for enough. There's too much *down time* on that side. It's their pleasure and delight to help us!"

"Remember that you can live a charmed life if you simply allow it to be that way," Choquette wrote.

Despite the session I'd had with Jan and Eia, and meeting my guides in a way that seemed quite convincing, all of this *still* seemed a little bit fantastic to me. And a little too . . . easy. But again, was this just because of the way that our culture had taught us to think? I *had* been experiencing a "charmed life" in some ways lately. Whatever I needed to continue my exploratory project had materialized just when I needed it. I'd been told, without asking, by a number of psychics, that this was because I had so much support and assistance from beings in other realms. As Christina Wright had put it when she'd pulled a card that accurately showed my current financial struggles and assured me that things would soon improve, "The guides are not going to pull the rug out from under you, sweetie, because you're doing *their* work too. It's your journey, and you chose certain challenges to experience here, but they're gonna support you."

Well, as I'd often found myself thinking throughout my explorations, if I *did* have such help available to me—if perhaps we *all* did—how big a fool would I be not to try to take advantage of it? And what was the risk in trying?

A while back, I'd been told by several of my Team members that my dear friend David was now serving as one of my guides. Maggie Moise, whom I'd asked to try to contact David after he'd died, had told me that he was helping me "to a degree I couldn't even imagine" with my project. "I know psychics always say that, like, 'Oh, you have guides on the Other Side helping you out.' But you really, specifically, *do* in David. He's your fairy godmother," she said, which made me chuckle because David, who wasn't gay but often joked that he *should've* been, because of his fondness for opera, musical theater, and John Waters movies, would no doubt have embraced that title with his usual great good humor. I hoped that, somewhere, he was.

Edward Ragosta agreed. When I asked him about David once, giving only his first name, he had said, with surprising firmness, "You really should dedicate the book to him. Or at least, include him in the dedication. Because he's helping you with it *a lot*." Well, I likely would have done that anyway, as he'd been one of my dearest friends, and I missed him so much, but it was great to have Edward affirm so strongly what Maggie had also said.

If David *was* helping me with the book, it made perfect sense. After all, David had been a writer and editor, and several times my boss—none of which I'd told Maggie or Edward. It seemed fitting to me that he'd be continuing to wield his red pen—or celestial editing software—from wherever it was he was hanging out these days.

After being told a few times that David was my guide, I started concocting little experiments to test this out. "David," I said one morning, "if you're there, show me, by day's end, an image of a piano." I'd chosen a piano because, after David had died, I'd had that memorable experience involving the upright piano in his mother's living room, which Maggie Moise had picked up on.

All day, the day of my test, I kept my eyes open, but no piano. That evening, I took a lovely Latvian dancer/choreographer friend of mine, Vija Vetra, out to eat at a Greek diner. I knew there was no piano there, nor did I hope to see one on our walk through the streets of Greenwich Village, so I figured, a bit disappointed, that my test hadn't worked; the day was almost through. But then at dinner, my friend Vija whipped out some photos of her students' recent dance concert in Latvia. There it was, in photo after photo: *a black, upright piano.*

Huzzah! I nearly knocked over my glass of wine craning across the table toward her to see it. Vija didn't understand my excitement, of course, so I tried to explain it, as I knew she was very open to the spiritual world and had had some remarkable otherworldly experiences of her own. She was pleased to have played a part in some way in bringing me the affirmation I was seeking.

How had she known to bring those photos? I wondered. Had David somehow arranged things so that they lay in her line of vision as she dressed for dinner? Could he do such a thing, the way, perhaps, spirits could manipulate butterflies or birds, energetically?

Of course, it could have been a big, fat coincidence. So I decided to try it again.

I asked David to show me, within the next twenty-four hours, a trombone, the instrument he'd played in school and in extracurricular bands and orchestras up through college. I was heading out for a weekend at the Shore, where trombones are normally not lurking about. I would have no TV out there, nor did I usually read newspapers or magazines, so I knew I was posing him quite a challenge. Indeed, the day went by, and no trombone. That night, I visited my friend Deirdre, and *she* suggested we watch a "movie on demand" on her huge, flat-screen TV, not something we often had done. I suggested a movie I'd never seen called *Ruby Sparks*, but a few minutes into it, there was some odd, static-like interference; the picture kept breaking up and skipping, much to Deirdre's surprise, as she'd not experienced this with her set before, until finally we gave up. Deirdre then suggested *Hyde Park on Hudson*, starring Bill Murray, and I agreed. I'd never seen it, either, and was a big fan of Murray's work. Not too far into the movie was an outdoor scene in a park in which a band was playing, and in it—insert fist pump here—*a man playing a trombone*!

Reader, I had to wonder: Had David somehow created the interference, monkeying around with the electricity, to guide us to a different film containing a trombone? Because the next night, I watched *Ruby Sparks*, and it did not contain one. But even if David *had* monkeyed with the energy to cause us to choose another movie, how could he know which movie Deirdre would choose? And what if she had not had that movie at hand? What if she'd had no movie that contained an image of a trombone? Would he have somehow jumped me to another reality where, as Rev. Kev had explained, the possibility of us seeing a trombone would have been more probable? What, exactly, *could* and *couldn't* a spirit do? I needed a field guide to spirit guides.

Now that David had passed my tests with flying colors, I decided to try it with Wallace. It felt weirder to me, asking to do a test with a spirit who hadn't been someone I'd known as a human—much more abstract. Still, Eia had said I'd chosen him as one of my particular spirit guides. Obviously, I'd known him very well in some other life or dimension. So if *any* spirit was there to help me—wherever the heck *there* was—I supposed it would be Wallace.

Still out at the Shore a few days hence, I took a long walk along the shoreline, picking up sea glass, sand dollars, and snail shells—my favorite shells, with their magical spiral pattern—marveling at the seagulls as they uniformly gazed, in clusters, out to sea, and chuckling at the quick-stepping sandpipers, who always reminded me of little wind-up toys. I thought about what I'd ask Wallace to manifest. A few weeks earlier, Griffin had emailed me about a song by the band REM. He knew about my explorations, though he didn't know that I'd actually begun accumulating song lyrics referencing the various topics I was writing about. I wanted to use them, if the cost wasn't too prohibitive (as alas, Reader, it proved to be), as epigraphs at the start of each of my book's chapters, but I needed more of them to make it work. Griffin had written simply that he'd heard the song, and that it had made him think of me, and sent a YouTube link so I could listen. Called "The Great Beyond," the REM tune was bouncy and catchy, and I loved the lyrics about looking for answers—after all, these days, that's what I was all about. As I waded into the gently rolling shallow water, the idea of these types of songs, about "esoteric" or woo-woo topics, came into my head, and I mentally asked Wallace to send me some.

A little more than an hour later, back at my brother's house and settled with my laptop on the now fully refurbished porch, I checked my email and saw that my friend Toni, an old writing-group pal who had no idea I was looking for songs about metaphysical topics, had sent me a link to a *New York Times* article. Entitled "Spiritual Seeker's Quest, from Blondie to Swedenborg," it was about a man named Gary Lachman, now a religion writer, who, as Gary Valentine, had been the bassist for the band Blondie. Apparently, at the time that he'd been with Blondie, Lachman had become fascinated with the occult, writing several songs about it. One of them, "(I'm Always Touched by Your) Presence, Dear," which appeared on Blondie's album *Plastic Letters*, was cited as an example. To quote Lachman in the *Times* article, "I think it's the only hit song about telepathy."

Astonished, I went to YouTube and looked up the song. There was Debbie Harry, circa 1978, in a fire-engine-red minidress, rocking out with her band to the catchy beat. Then I Googled the lyrics, which were clever, referencing "psychic frequencies" and "outer entities." It totally fit the bill.

Well, when you're hot you're hot, and Wallace, it appeared, was *smokin'*! It inspired me to try again. To produce an email with a song recommendation was one thing; like the image of the trombone in the FDR movie, it was something somewhat intangible. To produce a *physical object*, though, would be quite another.

"OK, Wallace," I said—on a Tuesday, as it happened—"if you're really there, send me a sign in the form of a *bill*, a one, a five, a ten, a twenty . . . or heck, a hundred! Whatever you can do." I'd found money on the street before, of course, but it was usually coins, and even so, far from a regular occurrence. By Friday I was back in the city, and no bills had materialized, so I was about to write off this particular experiment as a flop. But on Saturday, as I was crossing a midtown Manhattan street, what should blow into my path but a slightly worn *one-dollar bill*? I pocketed it, noting that Wallace, if indeed he had sent it, was, to put it nicely, frugal.

Well, I hadn't specified, had I? I decided to try it again.

"OK, Wallace. This time, please send me *twenty*. Either a twenty-dollar bill, or, well, just *twenty dollars*. However you can do it." I decided to give him a little leeway this go-round. After all, how easy could it be to manifest a twenty-dollar bill on Manhattan's streets? Even if Wallace *could* do it, New Yorkers being New Yorkers, and times being what they were, someone else would likely edge me out and snatch it up first.

I happened to see my friend Frankie that evening at a friend's birthday party held in a Flatiron District restaurant, and I told him about my latest endeavor.

"You have a ghost that can produce bills out of thin air?" he said. "Give him my address! Tell him I accept Susan B. Anthony dollars and Krugerrands, too, if that makes it any easier." He snickered.

"Not a *ghost*," I corrected him. "A *spirit* guide. *My* spirit guide."

He sipped through a straw from his large goblet of ginger ale. "OK, so tell me this," he said, affectionately poking my arm. "If people have spirits who can help them do anything, why not just ask them to pick the upcoming Powerball numbers and cash in?"

"Good question," I said. "But actually, I *do* think lots of people feel that 'spirit,' in whatever form, has helped them to get all kinds of things. I mean, look at all those Oscar winners who thank God or Jesus in their speeches for their success."

He gave his now nearly empty glass of ginger ale a loud, obnoxious slurp.

Anyway," I said, "what harm is there in asking your spirit guides for help? How else can you find out if it works?"

"I'd sooner eat marked-down sushi!" he gleefully responded. "I'd sooner eat a Hudson River trout! I'd sooner ask an Indian guy to recommend a steakhouse . . ."

Luckily, just then, the birthday cake arrived, or I'm sure Frankie'd still be there ad-libbing.

My uber-skeptical friend's joyful mockery notwithstanding, I continued to keep my eyes peeled for twenty-dollar bills or windfalls the equivalent thereof. But two days passed with no sign of either. On the third day, I treated myself to breakfast at my favorite Village café, the now sadly departed Sweet Revenge, reading a book about Houdini and his friendship with writer Arthur Conan Doyle, creator of Sherlock Holmes, and a member of the British Society for Psychical Research with an avid interest in Spiritualism, as I ate. Afterward, when my waitress put through my credit card, I was startled and a bit embarrassed to find it refused. The card was all paid up, with no balance, so I wondered what was going on. As I fished in my wallet for another card, not having enough cash on hand to cover my bill, a young man waiting to order who'd overheard what had transpired whipped out his Visa card.

Gesturing toward my bill for the breakfast, he waved his card at the waitress. "Put that on here. And a large coffee, for me, please, to go," he said.

"*What?*" I looked at him in surprise. He was impeccably groomed and dressed in what looked like an expensive, even bespoke, business suit and cool, mirrored aviator shades, but couldn't have been more than twenty-five.

My waitress looked equally surprised. "What?" she echoed.

"Put *her* bill on *this*," he repeated, handing her his card.

I looked him fully in the face, or as fully as I could, given his mirrored shades, which of course simply reflected my own image back. "That's so kind. But are you sure? It's *not* inexpensive!" Probably about ten times the cost of his coffee, I thought.

"I'm sure," he said.

"Thank you," I said. "Wow. And they say New Yorkers aren't friendly."

He smiled as the waitress handed him the slip to sign.

"I hope it comes back to you," I said, extending my hand. "I'm Anne."

"Graham," he said, and shook it.

"Well, Graham, today you're my guardian angel. Thanks again."

Once he'd signed the slip, received his coffee to go, and left, I realized I wasn't sure whether he'd added a tip. Probably he had, I surmised, as there was always a blank space on credit-card slips for writing a gratuity in. Still, I didn't want to take a chance on stiffing the waitress, so I found a few singles in my wallet and left them on the counter.

As I stepped out onto the sidewalk, I felt elated, and then positively giddy as it hit me: My bill, I realized, if one *were* to add a 20 percent tip, as I normally did, would come to twenty and change. If the kind young stranger had added in a tip, as he likely had, being the generous soul he obviously was, *there was my twenty dollars!*

Was it merely a coincidence? Or had he somehow been Wallace incarnate? Or an angel *sent* by him to do this errand—being that spirits apparently couldn't walk among us as angels apparently *could*, and angels being messengers and all. So maybe the guy *had* looked more like one of the "Men in Black" than an angel. But the next time I tried that credit card—with no call to the fraud division, no reactivation request made—it worked just fine.

I decided to test out my angels specifically too. Sonia Choquette had said in her book that the angels of ministry liked to bestow presents. Sometimes she asked them to surprise her with gifts—which they evidently did. Well, lacking a man in my life to do it, this sounded good to me. "Dearest angels of ministry," I said aloud one morning, "please surprise and delight me today with many gifts," thinking as I often did these days what a good thing it was that I lived alone.

I'd received an invitation to the Upper West Side home of my former writing-group teacher and her husband for her birthday celebration that evening. When I arrived at her penthouse apartment, she ushered me into her bedroom to try on various items of clothing she could no longer use, including a beautiful, soft-black leather jacket. I'd never owned a leather jacket before, though lately I'd had the yen for one. To my great surprise, because she was a good deal smaller than me in frame and height, it fit nicely. The other item was a pretty tunic top, which fit too. It had been *her* birthday, but I'd made out like a bandit.

And it wasn't over. That same night, I slept at the nearby apartment of my friend Bonnie, who'd also attended the party, and whose brother had seen the ghost of their Uncle Rudy on the farm. She sent me home the next day with a stack of books she no longer had room for on subjects that I was writing about, from kundalini to the science-spirituality bond. Truly an *abbondanza*!

That night I lay in bed, considering all that had happened. Had I really had such resources, such high-level helpers to call upon, at my fingertips and been ignorant of them my whole life? My test results had been quite powerful.

Of course, this begged a new question to be explored: Were there times when these tests *didn't* work? My sporadic experimenting over the course of several weeks had revealed that there were. But more often than not, Reader, they did. And often in such startling ways.

Did the fact that my tests at times didn't work mean that guides and angels didn't exist? Who could say? If they *did* exist, did that necessarily mean that they were obliged to help me each and every time I asked? What was in their job description, when they took on one of us hapless humans, and how many humans might a guide or angel take on? And just because they might be functioning at a higher level of consciousness, did it mean they didn't have their own limits, as we humans did? Or was there more to this than that? Were certain requests denied for other reasons? Karma? Lessons to be learned? Contracts to be fulfilled? Unforeseen and unwanted outcomes, even, to be avoided? Perhaps what we asked for might not always be in our best interest. If so, would our helpers step in to ensure that certain things we wished for might *not* be delivered?

Who could say?

One thing was certain, though: My experiments had inspired me to attempt to make better use of the guides and angels that might be available to me.

Yet even that thought prompted still more questions! If so many helpers were truly on tap, and eager to lend their assistance, why had they never let me know they were there? Was it one of those *Wizard of Oz* scenarios, where, like Dorothy, I had to "find them for myself"? And if so, *why?*

My questions were, as usual, never-ending. But that just meant I had more exploring to do. I obviously never minded that.

And now I could do it dressed in leather.

14

ADVENTURES IN
PSYCHIC DEVELOPMENT
✳ OR ✳

Sense and Sensitivity

I GREW UP ENVYING PEOPLE WITH ESP, THINKING THAT THEY were special; gifted; unique. It was as if they breathed some rare, exotic air that the rest of us did not, and I wanted, more than anything, to walk among them, inhaling those heady, esoteric ethers too.

If you ask professional psychics, though, to talk about their intuitive abilities—and believe me, I have—they will very likely tell you that *all of us* are psychically gifted. But just the way some of us hit the world with more of whatever it takes to break dance, dunk a basketball, belt out a show tune, crack computer code, or write in iambic pentameter, they will say, some of us are simply born with a more *developed* psychic sense than others. They'll point out examples of things that happen to most of us once in a while: knowing who's calling before answering a phone, say, or thinking of our childhood friend Buki from Camp Babawawa, only to have him pop up on *America's Funniest Home Videos* hours hence. They'll also tell you that, were you to attempt to develop your own intuitive ability, with training and practice you'd likely soon find it noticeably improved.

After embarking on my explorations, I heard from a number of my Dream Team members that I possessed very good psychic skills. While hearing it always thrilled me, I often found myself questioning it too. It wasn't exactly that I didn't believe my Team members, but back when I'd been a child, pointedly experimenting with my ESP cards, I hadn't, to my dismay, seemed to possess any extrasensory smarts at all. Granted, that had been many years back. And perhaps those cards had not tested my particular *type* of psychic gifts. But I certainly hadn't ever experienced any kind of regular, daily, spot-on intuition.

I *had* frequently had that sense that I could feel other people's feelings. And I'd had sporadic "psychic flashes" with phone calls and such, and even a few more surprising things. I'd once had a distinct sensation, out of the blue, that a friend of mine who was single at the time was pregnant, only to find out within days that, quite unexpectedly, she was. Another time, I had a "feeling" a friend had whitewashed a brick hearth in her living room; the next day I visited and found that indeed she'd done it, though she'd never mentioned the idea to me.

And then there was one more incident that had really knocked me out. As I was heading down the steps of my apartment building one afternoon to get my mail, I had a flash that a friend who lived halfway across the country, with whom I'd not been in touch for many months, had sent me a letter, and that inside that letter was a check. A little backstory here: My friend had married a man whose father had made a fortune, so she and her husband had come into a goodly chunk of change. I, on the other hand, was constantly struggling financially, laid off from one job after another. While my friend and her husband were generous people who'd hosted and entertained me in numerous ways, they'd never sent me a check, nor in any manner flung any actual cash my way—nor would I ever have expected it. When I got to the mailbox that day, though, there was a letter from that very friend, with a very generous check inside from her and her husband—far beyond any monetary gift I'd ever received.

I stood there holding the check for a minute or two, turning it over and over in my hand as if expecting it to "poof" out of existence, or turn into a pumpkin like Cinderella's coach at the stroke of midnight—or, given its size and shape, perhaps a summer squash. I was truly having trouble processing what had just occurred. Once I did, though, I felt a sparkly glow of delight course through me, not just because of the unanticipated new stash of cash, or the kindness and generosity of my friends, but because I'd somehow managed to "see" it! Or "feel" it. Or whatever it was I'd done.

Of course, the Jiminy Cricket part of my science-trained brain had to question it too. Short of using terms like *psychic* or *intuitive*, how could one explain an experience like that?

At the time, I had posed the question to my youngest brother, whose work dealt with probabilities, or odds, when we were both visiting at my mother's house one day. "Think about how many times you've had a thought like that, and it didn't happen. Probably thousands of times, right? So, this is just the one time in a thousand, or whatever, when it did," he said, in his supremely logical way, with a bit of a grin for good measure.

Well, I took his point. But actually, I *didn't* have thousands of thoughts like that. I did find myself *wishing*, now and then, for money, along with all sorts of other things: a bacon-lettuce-and-tomato sandwich, skinny jeans that allowed for hips, Johnny Depp in my Christmas stocking. However, this wasn't a wish. It was just a very precise and clear impression, a *knowing*, if you will—sudden and direct.

But assuming these several incidents *were* psychic in nature, they were still just that: several—a small handful in a rather lengthy life.

And yet, was it possible that I possessed a reservoir of something I was simply not yet tapping into? I found myself wondering about this one afternoon, back in my Village apartment. After all, I mused, Katarina hadn't really been aware of *her* gift until Patricia Masters had called her attention to it and told her to start practicing. Nor had Janet Alm been aware of her abilities until her deceased mother started chatting with her in her head.

I'd finished up my tests with my angels and guides, which had proved quite satisfying, and I hadn't signed up for any classes or workshops, and had no interviews with practitioners slated. Sam had been very busy with some new commissioned projects, and I was still trying to remain laid-back, to let him take the lead, and give him his space . . . and then some. And so, with a lull in my often jam-packed schedule, and intrigued by my Team's belief in my potential abilities, I decided to look for a book about developing one's intuition.

Never finding book-browsing as effective or enjoyable online as it was in person, I headed to my local Barnes & Noble—one of the few, alas, left in Manhattan, Reader—and found *Practical Intuition*, written by Laura Day. I liked the title, so I pulled it off the shelf, opened it, and read the Introduction by actress Demi Moore. Intrigued, I purchased it, thinking how thrilled my childhood self would have been with the mere existence of such a guidebook, and was soon settled into my threadbare armchair, ready to learn, as the back cover put it, to "unlock the remarkable power of (my) mind."

Over the next few weeks, I worked with Day's book. It contained exercises designed to help the reader develop his or her intuition—which, Day said, all of us were born with and unwittingly used all the time—"to bring the unconscious data it supplies to a place where your conscious mind can interpret it." This, she said, took "work and guidance."

The exercises were easy and fun. Many had to do with paying attention to my sensory impressions—what I was seeing, feeling, hearing, smelling, etc.—and then noticing what I was noticing. Because, "Just what if," Day asked, "you notice what you notice *for a reason?*" According to Day, everything we noticed had significance. Therefore, everything we noticed could be interpreted, and had "an application and a meaning in the future." Further, she asserted, *our subconscious mind actually directed us to those things that we noticed*; out of the ever-changing mass of information constantly bobbing and swirling around us, it plucked out what was important and called our attention to it. In other words, our subconscious was supplying us with answers all the time in the form of the information we registered. "The trick," she said, "is knowing what question the information is answering."

So, we constantly got the answers, but had to figure out the questions? Life as a sort of marathon episode of the TV game show *Jeopardy?* It was a provocative notion. In fact, I thought, the *subconscious* was *in itself* a provocative notion. I Googled it and found that the term *subconscious* was defined by Wikipedia as "a reservoir of material that was once conscious but has been forgotten or suppressed in the mind." This reservoir was thought to be accessible via dreams and hypnosis. Sometimes things leaked out of it when we least expected it— hence the term *Freudian slip*—usually things that were embarrassing, because they revealed true feelings we dared not express. In this sense, it was as if the subconscious was trying to "out" who we really were, or at least trying to clue us in about ourselves.

So, if what Day was saying was true, was our subconscious also continually trying to clue us in about things in our lives and the world around us?

A bit more than halfway through the book, Day mentioned that she'd successfully used her intuition to pick racehorses—and that all of us could do so too. My skeptical friend Frankie had often asked me why psychics couldn't pick winning LOTTO numbers; Day noted that, while she wasn't good enough to pick a winning lottery number *yet*, she was sure it could be done.

I brought the book with me while paying a visit to my mother. Sprawled on her living room couch reading as she worked at the *Times* crossword nearby in her recliner, I came upon an intriguing exercise. The author wrote that, a few pages ahead, we'd find a list of nine horses running in an imaginary horse race. Asking us to use *only our intuition,* she instructed us, *without looking at that list,* to write down our impressions of the name of the winning horse.

So here at Day Raceway, we weren't even getting the usual roster of horse names to *choose* from, which would be challenging enough;
we were starting from—no pun intended—*scratch*! What were the
chances? Glancing over at my mom, I thought of my Sicilian grandfather, Sal—her father—who'd spent many an afternoon at the OTB,
as Jennifer Hicks had pinpointed in our message circle, wondering if
I might have inherited some of his horse-picking genes. Then again,
poor Grandpa rarely won.

Aided by Day's techniques, I scribbled down the images that came
to me as horse names on a yellow legal pad. *(Gentle Reader, please note
that, so as not to spoil this exercise for those of you who have not yet read this
fantastic book and tried it for yourself, I've changed the names of the horses.
I have done my best to retain the essence of the way I received the images
involved. And for all of you who HAVEN'T yet read it, I'd recommend
you stop right here, gallop on over to your nearest real or virtual bookstore,
and grab yourself a copy!)*

After I'd written about a dozen horse names, I looked over my list.
Halfway down, I'd written the name *Silver Skates*. What I'd actually
gotten was an image of a girl with her feet clad in an old-fashioned
pair of ice skates—the kind you might see in an illustration of Hans
Brinker in the famous book by Mary Mapes Dodge, with blades that
turned up at the toes—gliding over glittering ice. I couldn't imagine
a horse being named *Girl in Old-Fashioned Ice Skates with Turned-Up
Toes Gliding Over Glittering Ice*, so *Silver Skates* it was. Something
pulled my pen to that name now, so for better or worse, I circled it as
my guess. I was pretty sure it would be for worse. The odds against my
guessing the name of any horse on Day's list seemed astronomically
high.

I then turned to the page that listed the nine horses—in no particular order—and Reader, as with that check in my mailbox from my generous friends, I couldn't believe my eyes! I'd gotten the *exact* name of

the eighth horse: *Silver Skates*! Funny enough, the name of the seventh horse, listed just above it, was *Glitter Girl*. It was as though I'd merged the two in my mind.

Next, Day instructed us to choose the name that most closely matched our impressions—so I went with *Silver Skates*—and then turned to another page for the names of the three actual winners. *Silver Skates* was not among them. *Glitter Girl*, however, was the "place," or second-running, horse! I was truly shocked.

"Almost all those who do this exercise are startled by how accurate their intuitions were . . ."Day wrote. *I'll say*, I thought.

Attempting to be a good investigative reporter, I launched myself off the couch and texted my youngest brother, the one who knew about odds, and asked him what the chances were of my coming up with any exact name on Day's list. He quickly wrote back that, as far as he knew, there was really no way to tell.

A few days later, I told my older brother, who happened to be visiting our mother with his girlfriend, about the exercise too. In his typical taking-the-wind-out-of-my-sails fashion, he said that the name must have been *subliminally embedded* in the book—an idea that had never even occurred to me. I knew about subliminal messaging in advertising —hidden symbols or information embedded in images, designed to appeal emotionally to the consumer. For example, an image in an ad for a brand of scotch might, if flipped on its side, resemble a nubile young woman with a come-hither look. I supposed that subliminal messages could also be inserted into the pages of a text-only book. For example, if the horse's name was *Monkey Bars*, the words *monkey* and *bars* could be made to appear over and over in the text, embedding themselves into the reader's brain simply by their frequency. So I flipped through every page, looking for the words *silver, skates, glitter,* and *girl*. But other than on the two lists I've mentioned, they didn't appear elsewhere in the book.

*

WHILE TYPING UP an account of my virtual "day at the races" back
home in the Village, I realized I would very much like to interview
Laura Day. I hadn't made any attempt to do so, though, when a funny
thing occurred. I was having a party—I've never been what you'd call
a "party girl," but I've always loved an opportunity to host one (yes, I
was a connector!)—and had invited my friend Larry. Larry and I had
gone to the same high school, though he'd been a few grades ahead of
me, so we hadn't known each other back then; we'd met many years
later at an alumni event and had just hit it off. Larry told me that my
party was the same night as his reunion at our alma mater, but promised to stop by beforehand. As the night drew closer, he emailed me.
Attending a pre-reunion gathering, he'd met a woman named Laura
Globus who'd graduated a year behind him, and a year ahead of me;
she was a professional *psychic* who worked in the corporate world, and
he thought we'd like one another. In fact, he'd taken the liberty of
looping her in on our email.

I wrote back to them both, inviting Laura to my party. A few days
later, she responded. Alas, she was heading to LA, she said—but perhaps another time.

As I began to close the email, I blinked as I noticed the name listed
in the "from" space: "Laura Globus Day."

"*Day?* Laura Globus *Day?!*" Could this be the same woman whose
book I'd just read, and about whom I'd just been writing? And she,
too, had gone to Stuyvesant, my Manhattan math-and-science specialized high school? Maybe because of her connection with Demi Moore,
I'd been picturing Day as a California girl. Not that—*duh!*—people
couldn't move across the country from where they'd grown up. Now
that I thought about it, I remembered that there had been a very cute
young man with the surname *Globus* in my graduating class; I hadn't
really known him, but we'd had mutual friends, and were actually
friends on Facebook. Could the two be siblings?

I Googled her, and up popped an article from the *Telegraph*, a British paper, published three years before: "Meet Laura Day: The financial psychic of Wall Street who predicted global meltdown." *Globus*, the article mentioned, was Day's maiden name.

Double shazam!

I wrote to Larry and Laura, and shared my story. Laura wrote back quickly: She was, in fact, the sister of the young man in my class.

Still trying to wrap my head around this bit of synchronicity, I searched for Laura's Web site and blog. She had a new book out, her site proclaimed, *How to Rule the World from Your Couch*. "In her new book . . ." it stated, "Laura Day teaches you or your company how to create success in any area by using your brain in unique and compelling ways . . ." Sounded good to me! I'd had that mind-blowing experience with the horse race exercise in her earlier book, but I hadn't really followed up with more practice. I'd been so busy researching other topics and getting enough copyediting work to pay my rent. And though ruling the world sounded exhausting, I ordered myself a copy.

This new book, I found, was largely composed of exercises too. I tossed it into my duffel bag, along with a notebook and pen, as I packed for a few weeks at the Shore, where I'd be overseeing some work again at my brother's house. The first exercise I tried, settled into my seat on the Jersey coastal line train as Manhattan's skyline flashed past me, was aimed at gathering information to answer a question of one's choosing. I pondered a bit, then posed the question, "Where will I be living a year from now?" I had no real plans to relocate, but I was open to it, and curious, and it was a simple question, which, I thought, should make the process easier.

Using Laura's techniques, which again had to do with picking up information using my various senses, I got the following impressions:

• The conductor's voice, over the train's speakers.
• The rumbling of the train, and also my stomach (hunger).

- Oranges.
- Kittens.
- A wicker basket.

I jotted the list down in my notebook, with no idea what to make of it. Day's book said that the answer to our question would be clear from the results. But I certainly didn't see it.

The next afternoon, as I was happily sipping coffee and writing in the Loving Cup—I'd missed the little town, with its old-fashioned main street lined with eateries and shops where people actually talked to one another—Young Ethan ambled over. I asked him what was new, and he began to tell me a story about his kitten.

"Kitten?" I asked. "Since when do you have a *kitten?*"

"I just got her!" he said. He whipped out his cell phone and displayed a photo of a small Siamese kitten, and quite a cutie. I told him I'd grown up with two female cats, and thus, in those pre–mandatory-spaying days, a house constantly filled with litters of kittens.

The conversation changed then, to a trip he was taking to North Carolina—Charlotte, to be precise. I told him I'd visited Asheville the month before, and what a fantastic town I thought it was.

It wasn't until later that day, while I was meditating in the little den at my brother's house, that my restless mind latched on to the Laura Day book and the exercises I'd done. *Kittens!* I thought. *Ethan's kitten!* And those cats I'd had as a kid that I'd been telling him about, the ones that were constantly dropping litters of kittens, they'd always birthed them in an old wicker basket that we'd set up in our linen closet, lined with an old towel we saved for just that purpose. So there was the *wicker basket.* And *oranges?* Well, as it happened, the precise section of my manuscript I'd been revising when Ethan had interrupted me was that funny little section about the strange, recurrent, unexplained smell of fresh-cut oranges in my apartment, which I'd been wondering if I should even keep in the book.

What else was on that list?

I jumped up, scampered to the bedroom I always stayed in, with an adjoining porch that afforded a glimpse of ocean, and found the notebook I'd jotted my exercise results in out on the porch. Right— the *conductor's voice, over the train's speakers.* Could that correlate to the fact that there had been music, with a vocalist, playing over the café's speakers?

And the *rumbling of the train and also my stomach (hunger)* . . . Well, I'd been at a *café*, hadn't I? In fact, I *had* been hungry when Ethan came over, and soon after ordered some soup.

But wasn't all this kind of a stretch? A definite, absolute maybe. At the same time, it was *curious*. How often did people bring up kittens in everyday talk?

Still, if all this was supposed to add up to an answer to the question I'd posed—"Where will I be living a year from now?"—I didn't get it. The only locations Ethan and I had talked about were Charlotte and Asheville, North Carolina. So, did that mean I was going to be living in one of those towns? My friend Katarina had told me, many years before, that she saw me in what she thought was Virginia, happily riding through rolling green hills, with a man. And several more of my intuitive friends, including Maggie Moise and Edward Ragosta, had seen me moving to or buying property in the South. Rev. Kev O'Kane had given me details about a romantic interest who was currently living a bit south of Virginia, and whom I'd start traveling regularly to see. I hadn't really wanted to hear that, since I was still wrapped up in Sam, but North Carolina fit the bill. Even if I did make such a move, though, I doubted it'd happen anywhere near so soon as a year hence.

On the other hand, could it mean I was going to be living *there*, in that Shore town, where the Loving Cup was located, and near to Sam; that I'd move *there* from the city, maybe to be with him? (Of course, Reader, I wanted to believe that!)

Or was it all just another big, fat coincidence?

Another definite, absolute maybe.

I stepped out onto the porch, sat down in the old metal "glider" swing that afforded the sliver-of-ocean view, and tried a few more exercises in Day's book. In one telepathy exercise, I tried to get my friend Frankie to contact me. That didn't work—at least, not immediately, as was my intent—and though I knew this stuff took time and practice, as Day had said, it put me off a bit, so I thrust aside the notebook and, lulled by that little snippet of blue, headed out for a walk by the surf.

The next day, though, I tried the initial exercise again, this time seated on a bench on the boardwalk; it was a bit cloudy but, at the beach, it was always hard for me to stay indoors. I knew this was a tough question, but still, I posed it: "What's the first name of this 'Southern Man' I'm apparently supposed to meet?" I took a bit longer with it this time. This is what I got:

- The sound of a plane overhead.
- Something about berries in a tree . . . an evergreen tree. The image I got looked like juniper berries on an evergreen branch.
- A bird, somehow connected to the tree and berries.
- Very strong sun, so strong it actually made me curl my head back and lift my arms and hands, which spread out in front of me the way a mime's do when miming a "wall" . . .
- So . . . somehow, a wall.
- A tiger.

I looked at my list and had to laugh, trying to connect the dots to assemble a man's first name from these odd bits and pieces. *Oy!* as we say in New York. *The sound of a plane . . .* Was his name, then, *Buzz?* Or was it perhaps *Juniper?* The attempts seemed ludicrous, but I kept on. Could his first name be *Tiger* as in *Tiger Woods?* And what about the *bird*? A first name of *Robin*, or maybe *Woody*? Feeling more than slightly insane, I gave up.

The next day, back at the Cup, I ran into Luke, a wiry older man with a silvery brush cut and a distinct Brooklyn accent who was, like me, a "regular." We'd become friends after discovering that he'd once worked with my next-youngest brother, as a fellow gardener/horticulturist, in a New York City park. As I wasn't a driver, and Luke knew that I liked exploring parts of New Jersey I'd never seen, he said that if it was nice out the next day, we could drive to a Starbucks in a nearby town called Shrewsbury; he liked sitting in their little outdoor mall. "Besides, I want to buy a canary at a pet store down there," he said.

What? A *bird*?! He was going to buy a *bird*? In *Shrewsbury*? I couldn't help but notice the word *berry* in the name. My interest was piqued.

"Love to!" I said, sparing him any long-winded explanation about the bird.

When I called Luke the next morning, he informed me that he'd actually bought the canary the afternoon before, and invited me to stop in and meet him, so I did. There in Luke's living room, in an old-fashioned standing cage, was my *bird*, in the feathers and flesh, a sweet, pale yellow canary named Plato.

Given the nice weather, we decided to keep to our plan. So we hopped into Luke's Jeep, adorned with bumper sticker and decals proclaiming his Vietnam vet status, and drove to the outdoor mall. I saw with a start as we entered that it was called The Grove at Shrewsbury.

The *Grove*! Now in addition to the *bird* and the *berry*, there was a *grove*, too, indicating *trees*, in the plural sense. And I couldn't help noticing that the day was not just nice, but blindingly *sunny*, thereby crossing another image off my list. As I did, I became aware of the unmistakable roar of a *plane* zooming overhead, likely heading to New York or Newark, not too far to the north.

Huh, I thought. *Now all that's left is the tiger—well, and a* wall. *If I see a* tiger *in Starbucks, I'll be a monkey's aunt.* A bird was one thing; a tiger, even in the wilder parts of New Jersey, was quite another.

Surprisingly, though Luke had specifically mentioned the outdoor seating, when we arrived at Starbucks, a rather large one, I noted, he said that he wanted to sit inside. He told me he'd get us a table and suggested I go up to the counter, offering to treat me to whatever I wanted, and handing me a twenty as he gave me his order. Coffee and goodies duly purchased, I turned from the counter and spied Luke at a table along one wall. I hadn't even thought of the fact that he'd chosen to sit along the *wall*, however, because, as I headed over, I glanced up to find a colorful print of a *Bengal tiger* staring back.

I stood stock-still for a second, as a smile crept over my face. *Wall: check. Tiger: check.* This was really pretty wild. Luke saw my expression and thought I was just happy being treated to my snack—and indeed, I was grateful, and I ate and drank it with aplomb. But a glistening of pure *glee* was passing through me, and it was more than the glee of a blondie and a grande macchiato!

Once that little reverie had passed, though, I had to ask myself: *How did it answer my question? Was the Southern Man going to be named Luke—or Plato—or Grande Macchiato?* The things I had "seen" were appearing in my life, but they didn't seem to be in any way connected to the question I'd asked.

A few days later, having returned to the city, I sat in my threadbare armchair and tried asking the same question. The following images came in:

- Steak.
- Cheese.
- A mousetrap.
- A piece of chalk, and then chalk on a blackboard.

- A gooey pink strawberry sundae, topped with whipped cream.
- The word *royal*, and then the specific image of a crown.

Again, they meant nothing to me. A few days passed, and *nada*. Another day or so later, I went to dinner on the Lower East Side with some women friends I worked with. When we got to the restaurant, a steak salad on the menu caught my eye: *Yum!* I didn't connect it to the word *steak* on my list, as by then I'd forgotten about what had seemed like a failed effort. The salad was decadent, laden with tender steak and creamy goat cheese, so when it came to dessert, I passed. My three friends, however, decided to share something called a Pink Pussycat Sundae. We all had a laugh about the name. It wasn't until the waitress plunked it on our table that it registered: *Oh my God!* It was the exact sundae I'd pictured in my exercise: pink ice cream and gooey strawberries, smothered in whipped cream.

When I got home, I searched for my list and was reminded of the *steak*, and the *cheese*, too. Though there'd been no *chalk* at the restaurant, we *had*, I realized, talked about *teaching* for most of the night: Two of my friends were teaching copyediting classes, and the husband of one, a professor, was searching for a new teaching job.

Could the *chalk* be symbolic? And could it also be that I was really reaching here?

Yes and yes.

But what about *royal/crown*? Then, *zing!*—it hit me: The big news at dinner was that one member of our party had quit her editorial job that very day at the publishing imprint *Crown!*

There'd been nothing said about mousetraps, or at least not that I could recall. Still, the image of that sundae wouldn't quit. No one in my life *ever* ordered strawberry sundaes: How many Manhattan restaurants even had them on the menu? It was downright weird.

But Reader, you're right: It still didn't answer the question.

I neglected Day's exercises for a few weeks after that. But the next time I was visiting my mom in Staten Island—now that she was alone and getting older, I tried to spend more time out there to keep her company, and help her get to doctor appointments and such—I decided to try it again. Posing my old question about the name of the Southern Man, this time I got:

- A lemon.
- Clouds.
- Chain links, as in a chain-link fence—I could see the crisscross pattern of metal diagonally crossing metal.
- Buildings, in silhouette—I couldn't see their features, just their outline, which appeared, for some reason, dusky purple.
- France.

Again, no conceivable answer to my question.

I was on the ferry a few days later, returning to my mother's after a workday in the city, when I started thinking about that latest attempt at the exercise, trying to recall the items on my list. *A lemon* was all I could remember. As I did, though, I realized that I'd brought some lemon slices to work that very day, in a plastic bag in my purse. I'd never done that before, but I'd been trying to cut down on coffee, and I liked tea if I had lemon.

That was interesting. *Yeah, but you probably had lemons on your mind when you decided to pack them this morning,* I mentally chastised myself, not the other way around. *You're just trying to make things fit the images that you picked up.*

As I was busy self-flagellating, though, a funny thing happened. I was sitting on one of the outdoor decks that line the sides of the older ferries. This type of deck had a sort of metal fencing at its perimeter, supporting the railing where passengers leaned as they took in the view. That evening, the sunset was spectacular. Clouds of purple, pink, and orange filled the sky. As I got up from the bench to lean on the railing, I thought: Wait, *clouds*—that was on my list. And there across the harbor were the *silhouettes of buildings* . . . against the sunset, I could only see their *dusky purple* outlines.

I sat back down with a *thunk*. What else was on that list? As I stared out at the bay's dark water, I realized that straight ahead, at eye level between the harbor and me, the metal fencing, painted Staten-Island-Ferry orange, was made of *chain link*—thin strips of crisscrossing metal, just as I'd envisioned during the exercise.

As I lifted my eyes to the Statue of Liberty, which we were now passing, I recalled the last thing on my list: *France!* Wasn't the statue a gift from the people of France, symbolic of our two nations' friendship? *Criminy!* This was starting to freak me out.

But again: What did these things have to do with my question?

I wondered if I was asking questions that were too hard to answer, or perhaps questions to which I wasn't yet supposed to know the answers. Or was I simply not yet skilled enough to bring in the answers clearly?

A FEW DAYS LATER, as I was perusing Laura Day's Web site, I saw that she was conducting a free workshop in downtown Manhattan, and signed right up. The event was held at a hair-styling studio, with the chairs pushed back to open up space for a combination cocktail-party-cum-psychic-development salon. Laura, who was gracious, down-to-earth, fun, and a vision in raspberry silk and heels, had provided a lovely spread of fruit and cheese, wine, and champagne for the several dozen attendees. Some of them had taken Laura's classes, including her "boot camp," a two-day training in intuition. Those who *had* were asked to identify themselves by tying a ribbon around their arm. Thus, they could assist us newbies as we practiced reading for one another while we mingled and drank. Though I'd heard it said that alcohol could interfere with psychic abilities, apparently Laura didn't agree; in fact, she cheerily tossed off, wine seemed to help her intuition flow.

We were each to approach someone and try and read for him or her, Laura explained. The person being read was not to respond, so that the reader's observations took the form of a nonstop monologue. Laura told the readers not to censor themselves, but to keep the words flowing. This, I gathered, was to prevent the thinking part of the brain from intruding; according to Day's books, that seemed key. In her books, she had instructed readers to pay attention to what they were *sensing*. This allowed the "noise" of one's conscious thinking to fade into the background, enabling the use of one's senses to access information.

Though I felt a bit awkward attempting to read for others, it was fun, too. Whether or not we were accurate was not to be our concern; in fact, we were not even to ask about that—though the first woman I read for shared with me that I'd been correct on several things. Still, I was surprised when, as Laura observed me reading for a second woman, she told me I was "very good." Could she tell that what I was picking up was accurate because *she* was picking up that information as she observed us too? Or was I just very good at acting the part of a reader?

Later, when I got her ear for a few minutes, I told her about my experience with the exercises in her book, and how I had been picking up things that later happened or appeared, but didn't answer my posed question. "You're not focusing specifically enough on the question. Try and focus in *very specifically* on what you're asking," she said.

That sounded simple enough. I was eager to give it a try.

✳

MY NEXT ATTEMPT took place back on the ferry, heading to my mother's house once more. I was starting to feel like a commuter again, as I'd been at various points in my life, with my cup of none-too-exciting, markedly American coffee—milk, no sugar—in a paper bag. Again, I sat on an outdoor bench. I'd chosen an emotionally neutral question this time, the answer to which I'd be able to prove right or wrong quickly and definitively. I placed my attention as fully as I could, lingering for a full minute, on my new and improved question: "What movie am I going to see when I watch TV with Mom at her house tonight?" This is what I got:

- Germany.
- Black-and-white footage, or photography.
- A cow, or cows in a field . . . especially, somehow, a black-and-white cow.
- A big bell.

What movie could all of that possibly describe? I wondered. *The Sound of Music* came to mind, though I knew it was set in Austria, not Germany, and I couldn't recall cows in it, or black-and-white footage, either—just a bunch of black-and-white nuns.

That night, I stretched out alongside my mother on her vast, king-size bed, bedecked with a battery of eight or ten pillows, to watch. I'd avoided the TV's "guide" feature, and hadn't looked at that night's TV listings anywhere else. There was a PBS show called *Doc Martin* (no relation to the shoes), which one of my brothers had recommended to us. It was about a curmudgeonly surgeon in a small British village who hated the sight of blood. My mother, who always wielded the remote and all its attendant power, was clicking around, and came upon it mid-episode. She allowed us to watch it till its end, and we did enjoy its quirky charm. Oddly, it ended not at the hour or the half-hour mark, but at forty-five minutes past. As I wondered what they were going to do with that stray fifteen minutes, a short film began.

We Are Germany, the title read.

Reader, a jolt shot through me. "Oh my God."

"What?" my mother said. I'd been telling her, in weeks past, about the psychic development exercises. So now, as *black-and-white footage of farmland* appeared on the screen—old photos, really, of farms and fields, *cattle* and plows—I explained what I had received during the latest exercise.

"*Really?*" she said, sounding incredulous.

"I'm telling you," I said. "Germany. Black-and-white footage. Cows, *black-and-white cows, in a field.*"

"Oh my God," she said now too.

The film turned out to be a documentary on early German immigrants in the United States: about how they'd made their living, and their way of life.

"All I need to see now is a *big bell*," I said. "That's the last thing I got." No sooner had the words fled my lips than the shots of farmland gave way to Christmas scenes; Germans were very into Christmas, I knew. And then it flashed onto the screen: a vintage photo of a smiling German immigrant family celebrating the holiday in their living room. Suspended from the ceiling was *a huge paper bell.*

"*And there it is!*" I shouted, raising my arms aloft like an Olympian champ.

"Now you're really scaring me!" my mother said. She did sound spooked, which made me laugh. Truth be told, though, I was scaring myself. When my Team members had told me I had very good psychic gifts, I hadn't totally believed them, though I'd wished it to be true. Yet now that I was seeing a bit of them actually coming to light—there was no way, I was certain, that I could have randomly guessed those particular images, *all* of which appeared in that one fifteen-minute film; the odds against that had to be enormous—it made me more than a little nervous. Not to say it didn't thrill me too. I felt giddy, almost high. But I had to admit that, for all my belief in intuition as part of our inborn nature—and I *had* come to believe that—there was something unnerving in actually experiencing it.

The rest of the short documentary played out on the set before me, but I couldn't take it in. My head was awhirl and I felt . . . well, slightly freaked out was the only way to describe it. Why, I asked myself, was I feeling this way? Was it that our culture kept these abilities so shrouded in mystery that bringing them into the light, even a little bit, felt like taking a forbidden peek behind the curtain at the Great and Powerful Oz? Or maybe that wasn't the right metaphor. After all, Professor Marvel had been perpetuating a *trick* behind that curtain. This was more akin to Dorothy learning about the Ruby Slippers, awakening to the fact that *she herself* had, all along, *possessed the power* she needed, the power to take her home.

Could it be that I, too, was glimpsing a small bit of my own ability to "come home" to who I really was, to some powers that might be in me, unacknowledged and untapped? Had a part of me always known they were there, and was that why I'd always been so interested in the invisible world? If so . . . why had it taken me so long to discover them?

I climbed off the bed and kissed my mother good night, assuring her that what had happened was completely natural—and likewise assuring myself. I thought of Janet Alm, who had been about the age that I was now when she'd started to experience her fascinating abilities, and began working to develop them, and about Katarina, who had been somewhere in midlife too, when she'd learned about hers. While most of my highly intuitive friends had told me that their abilities had surfaced in childhood, perhaps some people needed to mature, or to have certain experiences, before their gifts—such as they might be— could fully emerge.

Or perhaps, on a subconscious level, my abilities had scared me— as they definitely had Katarina—and I'd suppressed them. Maggie Moise had once told me that I was afraid of my own power, that I was only using a fraction of who I really was. Might that have included my powers of intuition? And if so, what other powers might I have, waiting to be discovered? What powers might *all* we humans have? And how might our world change if we all, collectively, stepped into them?

I pondered this possibility as I stood brushing my teeth. A world, I speculated, where we were all, actively, highly intuitive—like my Dream Team members—might ultimately mean a world of utter transparency. In such a world, I mused, relationships would be transformed—no cheating on a partner without getting caught!—as would institutions of every sort, from financial to religious to governmental. Lying, corruption, and cover-ups would ultimately disappear. And how effectively could wars be carried out if weapons and attacks could largely be "seen" and avoided? It was, to me, an exciting potential reality to imagine.

In any case, I concluded, coming back down to Earth from my imaginings, it was time for me to step into my own innate abilities, such as they might be. I would put in the work, and the practice, and see if my Team was right.

As I flipped off the bathroom light and padded down the dark hallway to my childhood bedroom, my thoughts drifted from these loftier matters back to the Southern Man and that question I'd been asking. Fine Southern men I duly appreciated—George Clooney, Owen Wilson, and yes, Johnny Depp—notwithstanding, the truth of it was, a part of me didn't want to meet the Southern Man at all, because of Sam. Was my difficulty letting go of Sam keeping the Southern Man at bay, delaying the meeting that so many of my intuitive friends had seen?

And then something funny occurred to me, and I couldn't believe it hadn't crossed my mind before: Could it be that the Southern Man they'd all seen was my *gay* friend Griffin? After all, he lived in the South, and we had, several times now, driven together through Virginia's rolling green hills, just as Katarina—the first to bring up the Southern Man—had described. My Team seemed to think that this man was a romantic interest, someone I'd not yet met. But could it be that they were seeing my very close bond with, and love for, Griffin, and interpreting it as a romance? If so, what kind of cosmic joke was *that*?

I was starting to see that psychic readings were a lot more complicated than I had once thought.

I climbed into bed, pulled up the rose-printed comforter, and lay there in the dark, thinking about it all. In my twenties, I'd taken that maiden European voyage, and the world had opened up to me; now I was taking a voyage of another sort, an inward voyage, involving my own potential abilities, and encompassing other realms and other beings. And what a fantastic voyage it was.

I didn't know where it would lead, or how it might change me, though I knew that it would; it already had. It had been several years now since I'd left my therapist, Melinda, and begun my exploratory project. As I continued to meet with my Team members, they'd often remarked on how much I had changed since our first encounter. "You're evolving at a very fast rate," Rev. Kev O'Kane had once told me. And "You're like a totally different person from who you were when I first met you," Roger Ansanelli had said. "You didn't come here to be the same. At a different vibration, you have a different experience. The higher we go, the more joy we experience, and share, because we *become* our joy by living it."

Well, I knew that he was right. I'd reconnected with that inborn passion of my youth, and through it, rediscovered my joy. And while I still hoped for a partner with whom to share my life, and trusted that it would happen—in the North, the South, or perhaps on the astral plane!—when the time, and I, were ripe, I no longer pined or suffered, or felt the sense of waiting for my life to begin. I was living my life . . . a life of excitement, of expansion, of fulfillment, of sharing. I was doing what I knew I was here to do, and hoping to inspire others to do the same.

"It's your time, sweetheart, spread your wings and fly," Christina Wright had told me at the end of my first reading with her. And "You're ready to spread your wings, dear," Jeffrey Wands had said.

Nice as it had been to hear it, I no longer needed to be told; I could feel it. Thanks to Frank Andrews, I'd lost my fear of flying in planes. And though I might not be quite ready to drive a rocket ship, as Roger Ansanelli had suggested, after all those years of flying my origami-rabbit "familiar" up, up, and away, I knew I'd finally taken off.

15

ADVENTURES WITH
MY DREAM TEAM
✶ OR ✶

In Your Eyes

IT'S A FUNNY THING ABOUT EXPERIMENTS: YOU CAN START off with a set of questions and the intent to answer them, only to find that the results raise more questions than you had when you began.

After nearly three years of working with my Dream Team on my informal experiment, I sat by the window in my Village apartment one balmy spring morning, pigeons strutting on the fire escape, their coos floating above the nonstop thrum of city traffic, and looked over the results. I'd started with a simple goal: I wanted to find out if, over time and many readings, my highly intuitive friends would come up with any common information. To that end, I had painstakingly recorded and transcribed each of my readings. Then I'd made a list, grouping similar information that my Team members had received into what turned out to be seventeen topics. There were actually more areas where they had said similar things—that my finances were difficult but would improve, for instance—but I discounted those as more general, albeit accurate, comments, and added to the list only the more specific ones. Now, for the first time, as I officially concluded my experiment, at least for now, I did a complete read-through of that list:

1. *My being a writer*: This had come up in my initial readings with Patricia Masters, Edward Ragosta, and Jennifer Hicks with no mention from me. "Writing is a form of soothing meditation for you, a cucumber eye-rest, if you will," Edward had said in my first reading, in his inimitable fashion. Roger Ansanelli had picked it up too, in that first workshop of his that I'd attended. And though she wasn't originally part of my Team, as I'd met her after beginning my experiment, Janet Alm had immediately zeroed in on my being an "author" too.

2. *My book, or actually* books, *about the invisible realms . . . and a possible movie tie-in*: Patricia Masters had memorably predicted that I'd write a book about people who did what she did, and Maggie Moise had asked in my first reading if I was doing a project about psychics. Later, she'd said that my book was part of a series. Jennifer Hicks had said in the message circle that my friend David was showing her "*volumes*," plural—indicating books that I was writing. And Roger Ansanelli had asked, "Are you writing the book . . . or *books?*" in my first workshop with him too.

"Do you still think it's one book?" Edward Ragosta had asked. "It's at least two. And there could be several more." Later, he amended that to an even greater number.

Rev. Kev O'Kane had told me that his guides and mine were concerned that I'd gathered more information than I knew what to do with, and suggested I shape it into not one, but *several* books.

And then there was Jeffrey Wands. I'd actually told him that I was writing a book. "It's about my explorations—" I'd started, but he cut me off.

". . . in spirituality!" he said, finishing my thought. "Yeah, there's actually a whole series. And one looks like it could go into a movie."

Similarly, "One of your projects may be made into a film. I'd be surprised if you didn't produce one," Frank Andrews had said.

3. *The fact that I'd "contracted" to write these books*: Four Team members had told me that my soul had contracted to do this work before I came into this life. When writing this first book took me far longer than expected, Edward Ragosta had delivered this message from his angels and guides: "You're not going to like this, but you're not going to be allowed to meet any more men until after it's published," he said. "They don't want you to get distracted any more than you already have been. They're saying, *you agreed to do this*, and they're holding you to it!"

4. *Writing and illustrating kids' books/painting/my love of color*: Edward Ragosta had seen me creating kids' books about spirituality, and the idea of writing for children had come up in my first reading with Patricia Masters, too. She'd urged me to do some illustration work for kids' books as well. And "I'm seeing colors and drawings. I felt the word *illustrations—drawing*s—as well as the written word," Frank Andrews had said.

"You *love* color," Roger Ansanelli had told me. For me, he said, it was akin to joy. "Painting, art, color: You have that in your 'file.' You should be painting! I see that you will be," he said.

5. *Working directly with children and/or doing healing work*: Seven out of ten Team members had brought this up, starting with Patricia Masters. Soon after she told me this, I was offered a job, out of the blue, in an experimental school program in which one of the children was severely learning disabled. "You will work with 'fragile' children. You will see the beauty of their imagination, and you won't consider them disabled," she'd said.

Dana Marie had suggested I use my "natural healing ability" with kids, doing reiki or other energy work, and Kev O'Kane had seen me "helping to bring out [kids'] light." Edward Ragosta saw me doing workshops with kids too.

Jennifer Hicks had picked up "a healing vibe" from me—a possible career. And according to Roger Ansanelli, I'd done work in a past life helping children, both as a doctor and as a shamanistic healer, and could do so again.

Finally, "If you told me you were a nurse, I'd say, 'Are you crazy?' Because you're all about the arts. But there *is* something of the healer about you," Frank Andrews had said.

6. *Past lives in religious orders*: I've written much about this, so I won't repeat it here. Four Dream Team members had discussed it, and while not officially part of my Team, evolutionary astrologer Patricia Bechdolt had talked about it too.

7. *My tendency toward reclusiveness, and toward self-protectiveness in terms of men*: Rev. Kev had warned me to watch out for my reclusive tendency, or I might not carry out the work I was here to do; Frank Andrews had mentioned my *I want to be alone!* vibe; and Edward Ragosta had warned me against my propensity to "stay home and hide," especially in regard to meeting men.

Three Team members had brought up my having donned a "suit of armor" with men—to quote Edward Ragosta. Jeffrey Wands had referred to my "barbed wire and alligators," saying I had to remove them to let men in.

8. *Producer/agent/"connector"/promoter/PR writer*: The idea of my being a producer or agent, or in some way putting people and/or projects together, especially in the arts, and promoting them, came up strongly with Frank Andrews and Christina Wright.

"Would you be interested in being . . . like an *agent?*" Christina had asked. "You're a '*connector.*' I heard that loud and clear. And you can also be a '*conductor.*' Not with music, but you can conduct artists about where to go and what to do. You can orchestrate things."

"You'd be fantastic as an agent, a manager, or working in PR," Frank Andrews had said. (He'd also said, see list item 2, that he'd be surprised if I didn't produce a film.)

Rev. Kev, too, had suggested that I seek writing work in public relations, saying that I'd be "not just *very good* at it, but *very, very, very* good."

9. *Living near the water, and the importance of that*: Patricia Masters had been the first to say it, using her "royal *we*": "We would like to see you living near the water." Similarly, *"Water's big,* so you've gotta *make sure* you're always near water," Jeffrey Wands had said. "But steer clear of the *Jersey Shore* cast!"

Dana Marie had picked up that I was phoning from New Jersey, with no caller ID on my phone. She asked if I was spending time near the shore, and said how good it was for me to be there. And from Roger Ansanelli: "You have *water* in your 'file' too. It helps you align, and helps you heal."

Finally, "I see you near the water," Maggie Moise had said. "There's a lot of water involved here. Almost as if you *need* to be near it. At the end of your project, you're going to end up living near the water. I see that it's more clean water, though, not like New York water. And not New Jersey, either!"

10. *Living on the Southeastern Coast (in connection with a man)*: Many of my intuitive friends saw me moving, eventually, to the Southeastern coastal US. My friend Katarina, while not part of my Team, had been the first, seeing me in a "triangular"-shaped state that started with a *V*, driving through "rolling green hills" with a man, and very happy.

Appealing as that sounded, I'd balked. *"Virginia?* I went to *college* there," I said. But she insisted this wasn't about my past.

Maggie Moise had seen me in Virginia Beach or the Chesapeake Bay area, buying houses and renting them out, connected to a man.

Edward Ragosta had seen me wanting to buy property too—"Maybe in the coastal Carolinas—either that, or Canada," having to do with a man.

Finally, Kev O'Kane saw me owning a house in the Carolinas, or as far south as Georgia or Florida. He said I'd start visiting a guy there, eventually moving there myself.

11. *My bad luck with (or bad taste in?) men*: This came up over and over with nearly my entire Team. "The guys you pick . . ." Frank Andrews had said in my first reading, "I mean, if a girlfriend came to you and said, 'What do you think of my boyfriend?' you'd say, 'Oh, he's a dud.' But it's very difficult for you to see it when it comes to the men *you're* with. You fall in love right away. Well, you don't fall in love, you *step* in it."

"Your maternal grandmother's standing here insisting that she's gonna find a man for you," Jeffrey Wands had said. "She thinks you're spectacularly talented but have 'terrible taste in men'—and that's a quote. '*Dys*-functional!'"

Jeffrey, Frank, and Dana Marie had all picked up that I tried to "fix" the men I fell for. And then there was Maggie Moise, who accurately saw the man-storm, which was partly about learning to heed red flags with men.

12. *Sam, my younger man*: I've written much already about what my Team members picked up about Sam. A whopping seven out of ten of them mentioned and/or described him, with no prompting from me. Everything they saw about him, his behavior, and the motivations behind it was accurate, according to what I observed and what he had told me himself. I'll just add here that both Patricia Masters and Frank Andrews had commented on men being *afraid* of becoming involved with me, well before I met Sam, which was, on a certain level, clearly the case with him.

13. *A romance with a "cop"*: Three Team members had seen me having a romantic relationship with a man who was, or had been, some type of law officer. "I can't imagine you falling in love with a cop," Frank Andrews had said. "But there's one in your cards. And he likes to be handcuffed!" Maggie Moise had seen him too, as had Dana Marie, who added that he and I had had a past life together early in the twentieth century, working together as police officers.

They all were in agreement that this man would be slightly older than me. I told them that I'd once dated an ATF agent, a bit older than me—but they all insisted that this was in my future, not my past.

14. *My "father issues"*: Seven out of ten Team members brought up my "father issues," starting with Patricia Masters. Again, I won't repeat what I've already covered, but I'll share these words from Jeffrey Wands, which echoed very closely what Patricia had said.

"There's a dad figure here," Jeffrey told me. "He adores you. You never got over the loss of him: I mean, abandonment issues. So, emotionally, that's why he stands here. You haven't been able to find anybody *normal* in terms of a man, and it comes from *that*."

15. *My mother's fears and anxiety*: Patricia Masters had brought this up, and it came up with Rev. Kev O'Kane, Jeffrey Wands, and Maggie Moise, too: "You're really prone to worrying a lot, and having anxiety about projects you undertake, because somewhere your subconscious is telling you that if you worry, you're doing a good job. It comes from the mother," she'd said.

16. *My health issues*: In readings a few months apart, I'd asked Jeffrey Wands and Frank Andrews if I had any medical issues brewing. They each said that I was quite healthy, and that they saw *only one*: a cyst in "the female parts," as one of them delicately put it. I had no history of

this type of cyst, but in my next checkup, there it was. And yes, aside from that, I had no physical ailments show up after that for a good long time.

17. *My own intuitive abilities*: Roughly two-thirds of my Team had said that I had very good intuition. Dana Marie had told me that I was "very clairsentient and clairvoyant," and "wasn't apart from" the people I was writing about.

"You'll start to use your gifts more and more, and have to rely less and less on people like me . . . because you literally will get the answers yourself," Kev O'Kane had said.

AS I FINISHED reading over the list, I sat back, gazing out the window and through the leafy boughs of intervening trees onto a small fountain that had been placed in the square there in recent years. The water had followed *me* this time, it seemed, and I was happy to have it. I pondered the results of my experiment; it had, I felt, proven quite provocative. As there was no one to share my satisfaction with but the pigeons, I enjoyed it on my own as I sipped my French Roast.

Much of the similar information I had received, I noticed, had been delivered in my initial sessions, when the readers knew little to nothing about me. Moreover, many of the readings had been by phone, so my appearance or expressions couldn't have been used to glean information. And very little of it, as far as I could see, could have been found out online.

Further, I realized, moving to my threadbare armchair to ponder more comfortably, there was this: While many of my Team members appeared to be doing something akin to mind reading, the results suggested that they *hadn't* been picking things up from my conscious thoughts—as many people who are at least open to the idea of psychic abilities believe. After all, I hadn't originally planned on writing more than one book on my explorations—in fact, I'd initially wondered if I'd have enough material for just one! I'd never thought of myself as a healer, or an agent or producer, and I'd certainly never thought of moving south! Yet my Team members had collectively come in strongly on those points.

As for the accuracy of their predictions, in many cases I couldn't yet say. Nor could I speak to the truth about my past lives, whatever my gut feelings might be. But in picking up on my traits and behaviors—and Sam's, too—they'd been abso-friggin'-lutely right.

Yet, for all the affirmation my informal experiment had offered that there seemed to be something *real* going on, it had raised some new questions too. For all the times when my intuitive friends had been so remarkably, so *specifically*, on target, there'd been times when they simply had not. So I had to wonder: *If these psychics were so psychic—and they truly seemed to be so—why did they get some things so wrong?*

Let me clarify, Reader: My Team had had *far* fewer of these misses than hits. Yet there had been a job offer, a script sale, and a trip to the Southwest, all seen by various Team members, which had not come to pass. At least, not yet.

And then there had been an odd variant on this: There were times when my intuitive friends had gotten things *sort of* right, but ultimately not. Once, for example, I'd been involved in a lawsuit about my apartment—an old-fashioned, "railroad"-style affair, one room leading to the next like railway cars, with sloping floors and steam heat. Over the phone, never having been there, Patricia Masters had described the place's odd configuration, the slanted floors—even the "burnt" odor currently resulting from a radiator leak. When she went on to tell me that I'd win my lawsuit, Reader, I rejoiced. And I did win my first round in court. But after my landlords appealed the decision, there was a change in a statute-of-limitations law, and in the end, devastatingly, I lost.

Beyond my great dismay at losing the suit, this had perplexed me no end: With all that Patricia had seen so accurately, how had she not seen *that*?

There were other such puzzling incidents too. Some years before my project, I'd had a reading with Jeffrey Wands in which—*shocker!*—I'd asked about love. "This next guy coming up, he deals in interior design. You'll like him, he's sophisticated. He's got a European thing about him," he said.

A few weeks later, I got a call from a coworker. "Are you open to a fix-up?" she asked. She told me about a man she'd met through a friend. "He's French, an interior designer. He travels a lot between Europe and New York."

Holy baguette, Batman! Jeffrey had gotten many hits before, but the specificity of this was *très* impressive.

My coworker gave this man, whom I'll call Sébastien, my number. He phoned me—he had a charming accent—and we made dinner plans. I was excited; because of what Jeffrey had said, I thought this must be someone special. Maybe I'd finally have a relationship that lasted a while, with a guy who wasn't seriously emotionally wounded or closeted or insane.

While I didn't feel an immediate chemistry with Sébastien, he wasn't unappealing. As we shared an expensive bottle of pinot gris—*his* treat—I found the conversation and company pleasant. At the end of the night, as we hugged—I remember his lingering lavender-ish scent, as if he'd been imported directly from Provence—he suggested we meet again. "Great!" I said, finding my excitement growing.

Sébastien told me he had to go on a short trip, but would call when he returned. And I found that I was looking forward to it. But the call never came. After several weeks, I phoned my coworker and filled her in. Chagrined, she did a little investigating. The friend through whom she'd met Sébastien said he seemed to enjoy meeting me, but beyond that, she couldn't say. And I never heard from him again.

I found myself more upset than I would have expected at his disappearance. Was it because Jeffrey had "seen" him so accurately? I had to admit, Reader, that it was.

And I had to wonder: *Why would Jeffrey have picked up on the guy if he was going to be "just not that into me"?* I wasn't in any way *blaming* Jeffrey, and he'd never specifically said this was going to be a serious or lasting thing. In the end, though, seeing as it had been such a short-lived incident, Jeffrey having seen it so accurately just seemed downright *odd*.

It called to mind an earlier time when Katarina had told me about a man she saw me meeting. He was "tall, but not *that* tall, and in very good shape," she said, with "a very likeable personality." His hands, in particular, were "very nice, with very perfect cuticles and nails." He liked to wear "brightly colored polo shirts," and she saw us in summer, he in a pink polo shirt and shorts. As for his hair, she saw none—which was odd, she said, because hair was usually the first thing she saw.

The "pink polo shirt guy" became a joke with my mother and sister; for *years*, I'd kept an eye out for him. And eventually, he did appear—shirt, shorts, and totally bald head!—another fix-up via a friend. And truly, we had clicked—in fact, I'd actually started to fall. Alas, after telling me how "life-changing" he'd found the times we'd shared, he'd vanished like Disappearing George and so many others, the back of his polo shirt pink as the metaphorical sunset into which he permanently rode off.

As with Jeffrey Wands and the Frenchman, Katarina had accurately seen this man in great detail. But both cases had ultimately resulted in non-events, calling into question for me what it was, exactly, my psychic friends were picking up, and why.

✳

OVER THE COURSE of my explorations, I *had* firmly come to believe that intuitive abilities exist. Impressive to me as the results of my informal experiment were, there had also simply been too many instances of individual Team members picking up very specific, accurate information about me during the past few years. But I'd also come to understand that these abilities are not what most people think. Despite what Patricia Masters had told me about there being many types of psychic gifts, if you ask your average person what psychics do, they'll probably say, "Predict the future." Yet most of my Team members stressed to me that they were "not fortune tellers"; that *predicting the future with total accuracy simply could not be done.*

I'd been startled to hear this. After all, I'd witnessed so many incidences where they had accurately predicted future events. Of course there had been some misses, but I had tended to chalk them up to something Griffin had once said: Given what psychics and mediums were doing—pulling in information *via an energetic field*, and in some cases possibly *from another dimension*, and then having to *interpret* it—it was astonishing that they were able to make sense of anything at all. As I've come to understand it now, though, the reasons that gifted psychics get things wrong are far more complicated than that.

For one thing, my Team members agreed that there was no such thing as a predetermined, unalterable future that was "written in stone," and could thus be accurately seen or predicted; rather, *possibilities* and *probabilities* were what they were picking up. Moreover, because we all had free will, the future was malleable, and determined by *all of us*—singularly and as a collective—according to, among other things, the choices we made and the actions we took. As Rev. Kev O'Kane had explained on that radio show interview I'd caught, and which I referred to in an earlier chapter, every time we made a decision and took an action, we jumped to a dimension where that decision and action were more probable. The future, as each of us perceived it, would thus shift according to each of our decisions and actions, so that it was constantly in flux.

Rev. Kev had also told me that the further away the event or person he was trying to "see," chronologically speaking, the less clear it was, because there were still so many permutations of potential outcomes that could occur. Thus, if he could see something, or someone, *clearly* during a reading, it tended to mean that the person or event was coming *soon*.

This whole idea of constantly shifting multiple potential realities reminded me of a movie I'd seen called *Sliding Doors*, starring a young Gwyneth Paltrow; I'll recount a little of it here, Reader, as it may make the concept of parallel universes or realities clearer, for those of you who may be new to it. *(And Spoiler Alert! If you'd rather not learn the very unique concept of this provocative film, stop here and skip a page or so ahead. But I hope you'll go and watch the film, in that case, and then come back and read this section!)*

At a point early in the film, which is set in London, Gwyneth descends into a Tube station and catches a train. We follow the action for a while as a man sitting next to her flirts with her. The film then flashes back to her entering the Tube station, but this time inserts an incident occurring on the platform alongside the track that causes her to *miss* the train . . . and we follow the now totally different action that ensues. The remainder of the movie switches back and forth between the two story lines, Gwyneth's character's two "parallel lives," which are entirely different—not because of a decision, in this case, but because of the random act of catching or not catching that train.

Parallel universes, I gathered from a bit of online research, were a notion taken seriously by many present-day physicists and cosmologists. Without attempting to explain the hypothetical theories and speculative models of parallel universes being tossed about on what some might call the "fringe science" front—by highly reputable scientists, however, at highly reputable places like MIT and Oxford—I *will* say that some are not unlike that basic premise of *Sliding Doors*. That is, they're centered on the idea that every time an individual is faced with a new possibility, that individual's reality diverges and splits off, like a fork in the road, into an alternate, parallel "story line." Thus, in that parallel reality, or universe, there now exists *another* individual who is an exact copy of the first individual, with his or her same features, history, memories, and so on—at least, up to the point at which the split occurred—and who, as with Gwyneth's character in the movie, is only aware of the particular reality or universe in which he or she exists. And yes, taken to its logical conclusion, this would mean that by the end of an individual's life, depending on his or her age, there would be, if not an *infinite* number of such copies simultaneously existing, then certainly enough to fill a few football stadiums or even a few dozen!

This idea that psychics are reading potential realities was merely a first step, I realized, in trying to understand what took place when an intuitive was attempting to "foretell." Assuming we all have free will, we must then remember that the people in our lives, or in our possible futures, have it too. This had been pointed out to me more than once by Maggie Moise—usually when I was in the throes of disappointment over a man. For example, Maggie had seen that George—the growly-voiced stage manager who'd ultimately disappeared—and I had a very good possibility of being together; of being, in fact, *partners*. But, she'd explained, when after quite some time it hadn't happened, *he hadn't chosen to pursue it.*

"We can't control other people's actions and reactions; we can only control our own," she said. So while we might hope to marry the man we're dating, or the charming Southern man that a *psychic* sees, it can only happen if the sum of his choices leads him there too.

So, one might ask—and I *had*—what was the best a psychic could do? Offer a sort of snapshot of what a person's future looked like at that moment? Yes, that was correct, according to Rev. Kev O'Kane. "When you get a reading, it's very much a product of the present time. Although I can tell of the future or past, the energy I'm reading is [that of] now, and may or may not change." Now, if the psychic was a good psychic, they could sometimes offer guidance as to how to make things happen or not happen a certain way, he said. "Sometimes you can say, 'If you take this job, I'm seeing you moving here; if you take that job, I'm seeing you living with a husband and children.' So the person then has a choice of which way they would want to live."

Now, that, to me, was not too shabby.

Most of the psychics I knew preferred terms like *intuitive counselor* to *psychic*, because that was their hope: to offer guidance to help a person move forward in the best way possible on his or her path. Kev had in fact once told me that the only reason to *do* past-life readings or regressions was to be of help to a person, especially to help that person heal in some way. The same held for psychic readings, he said.

"According to Edgar Cayce, 'If what we predict *does not come about*, then we have done our job as psychics.' Meaning that our job, as he saw it, is to *warn* of the future, so that people can do something about it. It might be more comfortable not to know the probabilities of what might happen, but then [that thing] will probably happen in all its gory detail. Isn't it better to have the opportunity to do something to avert that potentially black future?" Rev. Kev said.

That statement of Cayce's fascinated me. It reminded me of the Ghost of Christmas Yet to Come in Dickens's *A Christmas Carol*, who showed Scrooge his own "probable future," chock full of sadness and misery, on that fateful Christmas Eve night, prompting him to make the necessary changes to create for himself—and many around him— a happier life.

✳

UNDERSTANDING THAT potential realities were what intuitives were reading was a game-changer for me. Not only did it help answer my question about why psychics who were usually unbelievably accurate occasionally got things wrong, it helped me understand what, exactly, a psychic reading actually *was*, and thus to better make use of it.

Beyond the whole question of possible and probable realities, though, I'd found still more factors to be aware of when evaluating a reading. Maggie Moise had once pointed out to me, when talking about love, that we have to be careful about readers picking up on our *wishes* and even our *thoughts*—or those of another person we're thinking about. "Because a reader may see and describe someone very accurately—say, someone they feel we're going to marry. But it might well be that they're actually seeing what that person is *thinking* about, not what he or she will necessarily *do*."

To quote Charlie Brown again: *"Aggggggghhhhh!"*

There was also the question, Maggie continued, of where a psychic's information was coming from. "When people channel, you have to ask, who are they channeling? And what is its purpose?" Though a devotee of Edgar Cayce, she pointed out that no one ever knew the source of his often highly accurate information.

Beyond that, too, an intuitive often had to *interpret* what he or she was receiving. Like language translation, this was a skill—or even a bit of an art form. I've written about psychics and mediums picking up information as symbols, the meanings of which they must decipher, ideally with the client's help. Often, though, a symbol's meaning isn't even clear to the client until well after the reading.

Frank Andrews once told me this story: "A guy came in, and I said, 'You're gonna sell three properties. I see three houses.' And he said, 'I'm not in real estate. We don't even own our apartment.' And I said, 'You're kidding me, because I see three properties, three houses, and then I see a big box, like from Tiffany's, with a huge bow on it.' And I said, 'You're gonna get a big present from Tiffany's.' Well, he just shook his head. But he called me back within a year. 'I'm a writer. I sold three scripts in Hollywood. They call scripts *properties*,' he said. 'Dumb me, I never thought of it when you kept saying *"properties."*' And when I got the call from the agent, I said to my wife, "Honey, we just sold three properties," and you know, I *still* didn't think of you until she said, "Oh my God, we just got a present from Tiffany's!" She used that expression. And when she said *"Tiffany's"—Ding-ding-ding!"* Frank paused. "Now, had I known he was a writer, I might have put the pieces together. I mean, when people make it a guessing game, it becomes kind of hard."

I took his point. And in part I bring up this example to stress, again, the usefulness of communicating with the reader. While we might want to "test" our intuitive friends—and I had!—it can work against us in getting the best reading possible, so I'd urge you to keep that in mind.

While this next example doesn't involve symbols, it does deal with the difficulties of interpretation. Christina Wright had once phoned me, concerned; she'd "seen" me getting hurt somehow. It wasn't going to be bad, she said, but I should keep my wits about me in dark, narrow spaces, like alleyways, where there might be vehicles with which to collide. Needless to say, I looked both ways before crossing after that. But *nada*. A few months later, though, I went to bed and then realized I'd forgotten to lock my living room windows. Barefoot, I padded through my "railroad" apartment's dark, narrow rooms, very much like an alleyway, and collided with my roommate's new metal scooter— indeed, a *vehicle!*—skewing my pinky toe out at a horrifying angle.

Reader, I yowled.

Fortunately, once a doctor was able to manually relocate the toe (*yikes!*), it didn't take long to heal. Christina had been right, in many respects—yet I hadn't been able to avoid the collision.

And then there's the fact that psychics, when doing readings, are interpreting things, or perhaps even intuiting them, through their own *filters*—their experiences, emotions, beliefs, and opinions. These can color what they pick up and the advice they give, as can illnesses, losses, and traumas the psychic may be undergoing—as many of my

Team members confirmed. This can help to explain why one may get differing or even conflicting advice from different intuitives within a short period of time, or a great reading from an intuitive year after year and then one that's totally off. And yes, it can be confusing, or downright maddening. And suppose we make plans or decisions based on something a psychic sees, and then that something *changes*—since, after all, it was only one probable reality? Suffice it to say, we can be treading in tricky waters.

And here's another wrinkle: Christina Wright had once told me in a reading that Dr. Jung didn't want her to give me too many details about a man she saw me meeting because he felt I might meet a "double" and mistake that man for him. It had made me laugh; I'd been known to fixate on details my intuitive friends picked up about some upcoming man—how many siblings he had, what he'd be wearing, what color car he drove. If anyone appeared in my life who fit even *some* of those descriptors, I'd start wondering if it was he. But I'd never thought of the possibility that I could meet a guy who *fit all of the descriptors* and still might not be the guy the psychic had seen!

So yes, Reader, my experiment had opened up a can of wriggling worms, leading me to see that working with intuitives was far more complicated than I'd ever imagined.

✳

EDWARD RAGOSTA once startled me by telling me that he saw the next-to-last chapter of my book focusing on the topic "Do psychic readings help more or hurt more?" Now, that was an intriguing notion—and a very unexpected one, coming from a psychic!

"It's important, because people need to know that it's not all rainbows and unicorns!" He chuckled.

The more I experienced in my informal experiment, the more I came to see that Edward's prediction—which I'd rather call an intuitive *suggestion*, since I very much doubt I'd have come up with it on my own—was really rather brilliant. Such a chapter would not only be helpful but was, I concluded, quite necessary.

Despite all the possible pitfalls of psychic readings noted above, I've come to believe that they *can*—with the proper understanding on the client's part, and the proper skill and integrity on the psychic's—help far more than they hurt. In working with my Team, I'd received useful, sometimes inspired guidance about my career; about writing projects; about love and relationships (though I didn't always take it!); about finances; about family matters; and, though some intuitives won't go there due to legal and personal responsibility concerns, about medical problems and health. I'd been given information that helped me understand myself better, and "homework," often in the form of exercises and guided meditations, to help me get out of my own way—and I swear, they really worked.

I've also come to believe that we all, to varying degrees, have psychic abilities, and that we can develop them—case in point my experiences with Laura Day's book. And Reader, you *know* I'm a big proponent of that. But it's a process that takes time and diligence. Even if we work long and hard at it, many of us will never hone our skills to the level an experienced psychic will likely possess. After all, we can study bricklaying or law, but if we need our chimney repointed or adoption papers drawn up, we're going to want to call in a pro. And then there is this: As we work on developing our intuition, consulting a pro can be a helpful part of the process in validating feelings or visions we've had ourselves.

In a reading with Maggie Moise, for example, about six months after she'd predicted the man-storm, I told her that it had indeed come to pass. I mentioned a man I'd been dating named Dylan. Things with Dylan had been kind of heating up, until he'd told me about a trip he was planning to take . . . with his *ex-girlfriend*. Reader, Dylan's ex had a very serious, probably terminal illness, which was terribly sad. But the fact remained, or at least it was my strong intuitive sense, that he'd never emotionally detached from her. Now he was going to Spain with her to visit her family, and while I felt compassion for her—and him—that big red flag was waving like a matador's cape.

Or was I being too harsh? Dylan was cute and funny, smart and sweet—so I was having a hard time walking away, despite my clear sense that I should.

I didn't tell Maggie any of that, though, giving her nothing but his first name.

"What I'm getting on Dylan," she said, "is you want to hang on to him. But there's something he said to you, about a trip . . . that *is* a red flag. Whether the trip is a metaphor or not, I'm being told that . . . he likes to have his cake and eat it too."

"Ha!" I said, truly bowled over. "No metaphor! You're definitely hitting it."

It was good to have my intuition confirmed. I hadn't always been able to "just say no" when it came to men—as by now, Dear Reader, you've seen—but in that instance, with Maggie's help, I could. And in the end, it proved to be for the best.

Over the course of my experiment, as I came to trust my Team more, I acquired a new habit in readings: At the outset, I'd ask to be told *what I most needed to know.* Sometimes it was surprising; other times, especially as I continued to develop my own abilities, it was just what I'd been feeling myself. Always, though, it was useful, and continually affirmed my belief that my Team's sources—whoever or whatever they might be—had my best interests at heart.

✳

THOUGH SHE WASN'T officially part of my Team, it happened that I'd set up an interview with Laura Day at the time that I was finishing my experiment. I brought up the question of how psychic readings could be harmful versus helpful, asking her to weigh in.

Like most of my Team, she was opposed to "fortune telling"–type readings, but had her own spin as to why. "Knowing what's ahead doesn't often help people change it," she said, as we sat in her loftlike Tribeca living room. "It often helps *companies* change it," she said, alluding to the fact that she did a lot of work for financial institutions. "But predicting for *people* about the future, what you often do is make them afraid. Instead of empowering them to make change . . . And no intuitive, no psychic is a hundred percent accurate. So, you don't know where the mistake is."

In fact, she really wasn't a fan of doing *readings* for individuals at all.

What did she do, then, I asked, when she worked one-on-one?

"I call it *intuitive coaching*," she said. "It really developed from years of reading people. You know, I just got an email from someone who said, 'You read me thirty years ago, and everything you said would happen did happen over the last thirty years.' Well, that was probably *not* a good thing." She smiled. "Because what you want people to do is be able to say, 'OK, this is coming up and, right now, I'm not sure this is what I want. Let's see if there are any benefits to it, and how do I *change* that course?' So now I do more coaching, which is engaging the person's intuition, along with mine, to create the best possible life. A life where someone's happy, where they're part of a community, where they're compensated, where they have the basic 'pie' needs met: companionship, passion, self-expression, economics, safe living, and the ability to support those they love, and receive support from them."

Maggie Moise had something similar to say. Long before I'd realized it myself, she told me this: "I see your book as an account of how you experienced this process"—meaning my project—"and how it's helped you. I see it as showing others that there *is* some *real benefit* to doing this type of work, meaning work with psychics and so on. For instance, when you're in a bind, when you really feel powerless, stuck, or trapped, you can use it to look for answers and get real results.

"Your book's not a self-help book, but then it *is*, because it drives the message home that maybe this stuff is not nonsense, that it can be helpful, *if* you know how to use it. That it's a tool we can use to better our life, if we know how to use it and not *abuse* it."

So, using intuitive readings—*and* one's own intuition—not as a way of *predicting* the future, but as a tool in *creating* it: That seemed to be what all these readers were really advocating. Their words, and my experiences, had led me to see how important it was to gain an understanding of how they worked, if I was going to seek their help. And also to see how crucial it was to work with *highly skilled* readers— preferably those who'd been recommended by someone you knew and trusted—who truly cared about helping their clients to heal, grow, and reach their highest potential. Intuitives like the ones I'd come to know and trust in my own explorations.

16

THE ADVENTURES
COME FULL CIRCLE
✳ OR ✳

The Unbearable Lightness of Being Patricia

PATRICIA MASTERS HAD ONCE PREDICTED, AS I WROTE BACK in the Introduction, that I'd write a book about people who did what she did, and about the invisible realms—which of course I did, many years after she'd passed on. As I began interacting with the rest of my Dream Team, and interviewing them—sometimes formally, sometimes informally—about the way they worked and how they understood their gifts, I found myself wishing she was still around so that I could include her in that way too. After all, she'd been my first psychic; my extraordinary experiences with her had paved the way for the work with which I was now so passionately engaged.

I knew I could extract information from all the taped readings I'd had with Patricia over the years. But it wasn't the same as being able to interview her. And then it hit me: I *could* interview her! I'd just have to interview her *from the Other Side*!

I got shivers at the thought. How cool would that be?

But would it work? Well, if I believed all this stuff I'd been experiencing was real, then I ought to put my money where my mouth was and try.

I set up a phone reading with Janet Alm. Jan had that remarkable ability to channel the energies she contacted sentence by sentence, often paragraph by paragraph, as I'd heard her do with Eia—which would come in handy if this next experiment worked.

When the appointed evening came, I gave Jan only the name *Patricia*—someone I'd like to try and contact, I said—and told her nothing else. My body felt charged, as if I'd just drunk three double espressos, but I was nervous, too. It'd been many years since Patricia had died, and though I believed she'd had some affection for me, I hadn't been a major figure in her life. Would she show? It would be doing me an enormous favor, if so, but was that motivation enough for a spirit? If she didn't, of course, it would be a tremendous letdown. But would it shake my belief in all these things I'd come to accept as real?

"OK," Jan quickly began. "I'm saying, 'Patricia for Anne, can you send me an identifier, please?' And I got a flash of a blue car, so I don't know if she has anything to do with that. But the more substantial image was of her placing a *book* into your hands, or *my* hands, or something like that."

"Oooh! That's *good!*" I said. I didn't know if Patricia had had a car, blue or otherwise—most Manhattanites didn't have cars, though Patricia had later moved to the DC area and likely had needed one there—but I was startled by how perfect the *second* image was, given Patricia's long-ago prediction about my writing the book, and how my experiences with her had been the first step in the journey that the book chronicled.

"OK, Patricia, can you send me one more identifier?" Jan asked. "She's laughing," Jan continued, "and saying, 'Anne *said* it was *good!*'"

I drew in a breath. That comment, the tone of it—it *sounded* like Patricia!

"Well, send me one, just for the heck of it, Patricia," Jan said, amusement in her voice. "OK, she shows me a hand, writing with a quill pen. I would interpret that as just being *writing*," Jan said.

I hadn't known *what* Patricia might use to identify herself: maybe a crystal ball or something symbolic of her being a psychic, or a pair of

ballet slippers because she'd been a dancer. But the images Jan mentioned were actually much more on point, in this present context, than
either of these.

"I think we've got her," I said. "Oh my gosh! Hi, Patricia!" I ventured.

"Well, in that case, Patricia, thank you for coming through," Jan
said. "Is there anything you'd like to share with Anne today?" She
paused. "She says, 'Well, no, Anne is actually the one who's asking all
the questions these days.'"

How right she was. I laughed, but I was really a little overwhelmed.
I'd orchestrated this whole thing with the somewhat pie-in-the-sky
hope that Patricia would come in, but now that it seemed she had, it
was difficult to process.

"'I am wide open and ready to talk, Anne,'" Jan continued, channeling Patricia. "She says, 'I'm very happy with your current book
project, because of course, from the Other Side, I have a very personal interest in this project.' She says, 'It's like you're almost writing it *for me*, and I'm very interested in and proud of the work you've
done. I'm fascinated at the way that you have gotten your mind
around this somewhat nebulous subject. Your writing is outstanding,
it's very clear and very . . . thoughtful, and . . . reflective. Your readers
will enjoy following your thought processes. Because the people who
pick up your book are going to be people who have thought about
this field themselves. And you will be opening up a few little doors
for them to let light into their thinking process. Actually, there are a
number of us over here keeping an eye on your project. And we feel
that you have done a lot of very good work, and pulled so many different strands together, that you've really created something that adds to
the discussion.'"

Reader, I was tickled pink! Patricia had a personal interest in my
project? That was far beyond what I'd hoped for or imagined. I had
to say, too, that her description was quite accurate, about letting my
readers in on my thought processes. As for pulling together many

strands—it was exactly what I'd been doing, as I was writing on so many different topics and taking excerpts from so many readings I'd had and recorded over many years. Jan hadn't read my book-in-progress, and didn't know that. Nor did she know that "Patricia" had any connection to my book at all.

"I'm putting my hand on my heart, Patricia," I said, "because it's *very touching.*" I paused, debating whether I wanted to explain to Jan, now, who Patricia was or not. There seemed no more need to withhold it, so I told Jan how the book I was writing very much featured Patricia, who'd predicted that I was going to write a book about people like her—and that in fact the Introduction started off by recounting that prediction. "So I wanted to ask her whether she had any thoughts or suggestions about what I wrote about her, and whether I had her blessing with it, actually."

"OK, she's smiling, and saying, 'You absolutely have my permission to share things about my work, and your reaction to it, and our conversations, and, frankly I'm honored to be in your book at all. I'm very proud of that.'"

"I'm so glad!" I said. I couldn't stop smiling myself. I flashed back to Patricia's long-ago words about my being generous to her; perhaps this was part of what she meant. "She had a huge effect on me," I told Jan. "She's one of the main reasons I began exploring all this stuff."

"It's so interesting," Jan said, "because now that I know she was a psychic herself, the things that she was saying to you make a whole lot more sense. My interpretation of the placing of the book in your hand, and the writing, when she said them, was that she was maybe an editor, or in publishing." She paused. "What else would you like to ask?"

"I want to tell her how much we all miss her. I haven't found anybody else like her, in terms of what she was able to do."

Jan laughed. "She's, like, fanning her face, and saying, '*Ohhh*, you flatterer!'"

"Well, it's true!" I said. "I'm wondering if she has anything in particular that she'd like to say, I mean, to the world; if I can be in any way
a mouthpiece for her?"

Jan paused. "She says, 'Wow, what an opportunity.' It's like, she's
kind of hesitating, as if she's thinking. OK, she says, 'If I had one message to convey to those who are in . . . ' Give me the words for that,
Patricia. OK, she says, ' . . . for those who are having a human lifetime,
it would be . . . ' I'm trying to be super careful on the exact translation.
She says, 'I wish that I could convey to you the incredible love that
surrounds you. You are virtually *swimming* in love, and . . . because
you are tied to your human incarnation, your mind is . . . your *brain* is
processing all the perceptions that are required for that existence, and
so you are distracted away from an awareness of the tremendous love
in which you exist.'"

"*Mmmmmm* . . . That's beautiful," I said.

"She says, '*That's it!*'" Jan and I both laughed. "'That's what I would
love to be able to share with human beings,' she says."

It was briefer than I expected, but the brevity of it lent it, to me, a
greater power—as if she was saying that, truly, this was *all* we needed
to know.

I asked Patricia what she was doing now. "I know there may not be
human language for the way things work over there . . ."

"She says, 'Oh, *pish-posh!*'" Jan said.

"You know, it's really her voice, her attitude! I've read that, with the
continuation of consciousness after death, the personality is retained.
Still, it's kind of wild to hear her sounding so much like herself."

"She says, 'We are not so different when we cross over as some
people might expect. So many of us in spirit are working on issues that
were close to our hearts in our human lifetimes, because they're issues
that are part of our . . . um . . . spirit interests,' I guess, would be the
way to say it.

"And what are *you* doing, Patricia?" Jan asked, jumping in. "She says, 'Well, I'm helping with young dancers, in particular young boys. There is so much support for all the darling little girls in their tutus that the young males who would be interested in dance often shy away from opportunities presented to them. And so there are, not a lot, but a few of us, in spirit, who are encouraging young . . .' She started to say '*young men*,' then changed it to '*very young men*,' then said, 'well, *boys* . . . who discover their talent and interest, to reveal whether this is their love in life. And perhaps it's not, but we want them to have the opportunity if they have the latent . . . *love* for dance.'"

"Now, does she mean boys over there, in spirit, or boys here?" I asked.

"She's showing me boys in ballet class now. And she says, 'I mean flesh-and-blood boys.' She says, 'There are certain individuals who, as we perceive it, have the potential for experiencing the love of dance. So we make it our . . . personal project to open opportunities to them.'"

"Fascinating." Honestly, Reader, it was. I was loving this. I'd obviously had mediumship readings before, but I'd never really used them to ask these sorts of questions; to try to understand how things worked "over there," and to verify things I'd read, or clarify them . . . or alternately, have them contradicted. To satisfy my long-standing wonderlust in a most unique way. I felt a bit like a kid let loose in a candy store, overwhelmed with the possibilities.

I told Patricia that I'd heard of people in spirit saying they were teaching on the Other Side, or working with young people there; but I'd never heard it said that they were somehow working with people *here*.

"Yeah," Jan said, "I don't usually remember things that were said once the reading is done, which is as it should be, because it's not my business. But sometimes when something is really funny or interesting, it does stay with me. One man, in spirit I mean, I remember that his son asked him, 'What's Mom doing over there?' And he said, 'Oh, she's running around, she's on all the committees and singing in the choir.' And the son said, 'Yeah, that's Mom!'" But, Jan said, there had also been spirits who talked about pet projects that involved interacting *with humans*. "One time, the person I was reading for was inquiring about their father or grandfather on the Other Side—he'd either been a surgeon or died of a heart attack, but this person in spirit showed me an operating room, with him standing at the patient's head, or more like floating a little bit, up in the air . . . and simply beaming down at the patient this beautiful golden light. He said he was now helping surgeons as they perform operations in earthly operating rooms."

"You know, I just realized that I *have* been told by psychics and mediums that some people I knew, who are now in spirit, have been helping me with my book . . . so, there you go," I said. "Patricia, I've been wondering, how are you, over there, able to influence things that happen here?"

Jan paused. "She says, 'One thing we can do is share ideas. We share many ideas with humans whom we love and care about, or those whose activities or welfare we are involved with. We can, essentially, give you a nudge in a particular direction that will cause you to decide to take a particular action.' She says, 'We in spirit can create a kind of opening by putting an idea in the right place, giving a little boy's mother the idea to take him to a dance show, or bringing to her attention an announcement of a performance that will trigger his thinking, *Wow, I wonder if I could try that.* That's how we can participate and support humans in helping them find beneficial paths and choices.'"

Holy heavenly helpers, Batman!

I felt like my brain was about to explode because there was so much I wanted to ask. "This is a personal question she may not want to answer," I said to Jan. "Did she sense that she was going to pass away when she did, and was it hard for her? Did being so in touch with the Other Side make it any easier when she had to go?"

"She said, '*That* is a very good question!'" Jan said. "She says, 'No, hon . . . ' Did she call you *hon*?" Jan asked.

Yes, I told her, she'd use terms like that, once she'd gotten to know me. She was really capturing Patricia's way of speaking, I said.

Jan said that was good to hear, and then went on. "She says, 'Interestingly enough, I did not have pre-knowledge or a premonition that I was going to pass at the moment I did. However, as I discovered myself out of my body, it was tremendously comfortable. I had loved ones around me, and angels and supporters, and I wasn't disappointed or shocked. Even though psychologically, as a human being, I was not prepared for it or thinking I might actually depart at that time, it was ridiculously easy.'"

It was so comforting to hear. I hoped that all the loved ones I'd lost had shared that same sense of ease when they'd passed.

"One thing that I wanted to ask . . ." I told Jan. "Patricia adopted two young children not that long before she died. That must have been so difficult, to let go of them."

"OK, she's saying, 'You have to understand that *I didn't leave them.*' She says, 'Do you know what I mean?'"

"Meaning, she's still with them," I said, moved again.

"Yeah. She says, 'My regret, of course, is for their pain, but I know that they are doing well, and are strong and good people, and are surrounded by love . . . and can certainly feel *my* love—*I love them with all my being*—and know I'm with them. You also have to understand the perspective that, as soon as I leave my body, I am simply in a different reality, or realm of perception, so that I know that they are fine. I can continue to help them and to some extent protect them, and because I have such a personal sense of utter well-being, I don't have the human being's ability to work up a lot of worry. And I can see how this sounds hard-hearted from the human perspective, but it's simply the way it is. And I know that where I am is where I'm supposed to be. My perspective now, to look back even at my own adopted children, is from a perspective of my love . . . the love that surrounds me . . . *and the love that their entire existence is made of.* And it goes back to that whole concept

that I wish I could communicate to my human friends and loved ones—
*how much love surrounds them; that there is nothing but love, the utter love
that the human world is made of.'*"

There is nothing but love. I felt that on some deep level I already
knew that. That I was being reminded of that.

"'It's very frustrating to know that, and to see that, and know that
my children and my loved ones have essentially a veil across their perception that makes their life so much more difficult than it necessarily
needs to be.'"

So she *could* feel a sense of frustration, I thought, even over there. It
was interesting to hear what a spirit might and might not feel. Again,
there was so much I could ask! But I knew I couldn't keep Jan there all
night, so I mentally rifled through my questions in an attempt to pull
out those that felt most pressing, or about which I was most curious.

During the course of my explorations, I'd learned a bit more about
the idea of the Shift—a shift in human consciousness—beginning
to take place on Earth; from what I understood, it involved all of us
humans connecting more to our higher self, and opening up more to
the presence of other realms. It was a notion I was very curious about.
I asked Patricia whether she felt we were "lifting the corner of the veil
a little bit," presently.

"She says, 'There's no question that the general population is more
open to the idea of energy and spirit, and you can see that in the pop
culture. There's still, of course, lots of resistance, but yeah, that was a
good description when you said, "lifting the corner of the veil a little
bit." It's gonna take a whole lot more lifting.'" Jan laughed. "'But there's
no doubt we're all moving in the right direction together.'"

"Well, that's good. I'm trying to make my little contribution."
I laughed.

"Also . . . she wants to say that, from her current perspective, she
knows *now*—and she says, 'which I didn't know, *then*'—that when she
did that very first reading for you, she was part of that process of spirit

communication in which your spirit guides gave her the information *to plant in your brain the idea of writing the book.* 'So that's how this kind of communication works,' she says. 'Spirit literally placed the idea into my mind, with the purpose that I place that seed of an idea into *your* mind.'"

Wow.

"'So it's not that it was my idea, or exactly my pre-cognizance, so much as a spirit at the time placing that idea into *my* human conscious-ness, with the purpose of me passing it on, so that it would be placed into *your* human consciousness.'"

"*Wow.*" I said it aloud this time. "*Wowwwwwwwwwww.*"

If I thought my mind had been blown during my first reading with Patricia, it was nothing compared with this.

Still absorbing that last astonishing nugget of information, I asked Patricia if there was anything I could do for her "over here." It seemed the least I could offer.

"She says, 'Oh, hon, you *are* doing so much to help move human consciousness of the reality of their existence forward, because as you gather information, and share ideas, and converse, all of that is spread-ing thoughtfulness and awareness. And not just awareness, but open-ing people's perceptions to ideas they might not have been open to before. So, just the process of you doing this, that process alone is creating energy that flows out into the world, and your findings, thoughts, and ideas travel through . . .'" Jan paused. "OK, she first said, 'travel through the *osmos.*' But before I said '*osmos*'—it hadn't even registered in my brain yet that that wasn't a word—she stopped me and said, 'Well, I don't wanna say "*cosmos.*"' And she's having this debate about what the right word would be. She says, 'I'm just try-ing to convey that the energy that you generate around this inquiring thought process flows from your spirit and heart and being to others, even others with whom you aren't having conversations. It moves through, shall we say, "the air."' She was gonna say, '*through space,*' but she changed it to 'air,' because she's making the distinction that she's not talking about the whole Universe, she's talking about other human beings."

Now, that was very cool too. I'd thought a lot about the idea of us all being connected, all being part of a vast sea of pulsating electromagnetic energy. It was a big part of Lynne McTaggart's highly acclaimed books about consciousness and the power of intention—she called it "the Field." I'd wondered if this was what was responsible for what some people called the "Hundred Monkey Theory": the idea that if enough people—or monkeys, as the story goes, originating from the work of some Japanese scientist in the 1950s studying the behaviors of free-roaming monkeys—learned something, a tipping point was eventually reached where *all* monkeys knew it, even those not in contact with the original "learner" monkeys. As if ideas, or knowledge, were indeed spread through the ethers, or the Field, somehow, from a single being, and communicated to—*installed in*, perhaps, to use an apt tech metaphor—*all* beings.

"I have to tell you, I'm just thrilled that we're having this conversation," I said to Patricia.

"She says, 'Well, I love that we can have it too, because truly, there's a tremendous amount of spirit interaction with humans that humans are just beginning to perceive. Um, generally the receivers of spirit information are not consciously aware of it. They do not recognize it as coming from outside themselves. They perceive it, as Jan often says, "as if it were their own imagination." And there's nothing wrong with that. Because in most instances, what humans describe to themselves as their own imagination is actually a concept, thought, or idea that is being transmitted to them from outside themselves. So in a way, that's almost the definition of my, quote, *own imagination*.'"

"Yes, I've thought about that in terms of writing," I said. "When you come up with a story, say, are you really *channeling*? Or, where is it coming from?"

"She says, 'Yes, that's very much the case. Spirit energy and information, and love, is being shared with you, and is blended, in your own . . . *perceptual faculties*, into a single . . .' She's moving her hand in a circle in the air, to say, 'one big mishmash. It's a creative process. It's just that humans don't see all the elements going into that creative process, going on in their lives *all the time*. And it's very exciting.'"

"I'm thinking that the word *inspiration* actually has *spirit* in it. Or at least, I think that's where that word comes from, etymologically speaking," I said.

"She says, 'Absolutely! I love that!'"

I realized that we were drawing near to the ending time for our session. It had whizzed by.

I sorted through my many remaining wonderings, zigging and zagging off in so many directions, like so many intersecting crossroads. Which to choose?

"I went to your service, Patricia," I finally said, remembering the truly unique celebration that had been held at Manhattan's equally unique Cathedral of St. John the Divine. "I'm sure you were there too." I'd heard from mediums that spirits loved to attend their own funerals. "It was honestly the best memorial service I've ever attended. All your friends who spoke and danced and performed—it was so moving and beautiful."

Jan laughed. "She's saying, '*I* was moved! At my own damn funeral! *I* was moved! What more could a spirit ask?'" I had to laugh too.

"Just one last question," I said to Jan. A part of me couldn't believe I was really going to go down this particular road with the spirit formerly known as Patricia, but I couldn't help myself. Maybe we humans *were* all swimming in divine love that we couldn't totally perceive; I could surely believe that. But the very *human* me, I had to admit, was still hoping for love of that very particular *human* kind.

After Sam and I had talked things through, I'd felt optimistic that our relationship would grow more stable. And for a brief time it had.

But while he hadn't quite disappeared, my Knight of Swords had been showing signs once more of becoming the Hanged Man.

In a recent reading I'd had with Maggie Moise, she'd told me that, while he and I still had enormous potential to be together, Sam, out of fear and feeling "not good enough," was not choosing that path. But, she said, he and I might well be together again . . . in a future lifetime.

A future lifetime?! I knew she'd meant it to console me. But much as I'd come to put stock in the reality of past—and future—lives, and much as I'd learned to be happy on my own, and come to love the life I was living, my heart still wanted what it wanted, in the here and now.

"I always used to ask Patricia about my love life," I said. "From where she is now, I wondered if she had any advice for me." I paused. "She used to get a little frustrated with me because I had such a hard time getting over men!"

Jan chuckled. "That's funny, as you were saying, 'I wondered if she had any advice,' it was like she was shaking her head and rolling her eyes."

I had to laugh again. As I waited for Patricia to respond, though, I felt nervous. Perhaps it was because I'd asked her this same question so many times when I was so much younger. It was an admission, really, that I was still struggling with this problem, two decades later, and I felt vulnerable just asking it. And then, I wasn't sure I'd like what I'd hear.

Jan began. "She says, '*You* are a hopeless romantic, and there is nothing the matter with that!'" She paused. "That's your whole advice, Patricia?" she asked. "She says, 'Well, the whole *Sam* matter is up in the air, so don't push it, enjoy it, don't *count* on it . . . but you never know! It's good to have love interests in your life.'"

"That's true," I said, startled that Patricia had *mentioned Sam by name.* I'd never said his name in the session, or in my chat with Jan beforehand. Further, the whole matter with Sam still *was* "up in the air." *Jan* couldn't have known that from me; I hadn't been in touch with her since my last reading, nearly a year before! I didn't imagine Jan would even have remembered Sam's name! Much as I had become convinced that the things I was experiencing were real, there were moments like this when it hit me anew just how different the reality I was experiencing was from the reality most of us had been taught to accept as . . . well, *reality.*

I realized that Jan was now bringing the session to a close. "Thank you," I said to her. The words felt so inadequate to express what I was feeling, the fullness in my heart. "And thank you, *so* much, Patricia."

"She says, 'You're welcome. Bless you.' She's smiling and nodding," Jan said.

"I hope that we can speak again, sometime in the future, Patricia," I added.

"'Anytime, my dear,' she says."

I said my good-byes to Jan, then exhaled a deep breath as I hung up the phone. It felt, in a way, like regrounding . . . like coming back to Earth.

I couldn't do much for a while after that call except ponder what had just occurred. It had been one of the more astonishing connections I'd experienced, not only because it was so touching, but because of what I had learned. And that was just the tip *of the tip OF THE TIP* of the metaphysical iceberg, I had no doubt.

Anytime? I thought, Patricia's last words echoing in my head. I could call on her *anytime?* That was all the invitation I needed. I'd definitely be connecting with Patricia again.

I had so many questions still to ask.

✳

LATER THAT EVENING, I sat in my threadbare armchair, listening to a recording of my latest adventure (yes, Reader, I'd now talked to spirits, sung with angels, and met my nonphysical guides, but I still hadn't managed to replace that chair!). What stood out most was what Patricia had said about her ability to *put the seed of an idea* into people's minds. If that was indeed possible, it would explain how spirit guides could manifest things in our lives: how someone at Bulfinch had thought to send me that amaryllis plant, when they'd sent my colleague, Chuck, a fruit basket; how my dancer friend Vija had thought to bring along those photos to dinner, with the upright rehearsal piano, the night I'd asked David to show me a piano; how my friend Deirdre had chosen the movie *Hyde Park on the Hudson*, containing images of a trombone, when I'd asked David to show me that; how my friend Toni had felt the urge to send me that article about composer Gary Lachman the very day I asked Wallace for song lyrics; and so on, and so on, and so on.

Of particular interest to me too had been what Patricia had said about humans not recognizing information given by those in spirit as coming from outside of themselves . . . but rather perceiving it as if it were their own imagination. I'd experienced that sense often during past-life regressions, for example, where, much as ideas and images seemed to pop, with no prompting from me, into my head, I couldn't help but feel I must be making them up. I vowed to be less dismissive, from now on, of that which seemed to be coming from "my own imagination." If it truly *was* a venue utilized by Spirit to communicate with me, I'd certainly be a fool to disregard it.

As the recorder snapped off, I looked out the window to where the day's last light was falling on the redbrick buildings in that particular way that always reminded me of an Edward Hopper painting. Why did the word *seed* ring a bell? I got up and pulled out one of my cases of research files: letters *A* through *M*. It was something Roger Ansanelli had said, about the book I'd begun writing. I pulled out his folder and pored through my piles of transcripts and notes. Ah, there it was! "You're planting a seed, so that others can follow. Remember, your name is *Newgarden*," he'd joked.

So Patricia had planted a seed in me, or my *spirit guides* had, *through her.* And now *I* would be planting it out in the world, a sort of Johnny—or Jenny—Appleseed of the Woo-Woo. It was true that, as much as people had popped up to help me with my project, in just as great numbers people had expressed an interest in the topics I was exploring: sharing their stories; asking about mine; wanting me to recommend practitioners and books and classes. I did seem to be, Dear Reader, without even trying, *sharing* what I was learning, bringing them all along on my adventures.

"WHAT ARE YOU writing about?" Kamile, a young Lithuanian woman who was waiting tables for the summer at the Loving Cup, asked me one blue-skied day at the Shore.

"Psychics and mediums," I told her, "past lives, angels, spirit guides . . . what you might call '*the invisible world.*'"

"Do you really believe in all that stuff?" she asked. Her cheeks flushed as she said it. "I don't mean to be rude!"

"Well, I've had experiences with those things, and I believe in *those,*" I said. I looked her in the eyes—lively blue-gray eyes—and smiled. "Do *you?*"

I could see that she was, at the least, very curious. I recognized one of my kind.

"I've always wondered about past lives," she said, smiling too, almost in relief. It was as if by my own admission I'd given her permission to admit it herself. We chatted a bit, her eyes lighting up as I told her a few stories. She asked me some questions, and I mentioned some books, the names of which she scribbled eagerly on one of the back pages in her pad. With another radiant smile—she had dimples!—she thanked me. Then, as a man at a nearby table beckoned, she turned away, pulling out the pen she'd speared through the bun in her corn-yellow hair. As I watched her take the man's order, I wondered if she might one day look back on this afternoon and remember it as the beginning of her own journey of exploration.

The afternoon light was changing, taking on its golden, early-evening magic. I shut my laptop, paid my bill, and headed to the boardwalk. As usual, just setting foot on it brought back memories of my time with Sam. Since that surreally wonderful conversation I'd had—via Janet Alm—with Patricia Masters, Sam had once again gone underground. I was disappointed, I was dismayed, I was, as my mother would put it, "fit to be tied." It reminded me of that movie *Groundhog Day*, where Bill Murray's clueless newscaster woke to relive the same day, with the same set of scenarios—at least at first—over and over. In that brilliant movie, of course, the character played by Murray *learned* from his mistakes, and from his series of "do-overs." But would Sam? Or better to ask, had I?

I remembered something Roger Ansanelli had once said: "You can't expect to get things from people they don't have yet to give. They haven't gotten there yet themselves." Sam wasn't on the same page as I was in terms of finding peace within himself or finding his place in life, no matter his feelings for me. My Team agreed—and told me in no uncertain terms that I couldn't put my life, or my heart, on hold. And for once, Reader, I wasn't. I'd stopped attempting to contact him completely, and had even unfriended him on Facebook, which had started gaining traction at about the time we met; I was learning my lesson, at least, in that. Still, I couldn't help wondering: *Was I really supposed to just walk away forever from the one man in my life my heart kept telling me, even after all that had happened, was "mine"?*

My explorations, and the time I'd spent at the Shore, had helped me in healing. Sam, in loving me, had been a huge part of that. I *had* finally moved past wanting to fix men, or thinking that I could. I'd even moved past feeling that I needed a man in order to feel happy—through following my bliss, I'd found joy and love in and of myself. But I hadn't stopped loving him. I wondered if we were together in some parallel universe, spun off in another dimension, living out the story of our road not taken here. I hoped that, on whatever road he'd chosen, he'd find the love and healing he needed for himself.

I made my way to one of the new boardwalk benches installed after the hurricane. It bore a plaque, as most of them did, in memory of departed ones who had loved this beach town, as I had come to, and taken in this view: beloved grandparents, parents, friends, siblings, and spouses. I would read the names as I passed, imagining these people and the moments they'd lingered there—fleeting moments; fleeting lives. Some days, in times of sadness or loss, those plaques could feel heartbreaking. But most days, I found them uplifting. They were testaments to joy . . . to love. To lives lived, and meaning and connection found. To the love of beauty—of the sun, the surf, the seagulls, the sandpipers, and the shore.

I sat and gazed out at the ocean. No matter how many times I returned, I never tired of that view. The three swaths of color—sand, sea, and sky—stretching out before me were ever-changing. Some days, the sea was a muddy brownish green, with crashing waves and dark clouds pressing down toward the horizon; others, like today, it was nearly turquoise, placid as a tub under a brilliant, cloudless sky. There *was* something about that endless horizon—it cleared my mind's clutter; soothed my soul. "What's so great about the beach?" one of my city neighbors had asked me once, as I happily headed out for a wintery weekend's visit. I could only laugh. If she had to ask, there was no explaining it.

As I inhaled the briny air and listened to the seagulls' cries, I thought about this beautiful planet—"*Gaia,*" as Roger Ansanelli called her. In his class, I'd learned a meditation sending her love and gratitude, asking her for grounding and guidance in return. It had become my daily habit. I thought of the abuses we humans had heaped upon her, and upon ourselves. Was there any way to reverse the damages done, to help her to heal, and perhaps in doing so also heal ourselves?

Many people felt that our species was a lost cause, our fate a dire one, already sealed. Yet, more and more, I felt hopeful. Through the research I'd done, and the things that I'd witnessed during my explorations, I'd come to believe that so much more was possible for us to experience here than we could ever imagine. And I couldn't help but feel that we, as a species, were beginning to wake up: not only to our own powers, but to the fact that we were, in a very real way, *all one*— and, beyond that, *all love*; that it was, as Patricia Masters had said, what our human existence was made of.

Could it be that the veil across our collective perception *was*, bit by bit, being lifted? My own certainly was. By simply following where the Universe led me, I'd learned, as Shakespeare once wrote, that there were indeed "more things in heaven and earth . . . than are dreamt of in [our] philosophy." And in doing so, I had vastly changed—and enriched—my earthly experience, and vastly changed myself.

I could say with all honesty that I no longer feared death—I now saw it as an adventure grand beyond imagining. I no longer feared failure or opportunities lost; there would be time enough to come back and try, try again. I no longer forced things, or fretted when they failed to happen the way I wanted or expected: I'd learned to trust the Universe, and my guides, and to "go with the flow" and "just say no" (well, *most* of the time!).

I'd committed to a daily practice of meditating; I knew it connected me in some way to God, the Source, the Creator—whatever term you wanted use—and that it helped me to receive whatever He/She/They wanted to send me, and I felt calmer and happier when I did it. I'd learned to take more time and patience with my loved ones (again, *most* of the time!), to cherish them while they—and I—were here, aware, too, that they would never *really* leave me, or I them; and that I also had a family in other realms, with whom I'd reunite one day. I'd totally lost my fear of flying—no small thing for me, Dear Reader, and an enormously freeing thing, at that! And I'd gained much more of a sense of myself (bring on the horses!)—who I was, what I was here to do, and how and where I wanted to do it—and that definitely included living by the water.

I'd started to develop my own powers of intuition, to connect more directly with my guides and access the guidance of my own higher self—the divine part of myself, as I'd come to understand it, that remained in the nonphysical. Realizing that this was something *all* of us had access to had truly changed the way I looked at humanity. It had opened up my mind to possibilities about our evolution as a species, possibilities that excited and inspired me no end.

And yes, Reader, I'd finally learned not to chase love, but to allow myself simply to feel it, whether it was requited or not, hard as that sometimes was. Because deep down, I'd learned that love was never lost, never gone; it simply *was*. It was the thread that held us together, across time, across lives.

And that was just for starters.

I gazed out at the horizon again. I could see why so many writers and artists had used it as a symbol of that which might be attained: that which could not yet be seen, perhaps, but was there, beckoning.

On my own personal horizon, there was much to look forward to. Griffin had invited me to visit him in the "rolling green hills" of Virginia again. He'd bought a pendulum, and we planned to try some experiments in divination together. He wanted to show me a DVD about crop circles that he'd recently viewed. I was more than eager to go.

My friend Meg had been doing some energy-healing work with a practitioner out in Colorado, whom I was dying to try. She'd invited me to visit her too, to meet him and try him out.

My skeptical friend Frankie had actually asked me to "fix him up" for his first reading with a medium. If nothing else, he said, it'd be good for a few laughs. I hoped it'd be a lot more than that.

I'd signed up for a class on channeling, another on the tarot, and yet another on astrology. I was reading a book on the Akashic Records, and some others on manifestation—conscious co-creation of our reality. And I was looking for an opportunity to do energy-healing work with kids, as several of my Team had suggested.

Reader, there was so much more out there to explore . . .

I couldn't wait to continue my adventures.

Bibliography

Alm, Janet E. *Woo-Woo: Becoming a Psychic at Fifty.* Morrisville, NC: Lulu.com, 2010.

Begg, Dieke. *Synchronicity: The Promise of Coincidence.* Asheville, NC: Chiron Publicatiowwwwns, 2001.

Bertoldi, Concetta. *Do Dead People Watch You Shower?* New York: MJF Books, 2008.

Browning, Norma Lee. *The Psychic World of Peter Hurkos.* New York: Doubleday, 1970.

Burnham, Sophy. *A Book of Angels.* New York: Wellspring/Ballantine, 1992.

Byrne, Lorna. *Angels in My Hair.* New York: Harmony, 2009.

Choquette, Sonia. *Ask Your Guides.* Carlsbad, CA: Hay House, 2006.

Combs, Allan and Mark Holland. *Synchronicity: Through the Eyes of Science, Myth, and Trickster.* Boston, MA: DaCapo Press, 2001.

Day, Laura. *How to Rule the World from Your Couch.* New York: Atria Books, 2009.

_____. *Practical Intuition.* New York: Villard Books/Random House, 1996.

De Bertodano, Helena. "Meet Laura Day: The Financial Psychic of Wall Street Who Predicted Global Meltdown." *The Telegraph*, November 7, 2008. https://www.telegraph.co.uk/news/worldnews/northamerica/3400109/Meet-Laura-Day-The-financial-psychic-of-Wall-Street-who-predicted-global-meltdown.html.

Extraordinary People: Season 6, episode 1. "The Boy Who Lived Before." Aired September 5, 2006 on Channel Four, https://www.youtube.com/watch?v=2Wh0OsVtdeE.

Hunter, Dr. Allan G. *The Pathway of Synchronicity: Align Yourself with Your Life's Flow.* Forres, Scotland: Findhorn Press, 2011.

Iacuzzo, Terry. *Small Mediums at Large.* New York: Putnam Adult, 2003.

Jamieson, Leslie. "Giving Up the Ghost: The Eternal Allure of Life After Death." *Harper's*, March 2015. https://harpers.org/archive/2015/03/giving-up-the-ghost.

Jansen, Gary. *Holy Ghosts: Or, How a (Not So) Good Catholic Boy Became a Believer in Things That Go Bump in the Night*. New York: TarcherPerigee, 2011.

Jung, C. G., Aniela Jaffe, ed., Clara Winston and Richard Winston, trans. *Memories, Dreams, Reflections*. New York: Vintage, 1989.

Jung, C.G., R.F.C. Hull, trans. *Synchronicity: An Acausal Connecting Principle* (from *The Collected Works of C.G. Jung*, Vol. 8). Princeton, NJ: Princeton University Press, 2010.

Klein, Robert. *The Amorous Busboy of Decatur Avenue*. New York: Touchstone, 2005.

Larocca, Amy, Vanessa Grigoriadis, Marc S. Malkin, Denise Penny, Deborah Schoeneman, and Rima Suqi. "Mystical City: Guide to New York's Psychics." *New York Magazine*, April 11, 2003. https://nymag.com/nymetro/news/culture/features/n_8624.

McTaggart, Lynne. *The Intention Experiment: Using Your Thoughts to Change Your Life and the World*. New York: Atria Books, 2008.

Moor, Jonathan. *Perry Ellis: A Biography*. New York: St. Martin Press, 1988.

Oppenheimer, Mark. "Spiritual Seeker's Quest, From Blondie to Swedenborg." *New York Times*, 13 April, 2012. https://www.nytimes.com/2012/04/14/us/gary-lachman-from-blondie-to-swedenborg.html.

Ostrander, Sheila and Lynn Schroeder. *Psychic Discoveries Behind the Iron Curtain*. New York: Bantam Books, 1971.

Peat, F. David. *Synchronicity, the Bridge Between Matter and Mind*. New York: Bantam Books, 1987.

Stevenson, Ian. "Concerns about Hypnotic Regression." University of Virginia School of Medicine (Web site). https://med.virginia.edu/perceptual-studies/concerns-about-hypnotic-regression.

Tucker, Jim B., and Ian Stevenson. *Life Before Life: A Scientific Investigation of Children's Memories of Previous Lives*. New York: St. Martin's Griffin, 2008.

Vanden Eynden, Rose. *Ask a Medium: Answers to Your Frequently Asked Questions about the Spirit World*. Woodbury, MN: Llewellyn Press, 2010.

Weiss, Brian L. *Many Lives, Many Masters*. New York: Fireside Books, 1988.

_____. *Only Love Is Real: A Story of Soulmates Reunited*. New York: Grand Central Publishing, 1997.

Acknowledgments

I would like to extend my deep gratitude to the following individuals, without whom this book would not exist, and without whom my years on this planet (at least in *this* body!) would be a much less fabulous and fascinating ride.

Thank you . . .

. . . to all the members of my family, both here and in other realms, for your love; for playing your parts in our mutual drama to the utmost; and for the experiences and challenges that helped me develop the skills and gifts I needed, this time around. Special thanks to my mother, Dorothy, for sharing the "weird stuff" she heard on *Coast to Coast AM* on sleepless nights, and for passing on her curiosity about things metaphysical, perhaps more so than she intended; to my late father, Bud, for the writing and editorial chops, and for being a guiding spirit; to my own "fantastic five," my siblings, for keeping me on my toes and teaching me to be a team player—and in particular to my sister, Elizabeth (aka Cookie), for putting up with my childhood séances and channelings; to all their "Non-garden" partners, for adding new flavor to our crazy family soup, and for all their help and support; and to my four darling nieces, Sarah, Emma, Ella, and Carli, for being the gifts that keep on giving.

. . . to all of the wonderful practitioners in this book, and your teams in other realms, who taught me so much and allowed me to write about my work with you, especially Maggie Moise; Jennifer Hicks; Janet E. Alm, Ph.D.; Dana Marie; Christina Wright; Rev. Kev O'Kane; Edward Ragosta; Laura Day; Frank Andrews; Jeffrey Wands;

Marianna Lead, MCC; and Roger Ansanelli. I am deeply appreciative of your generosity with your time and talents, and look forward to our further adventures! Heartfelt thanks to Edward Ragosta, for gifting me with the book's main title; to Rev. Kev O'Kane, for spot-on guidance on the subtitle and cover art; and to Janet Alm, for the image of "reaching for the stars"—and ditto to all of your helpers in Spirit!

. . . to the late, one-of-a-kind Patricia Masters, for "planting the seed" so many years ago, and for allowing me to interview you from "beyond." You're simply the best, and I look forward to more. And to David Maurice Sharp, for the introduction—I frankly don't know if any of this would have happened without you; for being one of my first "woo-woo curious" friends; and for letting me share your story.

. . . to David Marc Fischer, for any and all guidance, editorial and otherwise, you've given me from wherever you are now, for your many years of loyal friendship, and for your continued presence and love; and to G.G. Fuchs, Dana Ann DeCarlo, and Edward Rogers, dear ones all, for coming through in spirit, again and again. You're always in my heart!

. . . to Cullen Stanley (of Cullen Stanley International literary agency), for your generous and expert editorial, artistic, and publishing advice, and for many years of treasured friendship.

. . . to Frank Santopadre, for being the funniest friend and foil; for being there when I needed you (in this life and other lives you don't believe in); and for letting me "channel" your words and humor in this book.

. . . to "Katarina," for your words of encouragement, which meant the world to me, and for the invaluable part you've played in my adventures, and my life! And to the late "Paul," too—not forgotten and in my heart.

. . . to my wise and dear friend "Griffin," for sharing your knowledge, lending your generous support, and being one of the few people I can always turn to with my "woo-woo" wonderings. It all means more than I can say. I look forward to our future "middle-aged road trips" (and "senior" ones!) . . . and more adventures!

. . . to the late Jeanne, Jamie, and the late Christopher File; Jake and Josh Reinhardt, and the spirit of "Bobby"; and "Rebecca"—for all your time and help, and for granting me the privilege of sharing, and participating in, your amazing stories.

. . . to "Marcus," for your excellent assistance and hard work in my quest to become a soap writer, and to "Madeleine," for the true graciousness and generosity of your offer.

. . . to all of the friends who gave invaluable feedback on various pieces and drafts of this book, and iterations of its cover, especially David Lott and Devan Sipher, my two earliest (God bless you!) readers; Angela Himself, who wielded the wisest of red pens; and Richard Willett, Howard Sterinbach, Shoya Zichy, Kim Roberts, Nicola Weir, Laurie Brand Blackstone, Matthew Hooban, Peter Cabot, Hilary Iker, Jake Jacobs, Linda Stults Myers, Clifford Lee Johnson III, Dina Luciano, Jenny Peng Windheim, Cynthia Patterson, Laura Duffy, Tommy Duclos, Ann Weil, Helen Fost, Danielle Sapienza, and Michael Dobkins . . . for going the distance, sharing your enthusiasm, and spurring me on.

. . . to Karen Minster, Diane Goldner, and especially the indispensable Michael Dobkins, for your help in navigating the otherwise daunting waters of self-publishing. To Karen Minster, too, for this book's oh-so-elegant interior; Michael Dobkins (and Henry Fielding), for the inspired idea for the Contents page; and Jeanne Schneider, Kim Roberts, and my father, the late Albert "Bud" Newgarden, for the wonderful cover and author photos. To Debra Nichols, for a truly stellar proofreading job. And to Laura Duffy, for your patience, time, and talent in creating the perfect, and perfectly beautiful, cover.

. . . to Michael Dobkins, too, for the name Star Garden Press; for unflagging and expert editorial advice; and for putting up with my endless emails and organizational challenges.

... to my lifelong friend Nancy Kechner, for enlightening me about the work of the Division of Perceptual Studies at our alma mater, the University of Virginia (*Wahoo-wah!*), and to Dr. Jim Tucker, for your generosity and time in answering all of my questions. I couldn't be prouder of the work of the Perceptual Studies team!

... to the brilliant Matthew Holtzclaw and Prakash Puru, for letting me pick your mentalists' brains so graciously. You guys are the coolest, and it's always a pleasure.

... to Perla Kuhn, Paul Kalish, Dan Benge, and Andrew Smith, of Fox Rothschild LLP, for being my legal angels. I'm so grateful for your extraordinary help and expertise. And to Danny Kuhn, for the inspired suggestion and always good-natured assistance.

... to Dr. Catherine Lindenman, Peeka Trenkle, Jake Jacobs, Kim Roberts, Harris Dillon, Tommy Duclos, Ann Weil, Roland Jones, Patricia Bechdolt, David Milne, Steve Priebe, Anne Brooks, Jeanne Schneider, Frank Bevacqua, the late Rita Rowan, Toni Wellman, Phyllis Salomone Collins, Karen Friedman, Alexandra and Lorraine Fuchs, Valerie Gilbert, Rich Metter, Diane Castiglione, the late Liese Fischer, Marny Skinner, Margaret Barranco, Mary Rose Morris, Angela Himsel, James Himsel, Jennifer Birmingham, Ida Picker, Barbara and Robert Schneider, Don and Mary Anne DeCarlo, Vija Vetra, Harvey Altman, Diane Aronson, Marla Del Collins, Roy Owsley, Rebecca and Henry Packer, Laura Schiller, Helen Fost, Christopher Beaver, Ainsley Burke, Karen Dillon, Lynn Johnson Minnie, Alice King, G. F. Black, R. Parsey, Frank Vinci, Carol and Al Lenza, Don Summa, Billy Finnegan, Robert Hrasna, James Cinclair, Sam Moore, Larry Welkowitz, Steven Frus, Rachelle Mandik, Jeffrey McAdams, Axel Aubrun, Chuck Fischer, Matthew Hooban, Jim Cooper, Neil Levy, Alec Ivanov, Paul Rátz de Tagyos, Michael Litchfield, Gerry Seidman, Nancy Ancowitz, Peter Cabot, Tom Leopold, Claire McKean, David Lott, Endla Burrows, Andrea Morse, Cheryl Payer, Jay Smith, Roger Smith, Joelle Hellebaut, Mary Lyons, Gloria Cahill,

Charlie Schulman, Ira Fox, Derek Slevin, Mark Gompertz, Bob Miller, Robert Martin Klein, and last but certainly not least, my youngest brother (you know who you are), for your thoughtfulness, generosity, enthusiasm, and assistance, on so many levels, and for being a part of these adventures.

. . . to all my friends, new and old, at the Jersey Shore, for making it my "happy place" all over again. To my brother David and his wife, Lorraine, for all my stays in your gem of a house; each visit was a gift, and I'm so grateful! To Ann Faris, Pegi Ballister-Howells and Tommy Costantino, and the late Mauro and Vicki Bacolo, for your kindness in opening your lovely homes to me; Adrian Bacolo, for continued generosity and kindness; Patrick Rochford, for spiritual camaraderie and caring; and Lee Morgan, for the "auditorium ghost" article, and thinking of me. To Amy Faris, Jake Jacobs, Dave Wrong, Nicole Strafacci, Jana Manning, Dan Jacobson, Robert Johnsen, Linda Stults Myers, and Janyce Lapore, for so many memories; all the wonderful workers at all the coffee shops and restaurants that served as my daily "office," especially "Young Ethan" and "Kamile"; and Erik B., for "owning it all."

. . . to all the authors, philosophers, scientists, musicians, healers, fellow explorers, and teachers in the realms of the metaphysical who are mentioned in this book. I'm grateful for your observations, creations, and contributions to this experience we call life, and appreciate the opportunity to share them with my Readers.

. . . to all my guides and angels, and any who have helped "on loan"—I've been told that you consider this *your* book too! And so it is! Thank you, thank you, thank you!

✳

. . . and to anyone who played a part in these adventures whom I may have left out here through sheer brain overload, my most sincere apologies. I am beholden to you all.

About the Author

ANNE NEWGARDEN was born and raised in Staten Island, New York City's "forgotten borough," where her fascination with the metaphysical began, and has been grateful for many years to call Greenwich Village her home. She attended Manhattan's Stuyvesant High School, and majored in English at the University of Virginia.

Anne has worked as a writer and editor in the field of children's educational and entertainment media; a copy editor/proofreader in magazine and book publishing; a personal assistant to a celebrated folk musician; a project coordinator in an experimental NYC public school classroom; and a concession-stand manager at an Off-Broadway theater, among other interesting jobs.

Her published works include *Christmas in New York: A Pop-Up Book* and *Christmas Around the World: A Pop-Up Book*, both with artist Chuck Fischer (Bulfinch); and *Becoming Jane: The Wit and Wisdom of Jane Austen* (Miramax) . . . with Jane Austen.

Anne loves strong coffee, independent movie theaters, sandpipers, small children, and expanding her consciousness, not exclusively or necessarily in that order, and has always been happiest by the water. She writes and plays, whenever she can, at the Jersey Shore.

Dear Reader,

Thank you so much for reading my book! I'm honored and delighted that you chose to spend your time joining me on my adventures.

If you're hungry for more, please visit AnneNewgarden .com and sign up for my mailing list.

You'll receive email updates about my upcoming books, articles, online and live workshops and events, and other news-y stuff. In thanks, I'll send you a free digital gift.

You'll also find my blog, where I'll be posting about new discoveries I've made in the world of the metaphysical that I'm excited to share, and a Resources section, with information on how to contact my Dream Team members and other practitioners who appear in this book.

If the spirit moves you (pun intended!), drop me a note in the Contact section. I'd love to hear about your own experiences and explorations!

Please consider posting a review of *Adventures of a Soul*, if you enjoyed it, with the online bookseller of your choice. I'd be most appreciative.

With love,

Anne

Lightning Source UK Ltd.
Milton Keynes UK
UKHW021829220822
407649UK00009B/1885